# A SMALL TASTE OF REDWINE

### CARROLL E. REDWINE

To: Janet Darryl & boys

I hope you enjoy this book

Carroll E. Redwine

Bloomington, IN  Milton Keynes, UK

authorHOUSE

*AuthorHouse™*  
*1663 Liberty Drive, Suite 200*  
*Bloomington, IN 47403*  
*www.authorhouse.com*  
*Phone: 1-800-839-8640*

*AuthorHouse™ UK Ltd.*  
*500 Avebury Boulevard*  
*Central Milton Keynes, MK9 2BE*  
*www.authorhouse.co.uk*  
*Phone: 08001974150*

*This book is a work of non-fiction. Unless otherwise noted, the author and the publisher make no explicit guarantees as to the accuracy of the information contained in this book and in some cases, names of people and places have been altered to protect their privacy.*

*First published by AuthorHouse 6/19/2006*

*ISBN: 1-4259-3363-7 (sc)*  
*ISBN: 1-4259-3362-9 (dj)*

*Library of Congress Control Number: 2006904357*

*Printed in the United States of America*  
*Bloomington, Indiana*

*This book is printed on acid-free paper.*

## Dedication

This book is dedicated to my loving parents, my knowledgeable mother Clarice Iva Cooper Redwine and kind gentle father, Adolphus Carroll Redwine

# Acknowledgements

Writing this book has been really an enlightening experience. Many friends, relatives, and helpful acquaintances have contributed to its content and the author is grateful for their sharing of their thoughts, memories, and expertise. A few of these fine folks and their contributions must be publicly and properly mentioned even though the writer will risk leaving out someone. Should this occur, rest assured that it was oversight and not in any way intended to offend.

Thank you and much kudos must go to David L. Redwine who generously and daily gave his time and wonderful computer skills to keep this project afloat. His patience and diligence plus his devotion to repairing his father's never ending screw-ups on the computer must have been a real challenge, as he not only had to continually repair the hardware, but teach and repair the software.

Thanks to Sgt. Kathy Miller of the U. S. Army Field Band and the archives of that great organization for the many helpful and purposeful letters, documents, and programs that authenticated and justified the tours, crowd numbers, music performed and the writers participation in this wonderful organization.

Thanks to D. Jane Bartlett for her help in remembering names dates and places, as well as partial help in editing the manuscript. Also for prodding the writer to continue when it appeared there was really no need to add more information and that the project was quite unimportant.

Thanks to Shirley J. Redwine and my four children for their patience and for providing the interest and enthusiasm that made the daily grind of this project easier. It is my hope that they are the real benefactors of my writing and will truly enjoy reading and passing along the many stories of the people in this book

# <u>Foreword</u>

It is the hope of the writer that present and future generations of his family will better understand how the family has come to task with its responsibilities and will not only enjoy knowing where the family came from, but will to some degree find it quite interesting. There were many omissions of unpleasant occurrences, as those present at those inopportune times will readily remember and some may question why the writer choose to ignore reporting on those issues.

Briefly, I must tell you focusing on the more positive times was much more to the nature of this family, we never dwell long on the negative part of any issue, and try to find the good, of which there is **always** some in every trial or tribulation. Please keep this in mind when reading and let your self laugh and enjoy this as much as the people did when it was occurring.

# Table of Contents

Dedication .......................................................................... v

Acknowledgements ........................................................... vii

Foreword ......................................................................... ix

Planting the First vines ..................................................... 1

Harvesting a Few Culls .................................................... 15

The Wines are Made From Many Varieties ....................... 25

The Vines Begin to Separate ............................................ 38

Some Sour Grapes ........................................................... 61

The Grapes Begin to Ripen .............................................. 67

The First Big Taste Test .................................................. 86

Licensing of All Future Vintages ..................................... 90

Two Bottles Survive Their First Crate ............................. 94

The Wine Drinks in California .......................................... 97

The Master Vintner Comes to California .......................... 100

Letting the Vintage Rest .................................................. 112

Redwine in the Vineyards of Europe ............................... 114

Getting Rich in the Insurance Business ............................ 189

We finish the Music Degree ............................................. 207

The Move to Broken Bow ................................................ 215

The Early Broken Bow Years ........................................... 222

Okie to Muskogee ................................................................. 251

On to Ft. Gibson ................................................................. 257

Rock Chalk Jayhawk- Lawrence Kansas- Our Next Home ........ 266

Rock Chalk Jayhawk ................................................................. 271

Oh Lord, We are Going to be Texans ....................................... 289

Broken Bow and the fulfilling of a lifelong Dream ..................... 332

Time to Move on to New Adventures in the Big City ................. 349

Sulphur Oklahoma Receives Benefit of Oklahoma City's loss .. 366

Recipes Listed Alphabetically, as to Food Type ....................... 399

A Few Thoughts on the Important Things ................................... 421

# A Small Taste Of Redwine
## Planting the First vines

The bitterly cold prairie wind howled menacingly through the rafters of the unpainted, dirt floor cabin as the local physician, Dr. L. D. Hudson of Dewey, Oklahoma went routinely about preparing the lovely young auburn haired woman, who was laying so indiscreetly on the families one and only small bed, as she was agonizing through the final pangs of childbirth, her hollow cheeks holding those obviously fearful, but courageously piercing emerald eyes that squinted tightly with each new round of pain, and opened mercifully, as the pains relaxed between rounds.

Clarice Iva Berryhill Cooper Redwine, who herself was born March twelfth, 1913 was descending into the valley of the shadows to bring forth a new life, a free spirit whose actions she would not always condone, but one she would certainly always love and for whom she would always care. This was a second experience for our delicate five foot four prairie flower, and she prayed that it would have a better ending, as only eighteen months previously; the spirit of her stillborn first child along with it's father's, left her to reside with the angels. Her husbands death was due to encephalitis and presently their earthly bodies lay in a grave beside her Grandfather Berryhill in the local Cemetery, his death was the result of a short, but deadly bout with pneumonia. The drafty cabin rocked as the January 15th, 1936 winds swirled the spitting snows around the barren unfenced yard, both were located on a high bank of Coon Creek two miles East of Dewey, Oklahoma on a Washington County Road, that passes in front of the old Dewey Portland Cement Plant. The cabin was located on the North side of this road about 200 feet East of a new bridge

1

constructed sometime during the 1990's. How could the mother of this fledgling, or her new son, who was soon to embark on such a wonderful journey, know that during the next three quarters of a century fate would present him, and for a half century, his bright and hard working mother with such adventures, that they would rival any dreamed by the worlds great story tellers, some of which were being formed in the minds of current men.

Presently, along with their whole nation they were experiencing economic hardships of a great world depression and regional drought that was so fierce, it caused dust storms, that daily blotted the mid-

*A.C. Redwine holding C.E. Redwine*

*C.E. Redwine at 12 months*

day sun into total darkness, and filled the mouths of area souls with grime, while covering some whole counties with a twenty foot deep, unyielding pile of useless sand. In less than ten years the globe on which they lived would be engaged in a massive world war that would

**NELLIE BERRYHILL**

## Berryhill rites set Tuesday

Mrs. Nellie Maude (Vulgamore) Berryhill, 84, area resident the past 62 years and widow of the late Grover A. Berryhill, died at 6 p.m. Tuesday in the Geriatrics Section of the Jane Phillips Episcopal Memorial Medical Center. Mrs. Berryhill had been in failing health for the past five years.

Funeral services for her will be 2 p.m. Friday in the Town and Country Christian Church with Mr. E. E. Butts officiating. Committal prayers and interment will be directed in the Dewey Cemetery by the Arnold Moore Funeral Service.

She was born Nov. 25, 1893 at Anness, Kan. where she was reared and educated.

She and the late Grover Alexander Berryhill were married at Wichita, Kan. on Aug. 25, 1911. They lived on a ranch near Liberal, Kan. until moving to Washington County in January 1916.

Berryhill came to this area with the Barnsdall Oil Company in early oilfield development and they lived on a farm northeast of Dewey.

Berryhill worked for the Dewey Portland Cement Company from 192? until retirement, in 1955. He died Jan. 4, 1963.

She then lived with her daughter Mrs. Clara Whittenburg, 112 South Choctaw, where she remained until moving to the Geriatrics section of the local medical center on Sept. 17, 1977.

She was a charter member of the Town and Country Christian Church.

She will lie in state from noon Thursday at the Dewey Funeral Home.

Survivors include three sons William Marion Berryhill, Rock Springs, Wyo., Lyle (Buck) Berryhill, superintendent of schools, Henryetta, and Earl Buford (Bud) Berryhill, rural Wann; four daughters, Mrs. Kenneth (Clarice) Thornton, Pawhuska, Mrs. Clara Grace Whittenburg, 112 S. Choctaw, Dewey, Mrs. Allene Ruth Stanton, Shidler, and Mrs. John (Betty Jane) Furnas, Phoenix, Ariz.; 19 grandchildren; 38 great-grandchildren; two brothers Ralph Vulgamore, Clearwater, Kan. and Everett M. Vulgamore, Wellington, Kan. and one sister, Mrs. Bessie Pickens, Denver, Colo.

result in the deaths of fourteen million people. How could they imagine that a fellow named Oppenhiemer with the aid of a few other men would learn to unleash unbelievable powers of good and evil from a particle that was so small it still had never been viewed by humans, but was only suspected to exist. Would they have believed that an image of whatever proportions one desired could be transported into outer space and anywhere one desired around the earth, or that man would step foot physically on earths' closest celestial companion and return to tell others about it. The proud woman on the bed with her gentle husband holding her hand was the daughter of Nellie Maude Vulgamore Berryhill, and Grover

*Clarice Iva Cooper Redwine, 1988 our wonderful mother, who went to be with A.C. Redwine and the Angels in July of 1991*

Berryhill. Nellie was the daughter of Agnes Vulgamore. Agnes was the Daughter of Great Great Grandpa Giggy of Indiana, a union soldier in the great American Civil War. Nellie grew up in Southwest Kansas (Anness) and spent considerable time in Abiline, Kansas. Grover whose father was John Wesley Berryhill and whose sisters were Don Chevally of Dewey Oklahoma and Ora Berryhill of Tulsa was the nephew of Susie Barrow of Oklahoma Indian Territory. Susie was reputed to have more than once aided the Daltons and Jesse James's boys and hailed from the Oxford Mississippi area, as did Grover and his father before him. Mother Clarice, who had very high expectations of herself and her children, was born in Aness, Kansas and came to Oklahoma in a covered wagon accompanied by her parents on the 12th of March 1913. The man holding the agonizing new mothers hand, agog with expectations of his first son was my father, Adolphus Carroll Redwine, son of Adolphus Cash Redwine who came to Indian Territory from Walls, Georgia, (Cash), was killed in an accident when his horse ran away at a church picnic and the wagon turned over on him, which led to his burial that same day in the church cemetery in (Bug Tussle, Oklahoma.), this account was related to me, Carroll Earl Redwine by my father who at the age of five witnessed the event along side his mother, Agnes Watts Wilson Redwine and three year old brother Earl Redwine and resulted in A.C. only finishing third grade as he went to work soon after in the local coal mines. My Dad's mother passed away when I was four or five years old and I remember attending her funeral at the Baptist Church in Wilburton. It was a warm sunny day and I played outside in the dirt, as they would not allow me to go inside. A very pretty lady came out of the church after the service, picked me up and said," What a pretty little boy," and I presented her with a handful of dirt.

I played my saxophone accompanied by my cousin Suzie Staton Gambino at my Grandmother Berryhills' funeral service, which was conducted at the East Side Christian Church in Bartlesville and I know Mom's mother to be buried in the Dewey Cemetery along with many other of my relatives; however; my mother and father are both side by side in the North end of the Pawhuska Cemetery in Osage County Oklahoma. My mother, the eldest of seven children born to Nellie and Grover Berryhill, had three sisters: Clara Wittenburg of Dewey, now deceased, Alene Staton of Caney Kansas and Betty Furnas of Phoenix Arizona. Mom also had three brothers: William (Bill) Berryhill now deceased, Lyle (Buck) Berryhill of Henrietta, Oklahoma and Earl Buford (Bud) Berryhill of Dewey. All Moms' siblings are listed here eldest to youngest as to gender. She was the oldest child in her immediate family and she was intelligent, and responsible to and for her parents. My father had eighteen siblings in what was a blended family of Wilson's and Redwines; although, none of them would tolerate your mention of such. They had no step or half brothers or sisters and delighted in telling everyone of this. I only knew my uncles, Jimmy Wilson of Dewey, Henry Wilson, Buddy Redwine and George Redwine of Red Oak, Oklahoma and Dad's sister Ada Redwine of the McAlester area, all deceased. To know more of these folks consult my brother Philip who spent a whole summer with them when he was about twelve years old.

My family moved from my birthplace East of Dewey to a three-acre home place located one half mile West and one-quarter mile

*Jane and Me*

North of Dewey, when I was about three years old. It had many cherry trees with forbidden fruits, which I readily sampled on a daily basis during the season. There was one special Bing cherry tree with fruit which Dad would not share with anyone other than my Grandma 'B', it was in the back yard and really off limits to my licentious appetite, that resulted in my being locked in the front yard many late spring days with my sister Janie (Delores Jane ' Redwine' Bartlett) currently of Richmond, Missouri, together we enjoyed making mud pies and feeding them to the neighbor kids, sometimes climbing the two cedar trees growing there to rob bird nests of their eggs to make our very special filling.

Once while my father scolded me for eating those forbidden cherries, my most cherished uncle, Albert Whittenburg jokingly admonished his nephew, reminding me that should I swallow the pits while devouring those luscious cherries, the resulting tree would grow out of my ears, a common thought among thieving children in those days. Sister Jane recently reminded me that there was

*Janie at 3yrs and me at 5yrs old*

a very special day when I had apparently helped myself to a great many of Dads' Bing cherries, which when swallowed a bit hastily, led to my running to the house screaming at the top of my lungs, " Do you see it, do you see it, oh what will I do?" while pointing to both of my ears with terror on my face, then being consoled by a mother who was really indignant with her brother-in-law Albert.

*Grover & Nell Berryhill & C.E. 1954*

My mother and father built a new home on this land in 1940,but did not get to enjoy it as shortly after finishing the house Dad had a major heart attack and was forced due his health to change his occupation from oiler at the Dewey Portland Cement plant to selling life insurance for the Metropolitan Life Insurance Company; and thus to relocate our family to a rental house in East Lynn Addition of Pawhuska, Oklahoma in Osage County. Since the job required my father to begin work in November, and I was in my first year of school at the Dewey Grade School, the family determined I should finish the first two months there before joining the family in Pawhuska. So I stayed with my Berryhill Grandparents until the end of November then transferred to the two room –grades one through eight- school in Lynn addition, where the big kids would daily beat up on the new first grader from Dewey; one time rolling him in the snow until his hands and feet were frost bitten, a fact which will not allow toleration of any cold on them without severe pain to this day.

Fortunately for me, Dad and Mom bought a house at 805 East 13th street in Pawhuska that spring, and I finished first grade at the newly opened Prudom Grade School, which due to its location was a really controversial facility; and although it was the newest and most up to date grade school building in the school district, it would only be open that one year, which forced me to attend second grade at Franklin Grade School. The Prudom School Building with all its wonderful new equipment would set empty for five years until Skelly Oil Company purchased it for a research facility. All this lost so that the little darlings who lived on the hill nine or ten blocks away would not have to walk so far, never mind, that the kids who lived on our side of the tracks would be forced to walk up that hill to attend school at Franklin.

I really didn't mind walking the four extra blocks up hill to Franklin as my walk took me by a very good turnip patch and pear orchard where for the next five years during the fall months I daily filched one of each for a little afternoon snack.

*Jane and Me at Franklin Elementary*

The one thing I remember most about Franklin was the darned sand burrs which were everywhere and hurt as much being pulled out as they did going in, and secondly, that during dry weather, my sister Janie and I would take a short-cut over the railroad tracks. This route to school took us by the Crownover Creamery and Charlton's'

Grocery Store in the 600 block of 13<sup>th</sup> St both of which were across the street from the Catholic School and Church where we enjoyed exchanging rocks and dirt clods with their students, especially since they were fenced in and could not continue the episode past a point we selected.

*A.C. Redwine with his four children back left, James Marion, Delores Jane, Philip Warren, and in front, Carroll Earl*

I continued to attend Franklin through the sixth grade during which time I delivered newspapers for the Pawhuska Journal Capital, a daily, and the weekly Osage County News. I took my first route at the age of eight, walking downtown to the paper offices from school at four o'clock, receiving my allotment of papers about four thirty, folding them with the other delivery boys, as we discussed that days' events and bagging them in the shoulder canvas bags used by all of us to carry them on our routes.

These conversations were very informative and kept me at the front of what was going on in Pawhuska, Oklahoma and WW-II. I still think my days as a news- boy were an important link in my up bringing, as they taught me many great lessons in fiscal responsibility and society's expectations as to business.

*L. to R. Jane, Momma Clarice, holding baby Philip, and me, Carroll. Picture taken shortly after Philip's birth in March of 1941.*

From the paper offices I walked east six blocks to Lynn Ave, where my route began. Then throwing papers I continued East to Boundary St. using Eighth St, then returning by way of Ninth, then walking the four blocks north to my house on Thirteenth. I usually got home about six p.m. each weekday evening for dinner, which we called supper; dinner was the noon meal! There was no Saturday edition, so that morning was used each week to collect from my subscribers and pay for my papers, which must be accomplished by noon, as the newspaper offices were closed after twelve each Saturday due to preparation of the Sunday edition, that I picked up at four thirty a.m. Sunday morning. This was the only morning edition issued, and after delivery of it; I was usually home for breakfast by seven a.m. and at Sunday school by nine forty-five, a required performance around our house no matter what else transpired each week. Our family attended the First Christian Church (Disciples of Christ) at the corner of Ninth and Prudom, on time or early and all sat together every Sunday.

Violet Willis a wonderfully wise and kind lady was my Sunday school teacher for most of my early years and a big influence on my social and religious education. At this point I will try to reflect on these grade school and preschool memories:

One of my most precious and revered memories was of the many wonderful hours spent with my father, who had big beautiful blue eyes that melted gently into the kindest round continence, always containing a

*My Father, AC Redwine donating time.*

special twinkle and I remember his wrinkled, but tender hands so like my brother Phil's.

I can still envision his left hand tugging at his left ear as with his right hand he would reach up to his red and gray checked flannel shirt pocket and gingerly pull out that pack of Camels or Lucky Strikes, tap them on the back of his left hand, and without touching the cigarettes, place the pack close enough to his lips to pick one out of the pack. Then with his empty left hand he would reach into his pants pocket and pull out the folding book matches, open them, and pulling only one from the attached dual line, scratch it across the rough lighting surface. Then cupping both hands around the lighted match to protect it from the ever present prairie wind, he would bring those lovely caring hands, full of fire, to the cigarette still dangling from his partially open lips. I would watch as he inhaled that long drag of tobacco and slowly exhaling like he had just entered heavens great gates, a giant puff of blue would engulf his wrinkled face and thin white wisp of hair. I can still smell that smoke to this day and sometimes I get a whiff of his good friend Franzo Philpot's‘ cigarillos. Franzo was Dad's most dear fishing buddy during my preschool days and during these fishing trips, a great many that I was allowed to accompany, some delicious moments were shared poaching fish from the most forbidden of fishing holes. We never fished on Property that wasn't "Posted" due to the fact these creeks and lakes were fished by everyone and had few fish left. Test Lake was our favorite; the water was clear, as the summer sky, cold to the touch even in mid July, required a long walk from the county road through a five-strand barbed-wire fence that was so tight that it would sing as we climbed very carefully over it. Test was really two small narrow lakes separated long ago by a concrete dam built by the local oil company. It was low to the upper portion, with water usually spilling over the dam, and six or eight feet above the surface of the lower body of water. The dam was impossible to walk across due to its narrow width and slick green mossy surface. Lined with tall, wispy, willows on its eastern banks, it had a high limestone bank on its western side, which happened to be the side closest to the fence and road. Sloping dangerously down this lime-stone bank; snaked a narrow, difficult to maneuver path, which led directly down to the concrete dam and to three small steps, that allowed a nice place to sit and fish if the cottonmouths were taking the day off. These steps were my fathers and my favorite seat on the lake. Test Lake was on the Montgomery Ranch which also possessed our favorite holes on famous Coon Creek...Ole' man Montgomery was a cantankerous fellow. and loved to run us off of his place, but our modus operendi was to get on his holes before daylight and out before his cowboys or he made their rounds about 8:30 to 9:00 a.m. (It got too hot to fish by then anyway;). On one of these many memorable trips to Test Lake, I enjoyed a particular side of my father, who was a very special man in every way. It may be interesting to the reader to note the preparation for these fishing trips and some idea of how they progressed: usually about 5:00 p.m., the evening before our trip, Dad, Franzo, and I would go to a small creek which had formed a small lake located just west of the cement plant about 1 /4 mile west of the old plant office where Dad and Franzo would seine about 6 to 8 dozen pond shiners which we would take to Franzo's home located next to the Katy tracks on Cement Plant Road. We would then pour them into two or three #3 wash tubs where they would rest until about 3:00 a.m.when after having a good breakfast which Franzo had prepared, we would put the shiners in three or four minnow buckets and load up our cane poles along with Franzo's rods, then head out to the Test Lake or Coon Creek. On this particular trip, Dad and I, who usually fished together (I couldn't swim): had not caught but two or three fish, but Franzo, who had not been saddled with a noisy five year old flailing the water and talking all morning, had a nice string of bass, which he proudly held up as he boasted from his perch on the high bank from which he always cast those damn rods half way across ole' Test, reaching out many yards to spots inaccessible to our trusty cane poles. As Franzo taunted Dad with his beautiful prize, he added salt to the wound by asking Dad if he wanted any of these fish, as Franzo did not have time to clean them, due to his work schedule on returning home…Dad thought a minute, then yelled to Franzo, "I'll help you with the fish."…Dad turned to me, and said, "Son you roll up our poles and gather our gear, I'll be back in a minute." He then left me and due to the high bank, I couldn't see him or Franzo, but in a few minutes, Franzo came to help me with our equipment. As Franzo and I rolled up the poles, we heard many loud splashes. Finally, we went up above and to our amazement, there stood Dad, taking Franzo's bass off the stringer and throwing each as far out in the lake as he could. Franzo didn't speak a word all the way home and didn't say goodbye when he got out of the car at his house. After Franzo got out and went in his house, Dad laughed so hard he bent over the steering wheel and tears ran down his cheeks. We had many great fishing days together until Dad passed away in February of 1964 at the young age of fifty eight due to a bad heart which he had tolerated for 24 years and a body full of cancer, the latter disease was discovered only three weeks before his death; oddly he had gotten a good recommendation from his physician only three weeks previously during his annual check-up. Some small things our fathers do stay with us as fond memories for as long as we live. Dad left us with such items as (practicing up for Christmas), a fun time that would come about anytime after the first cold spell in the fall and included dad bringing home such unanounced goodies as chocolates, special cheeses, nuts,--even once in a while a coconut, which he would help all the kids drive a nail into and drink its juice then break open with a hammer and pass its meat still in the shell around for each of us to nibble. He also loved to play cards or any games such as checkers, dominoes, monopoly,or Etc. which he used to teach us to compete and to read as well as to make change and count.

# Harvesting a Few Culls

My grade school days at Franklin were also World War II years filled with special memories of rationing of all staples, stamp books that allowed only five pounds of sugar per month, if the store had it and you had a stamp. Same for gasoline, five gallons per week, tires (1) per year per family, so the trips back to Dewey were fewer and fewer. Herseys or other candy or bubble gum were as scarce as hen's teeth and if you could find them, usually not for sale, as the store owners kept them for their families or

*L. to R; Philip, Carroll, James and Janie Redwine*

special customers, which did not include the Redwine's, their being new to town and living on the "wrong "side of the tracks. My Sister Jane reminded me that we also did not get butter, as a terrible tasting congealed substance called Oleo replaced it. Oleo was dispensed in one-pound plastic bags, which included a capsule of yellow color that the consumers were expected to squish and work into the Oleo. The resulting concoction had the consistency of butter and the taste of putrid lard. However, being a paper boy had real advantages, as we boys in this business usually heard about new shipments of all goods in Pawhuska before they were announced publicly, allowing us to usually be first in line for wanted items. I clearly remember hearing the radio broadcast announcing the death of Franklin Delano Roosevelt while playing on my front porch, as my mothers' friend Angie was visiting. After the announcement, my mother cried, as did her friend. During those war years, man hours and materials were vital to saving our nation, so we stripped the tinfoil from gum wrappers, saved and collected waste paper, traded toothpaste tubes for new ones, rolled string in balls, and in general conserved every material in vast quantities. All foods and useful items were included to aid the war effort, and we did it happily and WE WON!

The main entertainment for the kids in our neighborhood was to meet together under the street light at the corner of 14th and Ruble after supper, throw rocks at the telephone pole and visit. This may not sound very exciting to the youth of today, but I assure you, we solved some real problems at these sessions. The guys who showed up regularly were the Blankenship brothers, Bill, Max, and Larry (also known as Shug!), the Redwine boys and sometimes Tommy Lucas, the football coach's son presently a judge in Cleveland County and rarely, although he was always welcome, little David Carson. Lucas moved in 1945 making room for a new coach, Lyle Yarbrough; who was a really good man, and his son Lyman became a regular, as he was more our age. Other fellows would drop by, but these kids were considered by me to be real friends.

When I was about 9 years old, I got my first bicycle; it was used, very big, and heavy. I damn near skinned every spot on my body learning to ride it. After about a week of beating myself up on it, my Dad took mercy on me and traded it for a lighter model which I immediately was able to negotiate, and furthermore to appreciate, as I no longer had to walk to get and deliver my newspapers. Being mobile also allowed me to get more customers, as I could sell papers at the hotels and restaurants for cash and still find time to deliver my routes. This fact introduced me to alcohol and gambling, as Oklahoma was a dry state and gambling was illegal, but a kid with a buck in his pocket and a bicycle for making deliveries to the hotel easily and quickly learned who the bookies and bootleggers were and which ones needed his services. The extra money really made a difference, as I was able to purchase better clothes and a better bike. However, after only about three weeks of my illegal profiteering, as so often happens in a small town, some well-meaning soul alerted the Metropolicy Man (Dad), who also was well known in all social levels of the community, to the fact that his eldest was knocking down the quick, but illegal and somewhat dangerous profits; He had a few choice words with me speaking ever so softly as he held that razor strap, and I quickly understood the message, that newspapers were all I'd be handling in the future.

By the year 1946, the war was over and the country was trying to absorb the G.I.s returning to the economy. For a year or so things went pretty well, but by 1948, my paper business was not showing enough profit to fit my style, so I took my first job down town. I started washing dishes for "the Greek's Restaurant; $3.00 per day, 7 days a week from as soon as I could get there from school until 1:00 a.m. I made $21.00 a week and supper, which was usually either a hamburger or a bowl of chili, but never both as the Greek was pretty "tight".

Most of my five years at" The Greek's" Red Lyons, a middle aged and well-traveled fellow, was the night manager and fry cook. Red, a tall, grizzled skinned fellow, with a tousled, thin head of light sandy hair that floated gently above his mostly unshaven face holding those kindly deep set emerald eyes, was a very poor family man, who I suspect, although it is only conjecture on my part was also prone to imbibe the long rested and carefully tended juices of many different fruits, and I really enjoyed his company. We fished together many times after working until One a.m. at the Chile Parlor. After closing the restaurant we would then take Red's old Chevy Truck to one of Drummond's Ranch ponds, where we would fish until shortly after sun-up, then he would take me home, so I could get ready for my sleepy day at school. On these trips ole' Red always had a flask with him but never offered it to me, as I was too young; however I suppose he did not consider me too young to make the stuff, as he took me aside one evening at work and asked "How would you like to make some home brew?" Asking a twelve year old kid such a question, especially one who had heard of the many delights available from this renown nectar, was like asking an inhabitant of Hell if they would care for a spot of ice water, and I jumped on the notion like fleas on a pup. Red being a seasoned veteran explained; there was some necessary equipment for this process, and I could begin immediately to be of service by adding ninety-six (four cases) of empty beer bottles to my pearl diving duties in the kitchen. Before we closed that night, I made old Red proud by figuring out how to clean them and complete my regular kitchen patrol without the owner, Ole Tom's suspicions. In addition that same evening, I made a trip to the Packing House Grocery to purchase the necessary ingredients which the master brewer, Red assured me would make a nectar fit for the Gods. However he did not tell me we were going to assemble them in my mother's kitchen, while looking over our shoulder for Mom and

Dad or any other family members, or that the makin's were to be in my house, while they bubbled into their final state. These facts he would relate when the time was more to his advantage.

Red arrived at my house the next morning about ten-thirty, shortly after my parents had left for work and my siblings had gone to Bible school at the church (I was too ill to attend), We made sure the coast was clear, and proceeded to concoct our batch. Mom had a ten gallon pickle crock which we cleaned, then carefully following what Red assured me again was an old family recipe, of which he obviously was very familiar as he had it memorized, we put about five gallons of water in the crock along with five pounds of granulated sugar, a can of brewer's malt, and two cakes of Fleischmann's yeast and proudly stirred the whole mixture with vigor. We covered our treasure with one of Mom's old tablecloths and hid our bounty in the back of the bathroom closet where no one in our family ever opened the door. Although at the time, I felt sure my parents would not discover our treasure, I now know after years of experience of using yeast in a kitchen or close by, they must have been well aware of our operation due to the smell of our brew cooking in the closet.

They must have had a good laugh about two days after Red and I put the mix together, but if so said nothing to either of us and about three or four days after our first meeting, Red showed up with a bottle capper, caps and the bottles I had filched from the café and cleaned while on the Greek's payroll. He even thought to bring a funnel, (what a guy!). We carefully filled each bottle, added a spoon full of sugar to each before capping, and even more carefully placed them back in the cardboard cases; to age into what was to be an exceedingly fine finished product, as the extra sugar would guarantee a highly volatile alcoholic content in every sip. I could tell we must have done well for ourselves by the grin on Red's face when, before we capped our first bottle, he scooped up a tin cup full, right out of the vat, and as he was swishing it around in his mouth, grimaced; then immediately grinned fully, as he gulped the remainder of the cup. Red had his amounts correct, as the liquid in the vat fit adequately into the prepared bottles; and after cleaning all the utensils and other paraphernalia, Red left with his half of the booty. I hid my two cases in the old shed that was on the back of our property, and had once been a garage, but was no longer used as such due to a very leaky roof and lots of scattered junk stored there in. Mom or Dad seldom visited the shed, so I considered it to be a safe place to store my booze.

This little caper took place around the first of June, and I had forgotten about it by the Fourth of July, when about four thirty a.m. on the morning of the Fourth, Dad aroused me from a deep sleep and asked if I would like to go fishing with him on Sand Creek, north of town. I rubbed the sleep from my eyes and set up, trying to hurry out of bed before he changed his mind when he surprised me with, "Son do you still have any of that home brew left that you and Red Lyons made?" Sheepishly, I admitted so; and he continued, "Throw it in the car with the tackle!" I stumbled out to the old garage in the dark, rummaged around in the junk and uncovered both cases of my forgotten brew, took them to the car and put them in the trunk, then after gathering our fishing poles and tying them on the car, we proceeded to one of our favorite holes on Sand Creek, which at that time was just below the ole' Sand Creek Grade School a bit west of State Hiway 99 six miles north of Pawhuska.

It was just getting daylight when we arrived at the pull off beside the Sand Creek Road, but it was light enough to see our way though the brush, so we took the poles off the car, picked up the minnows in their bucket and the two tackle boxes and fought our way down to an open spot on the sloping sandy beach. While I got the poles untangled, and baited; Dad went back to the car and brought the Home Brew (both cases), down to the creek, and leaving me to finish setting the lines, he put both cases in the creek to cool out. Just as it was getting good and light and after we had caught a couple of small fish, he raked a couple of the bottles from the water, popped the tops off each, and while he sampled one, held the other out for my approval. Taking the brew bottle from his lips he wiped the drippings with the back of his hand, and congratulated me on the great taste of the stuff and laid down on the cool sandy bank to finish his drink.

Well, to make a long story short, by about five p.m. and after no food and consuming most of one case, neither of us could walk, and we certainly could not drive, so we had to do some serious fishing for about three hours; then rest for about two more until we sobered up enough to go home, arriving there at around midnight, so as to avoid Mom's wrath, and anyone else' s awareness. I don't know what happened to the rest of the brew we left in the creek, but I hope someone (stumbled on to and enjoyed it). I do know that was my one final experience with fermented juices for a long time.

I held this job with ole Tom for five years, working my way from dishwasher to waiter, then to fry cook before quitting to go to work at the Servall Food Market as a butcher's helper and food bagger. That ole' Greek, Tom Gavellas was a very good friend and taught me much, mostly how to survive on very little and work very hard for obtaining whatever you want. It's available if you want it bad enough.

The owner of a local market , food store and my next boss, was said by some local folks to be a mean progeny of a solitary queen in a deck, which consisted entirely of Jacks, and who had laid next to everyone of them, as her quest shuffled her blindly, but incessantly for that ever elusive king, but I found him to be a real mentor. He taught me many very valuable lessons from not trusting everyone to looking for excellence in all that you do. He showed me how to break down a side of beef, taught me the names of every cut of pork and beef and how to prepare them properly, both for sale to the public and for private dining. In addition, after I learned to run his meat market, the next year he moved me to produce and then to the groceries section. This knowledge has paid real dividends throughout all my years, especially since he was so demanding in the way he expected me to handle and maintain every item in the store (always placing the customer's rights and desires first)! He paid me really good, (35 cents per hour!) for 12 and 14 hour days when I was out of school, 6 hours on school days, and he was closed on Sunday, so I could attend church and deliver the Tulsa World to my customers.

At about this time, 1949, and during my Servall Grocery adventure with Crawford Norman, since I was free from my work there about 6:00 p.m. each evening, I took a second job.

The three movie theaters of which two, the State Theater that was located at the corner of Kihekah and Main, and the Kihekah that was located across the street one store front east, and south of the State, were still running films seven days a week. Each ran two matinees beginning at 1:00 p.m. and two main shows beginning at 6:30 pm for the State and 7 p.m. for the Kihekah. Both main showings ended, depending on the various lengths of the films, about 10:30 or 11:00 p.m., and this was when my second job began. I changed the show bills out front of each theater, this I did on Saturday night, Sunday night, Tuesday night and Thursday night just before each evenings production was over, so that the patrons coming out of the movie could know what would be presented as the next feature.

For these 15-20 minutes of my valuable time, the manager of each theater compensated me by allowing my free attendance at any and all showings. So for about three years, I saw every film that came to town, many of them more than once.

There were three theaters operating from time to time during the 1940's in the town of Pawhuska; the third one was known as the "Ritz" and was located across the street from the Pullman Café on Main street. This, as I remember was the two hundred block on the North side of Main, three doors East of the alley. The Kihekah theatre was one of the first grand theaters west of the Mississippi. In operation since the early 1800's, the original building was used as a hotel and was known as the Pawhuska House. It was purchased by a Mr. Byzantine in the late 1880s and was refurbished over the next three years, and then it was reopened as The Byzantine Theatre, one of the most highly regarded stages in the west. Although it fell into disrepair due to neglect by its owners in the 1960's, the city recognized its historical value and purchased the building after which the local high school shop class came to its rescue, restoring it to its original stature in the 1980's. This was done mostly with private funds, I understand. It is worth the trip to visit this fine old building. My family and the Red Red Wine Band performed in the newly renovated Kihekah in1996, which is now titled the Byzantine

Theater, to a standing room only crowd that treated us generously to a standing ovation and several curtain calls at the conclusion of our performance. The "Ritz" is presently a privately owned lounge, it served as the local Elks Lodge for some years after its closing as a theatre in the fifties, and the "State" was demolished in the sixties. Although the Kihekah continues to serve the community well, no films are presented there, as the equipment necessary for showing them was antiquated and so was removed.

Osage County, Oklahoma receives about forty to fifty inches of rainfall per year, and the sky is clear and blue most of the time. The tall Blue Stem prairie grass, native to this part of our beautiful nation waves like the farmers' planted wheat in the soft gentle breeze; and although temperatures can reach as high as 110 degrees in the shade on a hot summer day, it feels cool in the shade------(if you can find a tree).

Blue Stem is rich in protein, and cattle are shipped from as far away as Mexico to enjoy it before we enjoy them; therefore ranching is big time money and a solid parcel of the local economy. Thanks to the cattle and their need for water, which is limited naturally in this county, fishing is really great in the small lakes and ponds built to water their stock by the local ranchers. The local stock ponds hold many nice sized bass, and this fact provided my Dad and me with many wonderful hours of relaxation, however, not without some duress, as most ranchers did not allow fishing in them. The lack of water and wealth of rocky soil on this intemperate rolling high plain, somewhat interspersed with thick, short, and extremely hard to travel on horseback, blackjack timber was the reason the Osages had been forced to inherit this land from their white brothers in Washington D. C.

# The Wines are Made From Many Varieties

In the 1800's the U. S. Government forcibly moved the Osages from their rich fertile lands which contained many game animals in and around the Central and Northern Missouri area near the Missouri and Mississippi Rivers (the word Osage means people of the middle rivers) to their home in the north eastern portion of what was then Indian Territory and is now Osage County in the State of Oklahoma. The thinking by the leaders in Washington at the time of the Tribes' removal being that the fierce and proud tribe would be decimated by the harsh climate and lack of game, as the native bison (buffalo) were fast being slaughtered by the white hunters at the time for their hides, and other types of big game did not thrive in this very arid land.

The tables were turned in favor of the Osages and faces were red in Washington when in less than thirty years after this theft of the Indians' Missouri lands and their terrible and deadly mid-winter walk to Indian territory, huge oil and gas deposits were discovered below the surface of their newly acquired lands. The Osages owned the mineral rights, which their treaty expressly granted them, as the Government had explored the area and according to their exploration failed to find anything of value,. They were looking for gold or other precious metals and therefore; did not consider oil or gas when making the treaty.

The Tribe quickly became the wealthiest group of people in the world at that stage of history. Their sudden great wealth brought these proud, but barely surviving people, both the comforts that such riches can provide, and predators in the form of schemers and shysters, who provided them with plenty of alcohol, drugs, and ways to steal their money and lands. This was done to the extent of marrying, then murdering some of the Indian women for their head rights. (See **THE DEATH OF SYBEL BOULTON**) and **OIL MAN (the life of Frank Phillips) and The People of the Middle Waters, by John Joseph Matthews.**

I remember seeing many Osages in their braids with very colorful blankets wrapped proudly around their shoulders and riding in their Cadillac's and Lincolns with the man in the back seat his wife in the front, as was mostly the case.

When I was very young I had many good Osage friends, a fact of which I take great pride and I've even been fortunate enough to have some of their beautiful art work hanging in my home. I've been recently reminded I grew up in a segregated community with "Colored Town" in the south portion and the Indian Village in the northeastern part, each with its own grade school, a black high school, and the Indian children attended our white high school.

I remember the Osage guys, as always the best athletes at our school and very dependable, honest, and kind gentle people. They also had many customs that were a bit different from the rest of the community, one of which led to a very interesting situation, and concerned their method of burial and their attitude toward the departed persons.

I think this method was influenced by the fact that the ground gets so hard both in hot and cold weather one needs a jackhammer to move it. Due to this and since they want to protect the body from wild animals and buzzards it was common in years past to prop the deceased's body in a sitting position facing East, to greet the rising sun and cover it with a pile of sand stones, that are quite plentiful throughout the county. It was this method used by his friends to bury old John Stink back in the late 1930's that led to the rest of our story.

Stink fell ill with the " Pox"(Small Pox), the worst gift his European neighbors brought to North America, and second only to their indiscriminate senseless slaughter of the buffalo, which was the plains tribes life blood, but a necessary evil if one is going to have fences, cattle, and farms, which was the **only** mind-set of the last three or more thousand years of men in the land across the sea, and which these same men and women considered their just and (merciful) destiny, and a concept which was in direct conflict with the Plains Indians nomadic existence. However, those are stories, which would, and have, filled many and by some, ignored pages. After a short and miserable bout with the Pox, "Ole Stink " appeared to be dead and was pronounced as such by the local physician.

Believing him to be gone to the happy hunting ground, his friends and family followed the custom earlier described, as they piled their rocks on his body and said their goodbyes, and considered his earthly journey completed, however Stink was only in a deep coma and after three or four days, he awoke from it to discover himself in the burial mound. John, whose illness caused much fever and stomach problems and therefore created strong sweat and vomiting about his body, was buried with as little handling as possible due to his handlers fear of the disease. After two or three days on the hot Osage prairie, well, let's just say one did not want to be downwind of ole' John, who being a strong and quite husky fellow freed himself and walked the mile or so to downtown; where he promptly created quite a sensation, scaring the hell out of everyone: and subsequently, as he was now considered a spirit, no one not even his family, would have anything to do with him.

My family moved to Pawhuska shortly after John's episode, and "Ole Stink" which was not his name originally still lived in a house (by himself)! His home was located across the street from the Southwest corner of the Pawhuska Golf and Country Club. When I was a boy, my buddies and I delighted in hiding across the road to get a peek at the" Ole Spirit Man", sometimes waiting all morning for just one glimpse of him doing his outside chores.

As for my Osage friends, their agency grounds were my favorite place to spend an afternoon in a pick-up softball, baseball, or football game depending on the season of the year and what the big boys were currently into. I also enjoyed watching their wonderfully colorful dances at the pavilion in Indian Camp, which was a mile square area that had served these people and their ancestors as a true camping ground since the late 1800's and was located only a short quarter mile or so walk from my home on Thirteenth street. The Pow Wow was held annually in the fall and our whole community was welcome on "open dance nights" other times non-Osages needed an invitation by an Osage friend, as I remember it. They may have been welcome all evenings and my lovely mother decided that an outsider not being welcome was an easy excuse and a sure way of keeping her son at home.

One of my Osage buddies was named Billy Hill, and he lived across the street from the old Prudom School building on the corner of Thirteenth and the street that ran in front of the school. I can't remember the name of that street but, I can remember that on more than one occasion we had some serious rock fights, that is until he popped me with a really sharp one and split my forehead open just above my right eye. He would be proud of the mark it left as I still wear it today (bringing blood was a big thing with young boys and scars were somewhat of a trophy), but mothers did not view these episodes with quite the same indifference, so after that we held to hiking, fishing, and baseball ---- and a few cob fights!

On one of our hikes in which we had set out to find where the sun came up in the morning, we were about nine years old at the time, we took no water, or food, and it was in the middle of July; by noon the temperature was over one hundred degrees. Hot, miserably dry, and really hungry, we stumbled onto old Bacon Rinds' Monument on the highest point east of our valley. (What a find!) Finding this was like a cool drink of water on this sweltering summer day to our two adventurers. It is still there amid the tall waving bluestem on that beautiful windy hill with the many native sand rocks standing as though sentinels protecting the monument and grave east of the city.

Bacon Rind was the original chief of the Osages who moved to this area, and it was for him, that the city of Pawhuska was named. Pawhuska means White Hair, and he was much revered by everyone. The town is cradled below two large hills, one to the north and one to the west with a narrow northwest exit route extending between the two hills. A large creek forms the cities' south and east boundaries. Known as Bird Creek, this major tributary of the Verdigris River and the surrounding hills, which form the valley, were said to be good protection from the tornados, which haunt the Midwestern plains, and the major reason this site was originally selected for settlement by the Osages.

In 1940 a major twister did slam into the area just southeast of the city on the southeast side of the creek in an area known as Lynn Addition, it killed two people and maimed quite a few others including Lois Jean Millicent, one of my early baby sitters, who lost a leg in the storm that also destroyed about twenty structures, however as far as I know the city itself has never had a direct hit by such a storm.

About one mile southwest of the city, Bird Creek is joined by another fairly large creek known as Clear Creek, which for many years was the chief source of water for the city. Due to the many high hills in the immediate surrounding area, Bird Creek above the city divides into three large tributaries known as Upper, Middle, and Lower Bird Creeks. Until the late 1950's, at which time a large dam was built by the city below the confluence of these creeks, about eight miles north and west of town, Bird Creek was the source of much flooding in the valleys around and below Pawhuska. This dam resulted in a much-needed new water source for the city and rural areas and a beautiful lake named Bluestem, which has also become a welcomed recreational area. Interestingly since the main creek channel flows through the town, the dam allowed for flood control and convenience of the water without need of an expensive pipeline to the city's' water treatment facility. Pawhuska also had an auxiliary water source in its beautiful City Lake southwest of the city; it is spring fed, and is presently used as a back up water supply and is the only lake in this part of the state stocked with trout, making it a major fishing attraction to tourists and locals alike.

I was aware of another segment of our community during these early years. Their skin was much darker than my Osage friends, or mine, and they resided wholly on the south side of Bird Creek where they were considered separate but equal. I never really understood this separate, but equal business, especially since their equality appeared to qualify them for jobs as dishwashers in the cafes, or elevator operators at the banks, or shine boys at the hotels, but did not seem to extend to positions with higher wages or prestige.

My parents made sure I knew this practice was unjust, and my dad took me along when he did business in this part of town. He considered it important that I met and played with the children of his clients, making certain I observed the squalid conditions that were prevalent. There was no running water, only one hand-dug well for the whole community, and their unpainted clap-board shot-gun homes sat only a few short steps from the deeply rutted dirt road, each carefully fenced with hog wire that leaned lazily on its gnarled posts, which until recently had been dressed with oak leaves. Since there was no running water, each home had it's own drafty outhouse in the back yard, with spaces so wide between any two side boards; that you could throw a cat through them without causing it to hiss, while you took your personal relief. However, each of these necessary facilities was decorated nicely with a quarter moon cut ever so visibly in the middle of the hinged door just high enough so that any one sitting inside could see out.

When I was about 10 or 11 my dad took me even farther into this community when we attended the Booker T Washington High School basketball games together, and I begin to be aware that these boys and girls had the same wants and needs as I did. Their teams were really good, and to my surprise they had their own school. Until I attended those games, it never occurred to me that the Black Kids attended school, as there weren't any at Franklin. It also amazed me how welcome all the fans and teachers made Dad and me feel, two white faces in a sea of black.

This brings to mind a much earlier memory of another water well in another black community.

My Grandma B. was a very special person in my life, and to this day my brothers and sister contend she only had one grandchild. That is until our cousin, Claudia Ruth "Suzie" Staton of Caney, Kansas and presently of El Cerritos, California made her illustrious appearance in the family.

Susie, as she was then known; came on the scene when I was about six, and we all thought she was the cat's meow, and we continue to think so today. I dispute my sibling's contention as to my place in Grandma's pecking order of grandkids, but not too heartily, as I truly relished the special relationship we enjoyed. I spent many nights with her during the years while my family lived in Dewey, Oklahoma. The Berryhill home place was located about one and one half miles east of the Dewey Portland Cement Plant on the north side of the plant road. My grand parents' place covered about three acres and was a true Okie farm. Due to necessity, they grew about everything they had on the table, except for the wild game and fish, which were also daily fare. The family butchered two or three pigs each winter and a calf, the meat of which was either hung in a smoke house a few steps from the main residence or taken into a frozen locker plant to be processed, packaged, and stored. The hams, bacons, and salt pork portions were rubbed with salt, spices, and sugar then hung up in the smoke house; where they were slowly smoked and allowed to cure into the most delicious meats a boy ever tasted and making the smoke house off limits to all kids. The frozen portions (mostly beef) were brought to the home from the locker in town in small amounts that would fit into Grandma's ice box, a process that required daily replenishing of the ice purchased at the rate of fifty to seventy-five pounds daily, from the dock at the locker plant, where it was cut from three hundred pound blocks covered with an old quilt and carted home.

My job during the butchering was to scrape the hair off the pigs after they had been shot behind the ear with a 22-caliber rifle, eviscerated, and hung on gin poles where with the aid of a pulley system, they were raised, then lowered carefully three times, for about one minute each dunking into a fifty-five gallon drum of water, that was heated by a wood fire stoked below the drum. This aided the cleaning of dirt and blood from the carcass, which was then lowered onto an old barn door where my job began. It was hard, cold, and wet work for a three to five year old on a midwinter day but was expected and accomplished, with some help from the young women in the family. After scraping the hair off the carcass it was dissected into manageable sections to be smoked or cured or both, with some portions especially the skin cooked into lard, a process that resulted in a by- product called cracklings, a delicious sometimes tough, but always available and (plentiful) kids' snack. Although these cracklings were used in making biscuits, cornbread, and other such foods, they were mostly eaten by the ravenous handful, warm; right out of the oven where they had recently had the fat rendered from them.

The Berryhill farm was considered a dry land venture, which meant it did not have its own source of fresh water, neither creek nor well, a fact that leads me back to the other memory of the well I

33

mentioned earlier. This next adventure within my wonderful journey concerned my association with and love for my mother's youngest brother, Bud.

My uncle, Earl Buford (Bud) Berryhill, was still in high school during my very early years of three, four, and five; Bud was my idol, he was a fine athlete, playing all sports at the local high school; and he was also a real cowboy, sitting tall and straight in the saddle astride his big sorrel horse. He was truly impressive, as he would rope steers in our pasture, sometimes even letting me ride behind him while doing so. That made me feel very special as we galloped wildly with the wind whizzing around our head, and bumped up and down crazily on the back of that big horse, holding on with both arms tightly around Bud's waist, scared to death to look down at the ever approaching and receding ground and oh, so close to falling off. Bud was a special uncle, but also quite mischievous, and he loved to tease his nephew. A few lines back, I alluded to the fact that this was a dry farm and fresh water was unavailable unless it was acquired elsewhere. Well, it was Bud's job in the family to hook up the wagon to the huge team of workhorses and drive the mile and a quarter distance west to the Nigger Town well where we got our water. The only well available in this area was located in the local black community, which was a row of ten or twelve homes sitting like a wart on the prairie, bathed in a continuous flow of industrial cement dust from the adjoining plant property. These homes, some made entirely of concrete, reminded one of small mounds of dirt and they decorated a north – south lane jutting north off the cement plant road, where the well was centrally located for the convenience of the communitys occupants.

Bud would haul three, fifty-five gallon oil drums to this well on the wagon, fill them with water from the well and haul his precious cargo back to the farm, and would do so about every three days. Nigger Town, as by now you have guessed, was an all black community, whose men folks worked at the adjoining local cement plant. At this time in our illustrious history, whites and blacks were almost always living in separate communities. I really liked to tag along on these trips to the well, and Bud took advantage of my enthusiasm for his companionship, using it to get me to do most any chore he choose on the days of the trip.

Being aware that I was somewhat frightened of the black kids, Bud would tell me they were really a tough bunch, and I should know that they were going to catch me away from the wagon if possible and KICK MY BUTT!!! He further explained that these kids were so tough that they could break a two by four board with their bare fist; and after making sure that he had scared the livin' hell out of me, he would present me with a solid solution to this dilemma, solid that is as the board he gave me with which to practice. Bud had me hitting it with my fist until I could break the two by four, or until my fist became a sore and bloody mess; and therefore, I'd be able to hold my own with the kids at the well. I can still recall the pain in my fist as my Grandma caught me practicing for the trip on one cold winter day, and after becoming aware of Bud's tricks, read the riot act to him. He sheepishly lifted his protégé on to the wagon and quietly drove us to the well, where on this particularly cold and blusterous winter day the spray from the barrels being filled from the four-foot long metal bucket froze on our hands and faces.

Another chore of Uncle Bud's was to milk the cow before and

after school each day, again I loved to tag along and watch him; he delighted squirting the warm milk at me from his position on the milking stool; he was very accurate with it. During those years, I really enjoyed fishing in the pond, which was about three city blocks from the farmhouse. I'd take a roll of twine that I'd saved from the meat wrapping, a safety pin fashioned into a hook, and a medicine bottle cork, and then I'd go fishing. Uncle Bud's scraggly dog, "ole' Whiz-Bang, followed me, and we'd catch a rabbit which I would cut apart, saving the liver and heart for fish bait and feeding the rest of the carcass to "Ole Whiz". Then we would spend the day, fishing at the pond. I couldn't swim, but no one worried about this since Grandma told me never to step into the water and this was a time when kids did what their elders told them to do without question. After all, it was widely known that they did this for your best interests.

I learned this the hard way as when I was about two years old, Grandma was frying squirrel and had a skillet full of boiling lard. She told me to leave the room, but I pulled the skillet from the stove and onto the left side of my face and body. I still have the scars on my upper left bicep after 65 years. However, I tended to pay attention to her after this incident, and she only spanked me one time after that I can recall.

She spanked me after her neighbor Bud Brown picked me up in his pickup on the main road to the well, where I had walked as I looked for my pocket knife, which I was sure I had left on the hood of Grand Pa's car and that he had driven to work at the cement plant. While she was visiting with Mr. Brown about my running off, as she called it, I hid in a cornfield across the road from the house on this very hot summer day, and she called me many times trying to get me to come inside the house. When she finally became concerned as to my whereabouts and came into the field, I being a great deal shorter; could see her through the stalks, but she could not spot me. I quietly led her on a merry chase, her yelling, "Sonny, Sonny, where are you?" over and over in that very concerned high pitched voice which grew higher, as she fought her way though the stalks in the boiling sun and me in the shade of the stalks, until I finally felt sorry for her and capitulated. A real mistake on my part, as she warmed my backside really good for putting her through this ordeal.

# The Vines Begin to Separate

In March of 1941 on the twenty- first day, and again on the tenth day of August 1942, God saw fit to provide me with two of the best brothers a man could hope for. The older was Philip Warren Redwine, born to our wonderful mother Clarice in 1941, and the youngest of our family, James Marion, gasped his first full breath in 1943.

*Left to right; Adolphus Carroll Redwine and his four children, Carroll E (front) and James M., Delores J., and Phillip W. (back)*

Thanks to these guys, my life has been a really great ride. We grew up playing, fighting, learning with and loving each other as few other men could match, and I'm proud to say, this is still the case. Their lives have been full and very fruitful with beautiful, healthy, brilliant children and caring helpful mates. And best of all, they all show their love for and tolerate me.

My siblings and I had many wonderful days together, as I earlier explained and as memories return, I will try to set them to paper and pen. Today, after five days of contemplation, the thing I remember most is these guys tearin'up my toys! Or griping because they were allowed to sit in the hot sun all afternoon with nothing to drink and just a hunk of cheese that was divided among them and Dad with the same rusty knife that was used to cut up the fish bait. I really never understood why they didn't enjoy these fishing trips; Dad always swished the knife in the muddy pond or creek before he used it on the cheese! Maybe it was because the cheese laid out in the heat until the oil was running out of it, and its color was deep dried up orange. They should have appreciated this as a lesson taught each of them in self-deprivation. To this day, my own kids think I'm part camel, as I can go many hours, even days, without water, all due to my Dad and those fishing trips.

My fourth grade year, the school system hired a band director by the name of Max Devlin. Max was young, single and fun to study with, so remembering that my Dad used to play saxophone and that it was still in the hall closet, I asked my parents if I could use it in the grade school band which Max was starting. Being very naïve as to what this would require, and thinking Dad's old sax sufficient for this project, they both encouraged my indulgence. Little did they know what a real dog this horn was or the moral fiber of Director Max who just weeks after being hired by the school was accused of giving some young girls in Bartlesville a bottle of alcohol; an action that resulted in ending my fourth grade band project. It was probably just as well, because I could not get a sound out of the old horn anyway.

When the next fall rolled around, Pawhuska Schools hired George Brite to build them a band program. George was just the opposite of Max in every respect, all business, a no nonsense brilliant teacher who immediately set out to turn the school band program into a winner, and providing the kids with an outstanding musical learning experience, but even Mr. Brite couldn't get a decent sound out of the old sax. So it was sent to the Saied Music Co. in Tulsa for an overhaul. When it returned it still did not play very good, but at least Saied had removed most of the green fungus from it and I began my serious journey into the wonders of music. One morning during my 7th grade year, I walked to early morning band rehearsal arriving about 7:00 am at the school band complex. As I walked closer to the instrument storage room, which was separated from the rehearsal area by about ten feet of side walk, I noticed that all the kids were standing around crying and the storage room doors were off their hinges. When the other kids saw me coming, some ran out to meet me, and sobbingly they explained that during the previous night thieves had broken into the storage room and stolen all the instruments, all that is except mine; they had left the old sax lying in its open, battered, and tattered case for all to see, lonely as a drowning rat on the table and embarrassingly blocking the front door. Shortly after this episode, my parents who for some reason never mentioned Dad's ole sax again, presented me with a shiny new Martin alto sax. I heard later that Saied would not take the old horn in on a trade, which was probably true. I performed and practiced on this horn through my junior year in Pawhuska High School when C. G. Arnold replaced Mr. Brite in the summer of my junior year. C. G. was a fine clarinet and saxophone performer and suggested I use his wonderful Selmer sax, as it not only played better mechanically than the Martin, but also was much easier to tune through out the instruments register. I was really flattered that he would loan me his personal sax and enjoyed playing it immensely, and I continued to use it throughout that fall season until one fateful cold winter morning I made the stupid mistake of placing the case too close to the radiant heater in the rehearsal room where I was using the sax for an early morning sectional. Boy, does old leather stink when it's smoldering! And old men get mad when you screw up their beautiful horn cases.

Oh well, I still had the Martin and it was a good thing I did, because that was the last time I ever saw C. G. 's Selmer.

**WILL APPEAR IN CONCERT** — These former Bartlesville students will perform during an afternoon concert by the Oklahoma State University concert band March 12. They are from the left Marjo Hettick, Frank McKinney, Tom Claiborne, Carroll Redwine, former resident of the city; and Charles Lee, band president at OSU.

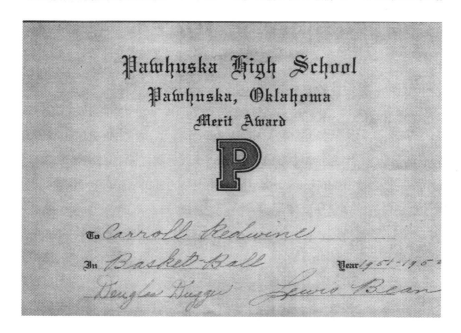

Pawhuska High School

Pawhuska, Oklahoma

Merit Award

**P**

To *Carroll Redwine*

In *Basket Ball*     Year *1951-1952*

*Douglas Bugg*     *Lewis Bean*

41

I entered Oklahoma State University in the fall of "54" and played the Martin in the OSU Bands and Orchestra through fall of "55". . In the spring of "56" Stanley Green, the OSU woodwind instructor and my private teacher, had the university purchase a new model Conn Sax, which he offered me to use in the University bands, as he thought it was better in tune than the Martin in their high register. I disagreed with this assessment of the problem, and my position was that my embouchure was incorrect, which caused me to bite too hard and therefore to play sharp most of the time. I know now that I was right; it was me and not the horn, although, the horn did cause a bit of the problem. I corrected this problem while playing with the U S ARMY FIELD BAND of Washington D.C. and using the army's' Mark VI Selmer instrument. I played the Martin Alto for twenty years after leaving the Field Band and while I gypsied around teaching high school Bands in Oklahoma and Texas. In 1973 while teaching at and managing the Seminole Junior College Music Department, I acquired my present Selmer Mark 7 alto, which I've used in many hours of performance over the last thirty years.

My 7th and 8th grade years were spent at the junior high side of Pawhuska High School. Aside from playing in the high school band, which was really fun and participating in all available school athletic teams, my claim to fame as I remember these years was when I got my butt busted for shooting the 8th grade history teacher with a paper wad propelled from a large rubber band. It was an accident, but I could not prove it; the kind lady had left the room to speak to the principal, and she reentered earlier than expected, just as I was trying to splatter a real juicy wad in the hair of a guy sitting on the front row by the classroom door. Oops! I could not stop the rubber band; it was in motion even as she turned to come in. She really got even though, as I received three licks from the principal for my indiscretion and many more at home when Mom and Dad heard about it. It was my one and only spanking received at school for disciplinary reasons other than fighting with Earl Cook, although I probably deserved many others.

The summers between these years were real hell for me. I spent my 7th grade summer lying on my stomach, naked in bed due to sitting down in a patch of poison ivy while fishing off a sandy bank of Rock Creek north of town. I did not know what the plant looked like, and it really inflamed my back, buttocks, and legs. The lesions were so bad that I lost a layer of skin from my whole backside plus spent a very miserable summer ruining Mom's sheets. My first agenda after getting where I could walk again was to learn what the damned plant looked like and be able to forever avoid it. My 8th grade year was even worse, as in May just after school had turned out for the summer, I was playing a tennis match with a good friend named Jack Heflin; when I discovered my left jaw was quite sore. It never occurred to me I might have the Mumps, so I continued to play tennis for about four hours; man was that a mistake. Adolescence, exercise and the Mumps are a real dangerous mix, and add in encephalitis, which at that time was a 99 to 1 chance of survival and there went another summer.

I was unconscious for four weeks, during which time my mother later told me I had fevers as high as 107degrees and continuous fever of some type for at least 21 days. However, this was not my entire dilemma, as during these horrendous problems my doctors also diagnosed a case of Pancreitus that further complicated them. When the fever broke, and I regained consciousness, I could have only sugar to eat. This meant a strict diet of candy and sodas with water, for the rest of the summer. To some this might sound great, but let me assure you after about three days with not even any nuts in the candy, a person gets mighty hungry for a piece of meat and a piece of bread, and the latter disease resulted in eventual Hypoglycemia and an immediate need to learn to walk again, as when I tried to take my first step from being in bed all summer, I fell flat on my face in the floor. The doctor had warned me about this, but I did not believe him until it happened.

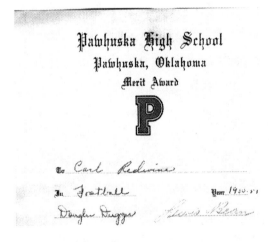

As a result of these two hellacious summers, I remember dreading the end of my freshman spring, as I was certain the summer held something very special for me. Before these past two summers I had a great memory; however; afterward I truly could not remember much and have had serious problems concentrating on memory- related subjects ever since. As I made efforts to improve my memory, I read the complete set of **Hardy Boys** mysteries, along with many other books during the two years following these trying summers. Studying music was really a help as it required diligence in both memory and eye hand coordination.

Those close to me will probably accept these past explanations as my excuse for a lazy mental attitude, and they will be accurate to a degree. I credit my physical recovery from this very serious situation to much

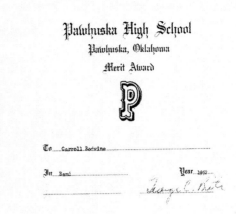

prayer by many family friends and my parents, relatives and the local clerics, as the medical community was flatly astonished by it. More memories of these years may come to me at a later date, if so I will try to include them.

I do remember winters of both years as great times, sledding down Flanagan Hill with my buddies from the top, which is eleventh street all the way past the First Christian Church, and one more block to 7th street. We always built a bonfire just off the southeast side of this hill in what was then an open lot at the corner of 10th and Flanagan Hill. It was a hard walk pulling the sled to the top, but it was a great ride back down.

My sister, Delores Jane Redwine Bartlett was eighteen months younger than me; she was born on July 23, 1937. Being older than someone does not necessarily ensure one of higher rank. This fact was never more obvious to me than when I would try to force Janie to do family chores, which our parents had specifically assigned, to the eldest son. My brothers learned very early on that "Janie" not Sonny, was in charge and nothing has changed that family tradition.

When we boys need a wise family decision, it is "sister" Jane we ring up. She is, and always has been, a wonderfully kind, considerate, extremely generous lady, who faces adversity head on, peering wisely beyond the immediate situation for a long term solution which is best, not necessarily for herself but for all persons involved.

If our parents had a favorite child, it was our sister due to the fact, she was not only the only girl child but was usually the one who completed her family tasks and who Mom depended on to get us boys to do ours. Her stories would fill many interesting volumes, and maybe she will see fit to put them on paper; I hope so. However, I will digress a little from my story to state just a bit about her. Jane, who was the picture of health, had hair of light spun gold that hung in long soft curls which framed an always smiling, endearing round

*Left to right; Phillip W Redwine, D. Janie Bartlett (Bud`s `mother), Carroll E. Redwine, Clarice Iva (our mother), and James M. Redwine. Picture taken outside Jane's home on day after Buddy's death*

face that held those large warm, sky- blue eyes inherited from her father, an adequate nose that was not too prominent, set above a lovely dimpled mouth and a very determined chin, all this mounted on a strong, but softly appealing body that as a young girl had all the right curves in all the right places. She was a very good student, has always made friends easily, due to both her outgoing personality and kindly disposition, played clarinet in the High School Band and graduated from High School in the top of her class. She married young, just after graduation, to Bruce Bartlett, who was at that time jumping out of airplanes for Uncle Sam and was stationed in North Carolina with the 82nd Airborne. So, sadly, our family wished her well, as she became a resident of the military establishment with her new husband. They soon had a little child, "Our Buddy," who quickly

*My mother, Clarice, me, and Daddy1954*

became my mother's first and most beloved grandson. She thought there was never a child quite like Buddy, and so we all did, as he was a very bright, talented young man who made friends quickly and loved the outdoors as few people do. When Buddy was taken from our family in a horrendous car accident, it caused a void never filled; his memorial is in the Richmond, Missouri cemetery and his mother and father regularly visit it to remember his life with flowers and many hours of attention to his memorial site.

Jane and Bruce had two additional children younger than Buddy, a beautiful daughter, Melanie, who along with her husband, John Gill, has provided them with two wonderful grandchildren and me with a delightful grandniece and nephew; whom, although I rarely get to see them, due to the distance between our residences, I love very much. John and Melanie are highly respected businesspersons each owning

*<< Sons of Phillip W. and Sarah Redwine left to right: Phillip, Frederick, and Ryan Redwine*

*<<James David Redwine at age eight and ten only son of James Marion Redwine*

their own businesses. Bruce Loren Bartlett, Jane and Bruce's younger son is one of my favorite people; he also is a highly respected and very gifted Nuclear Engineer with the Government's Nuclear Regulatory Commission. Bruce Loren is currently married to a lovely lady by the name of Donna, whom he met while working in the Chicago area. They have a great life together and are quite busy as Donna has two children from an earlier marriage and two delightful grandchildren. Bruce Loren's first marriage to a high school sweetheart produced no children and ended in divorce.

Jane has not only a brilliant mind, but a tenacious attitude, a facet she exhibited throughout her life and especially when she drove from Richmond to Warrensburg, Missouri daily for 4 ½ years and studied for a Bachelor and Master's degree in English and counseling, all the while keeping her family in good stead. She has used this knowledge well, teaching at the college level for many years, serving on many boards and generously helping many young people to obtain their education, sometimes taking them into her home. She and Bruce provided them with food and shelter along with much compassion and understanding while encouraging them in every manner to build a better life. Jane and her family are blazing stars and beacons of brilliant light for all with whom they come into contact, a lighthouse that has and still is keeping many from the rocks of life's tossing waves.

After my father died in February 1964, my mother was very despondent; hoping to ease her pain, Jane called her every morning at 7;00 a.m. until Mother's death 29 years later. They had a great relationship. So if you want to know the real story about most anything in our family, **contact Janie.** (I'm sure a good bean story will come from this segment later.)

My brother, Philip Warren Redwine, made his family debut on March 21, 1942. Phil always was, and to this day remains, a kind and considerate gentleman, who as a child was jovial and really fun to play with, a facet of his that I observed brought him many friends. However, never mistake him for one easily swayed, he has always had that determined "Redwine" jaw and is the most tenacious yet patient of adversaries. Although he always tries to see the other's position, you don't want him against you, as he just never gives in; and with a wonderful intellect along with his persistent attitude; he is a formidable force to face on any issue. We had many wonderful days while growing up, playing and learning to play baseball, which we Redwines consider our game. At least we did in our younger years. Phil and his boys are fine athletes and enjoy golf

One story I would share with you about golf, Phil and myself;

took place quite a few years back during Phil's sophomore year in Pawhuska High School and on one of my furloughs from military service. Philip was anxious to show his big brother, who was touring the world as a performing musician, that he also was very accomplished in a different area. He had worked really hard for about two years, selling shoes every Saturday at the J.C.Penny store. He had diligently saved his salary during that long many Saturdays and proudly showed the author his new golf clubs, which he had used on his Sunday afternoons to learn the game. He asked if I would like to go up to the Pawhuska Golf and Country club where our parents had a membership and play a round of golf. Naively, I thought I could just pick up those beautiful clubs and play, so I quickly agreed. We got to the first hole about noon and no one was in front of us, so Philip kindly tried to explain how I should position body, club, and ball to drive the green. I listened, not very intently, as he showed me how to use his nine iron and then generously handed me the club to hit my first golf ball. I stepped up to the ball, with all of the confidence of one who knows everything about everything and promptly struck the ball 154 yards to a hole in one, thinking, Boy what an easy game. I have this situation under control. I began rubbing in the fact Phil took a 4 on this par 3. I stepped up to the second tee box and asked Phil for his only wood. A reluctant look came across his face, but his generous nature and love for his older brother got the better of his good sense, and grinning he handed me his wood. I addressed the ball on the tee, realized this was a par 4 and a much longer drive to hole #2, so I really put some effort into my swing. About three-fourths of the way through it, I felt a real thud. Mother earth separated the woodenhead from the graphite shaft of Phil's club; the ball never moved, but the head of the club flew about 20 yards in front of the tee. Sheepishly, I handed the broken shaft to Phil, who at first had this incredible look of disbelief, which slowly dawned into a look of real frustration. It was some years later before I realized the gravity of my actions. The reality of the cost involved came to me when I went to buy a set of clubs for my youngest daughter, Tonya, who as a High School team golfer at Seminole won the Oklahoma women's 3A State Golf Tournament Championship in 1981-82.

The reader should be made aware that Mom and Dad were God fearing people who came from a long line of family with similar background, so it is easy to understand both of them wishing that at least one of their sons would go into the Christian ministry. It became obvious early on by my many transgressions before finishing my high school graduation that yours truly was not the peg for that hole; and therefore, Dad began working on brother Phil at an early age to take up that cross. Phil tried hard to please Pop, even to the point of spending his college freshman year at Phillips University, but Phil knew this was not his true calling even though his faith was quite strong. So after visiting with Dad, he transferred to Okie State his sophomore year and changed his major to premed. At OSU he met Sarah Redwine from Spiro, Oklahoma and eventually they married in June of 1964, both worked hard over the next few years, obtaining Phil's law degree from OU, that little school in Norman that claims to have a football team.

Phil and Sarah have three sons: Phil Jr. who is married to Dedra, and together they have two lovely daughters named Haley and Brook; and one son Philip the third. Fredrick, who along with Phil Jr. has a law degree and is currently working in Nashville, Tennessee and

Ryan who together with his wife and their two sons Bryson and Tillman recently completed his studies for the Baptist Ministry at the seminary in Ft. Worth and has accepted a church position in Reno, Nevada. Both Ryan and Stacy have undergrad degrees, which they recently completed. Dad finally got his full time minister, and "boy" would he have been proud, no one in the family could be, or is better suited for the job.

As with my short biography of my siblings, this extremely short description of their families in no way begins to cover their tremendously wide and varied accomplishments, but in some short manner does alert the reader to their names and the relationship of them to me, and I hope any one reading this will encourage my siblings to eventually put keyboard to paper and expand on their particular stories, as each is completing a magnificent journey.

Our baby brother, James Marion Redwine was born August 10th, 1943 and has resided in the Evansville, Indiana area since receiving his undergrad and law degrees from Indiana University at Bloomington. He has practiced law in that area for some years and is currently serving his fourth term as Posey County Judge, an elected position for which he must be doing something right, as he has not drawn an opponent in the past two elections. An avid golfer, he gets his best tips from me. Jim, as he is known to the family has one son from his first marriage, James David; although, we all know him as jimmy is a lieutenant colonel in the regular army of the US of A, is a West Point graduate and has successfully completed every strenuous school our army has to offer. In so doing; he has had a meritorious and consistent advancement though the Army's officer corp. All this while married to his beautiful and talented high school sweetheart

Gina. Together they have given the Judge two fine grandchildren, Nicholas a grandson and one year old granddaughter Elyse. His honor is currently married to a vibrant witty and kind lady, Margaret Dunn, who is well suited to our lil' bro. Peg and Jim spend many hours skiing and hunting golf balls, which, when they find the dirty little critters, they promptly bash again with their expensive clubs. Best of all, these two are regulars at our family functions even though logistics sometimes make this difficult.

Jim and Phil, my younger brothers; and I spent many wonderful hours together as young boys. Our favorite games were always involved with a baseball, either hitting fielding or throwing and catching or just playing a pick up game with our buddies and generally learning the fine points of the game.

I was on a performing tour during Phil's' senior year but fortunate to be living in Pawhuska during Jim's. Jim sang in the First Christian Church choir which I directed that year, and he religiously took my three year old daughter to Sunday School every Sunday, a task that later I will have more to say about, and he played outstanding football and baseball on some of the local schools historically best squads.

The Husky Football team was amazing that year and won each of their first seven games of the season, coming from behind to win with less than five minutes left to play in every one. A couple were real nail biters with the home team winning in the last thirty to ninety seconds of regulation. However, it was the eighth game of the season that will stay in my head always for it was very special. Pawhuska had entered the season ranked low in the league by the Tulsa World and other state pollsters; but due to their many last minute heroics was by the eighth week of the season in the top ten behind number three, Claremore's' Zebras. Claremore, a bedroom community of Tulsa, was considered a shoo-in for the district championship. The Zebras had a tandem of guards up front, both rated as college division one blue chippers and supposedly the four fastest backs in the area. Claremore was considered by most pollsters and many folks in the state to be an excellent prospect for the 3A State championship. They were bigger, faster, and more experienced than the Huskies, and according to articles in the area papers, certain to break the fantastic string of luck Pawhuska was experiencing. This line of thinking was so prevalent that on the day of the game, which would be played in Pawhuska, the visitors were ranked as eighteen point favorites with talk of how good the Zebras were and how they could possibly be our first loss of the season buzzing all over town. It was a wonder we needed to play the game; however, someone forgot to tell the Huskies team, and they worked really hard all week on a special plan to defeat this fine team. On the practice field and in the classrooms, the school kids and especially the football team was daily gaining more confidence; it appeared a gigantic upset was in the making, but it only appeared so to the locals.

Friday, game day, dawned as a beautiful Indian summer day should, with a lazy blue haze covering the fields and mixing gingerly with the sparsely dressed trees still displaying their brilliant gold's, reds, and browns of late autumn with not a menacing cloud in sight. The sporting Gods were with us; Claremore's' size advantage would not be aided by a wet field, and the beautiful weather held throughout the day and evening which was cool and therefore an aid to our fewer numbers of personnel. For the first time this season, the weekly pep rally was held, not in the school auditorium, but downtown on

Kihekah at the north end of the triangle building. The high school band gathered closely around the monument dedicated to what was the first Boy Scout Troop in North America, which we are told, was organized in Pawhuska. Then the cheerleaders began performing noisily, facing northward up Kihekah in front of the band. When the team showed up about twenty minutes later, pandemonium rained, and the nearly five hundred kids and town's people came together in a rousing chorus of Illinois Loyalty, the traditional Huskies' fight song

After the crowd heard from the teams leaders, Jim included and the girls and coaches led a few more cheers, the team, obviously in great readiness for tonight's' battle headed out for their evening meal and other game preparations. As a graduate of Pawhuska High School, I'd been to a number of pep rallies, but I must say that one "Took The Cake".

The stands began filling up early; most folks couldn't find a seat after 7:00 pm for the game that was scheduled for 8 :00, and fans were standing three and four persons deep in some areas behind the protective fence around the playing field. The atmosphere was electrified with the expectations of both teams and their followers, but the Huskies must have received the greater charge as they received the opening kick-off and scored in three plays. Then after kicking to the zebras who made a first and ten on their first series of downs but bogged down after two additional running plays and a mishandled snap, the home team scored twice more on two long drives before half time. However unlike past weeks when field goals and extra points had been automatic and in some cases the difference in the winning ways of the Huskies, the team failed to score any of the extra points after these three scores due to either missed kicks or mishandled snaps from the center to the holder; and Claremore, who had entered the game an eighteen point favorite, found themselves eighteen points behind at the break.

Although elated with the present score, no Huskies fan or player felt secure, as Ole Claremore with its vaulted offense and superior experience throughout the team could still claim a victory, and we all were well aware of the possibility of such an ending to this magnificent beginning.

The second half began with the Zebras on offense; it was their third down and about three yards to go for a first and ten. The stands were hushed as they came out of the huddle and quieter still as the players lined up; the ball was centered to the Zebra quarter back, as those giant guards looming ever so huge over our light line pulled to lead the backs around the left end of the Huskie line. The visitors' quarterback faked a lateral to his right halfback and tossed the ball left to his other halfback, but to his utter amazement his omnipresent offensive guard had missed his block on the quick and crafty Huskies line backer who took the ball out of the air and even though he was the slowest man of the eleven home team players flying around with such reckless abandonment, he raced the thirty-five yards to pay dirt with the Claremore QB and one of the Zebras linemen hanging on him as he crossed the goal line. That crafty linebacker broke those Zebras spirit and the game wide open with that one big play and the final score was 36 to 0 in favor of the locals. That linebacker was my lil brother Jimmy, now his honor, The Judge.

However, not all situations went this well for my mischievous sibling who was fond of teaching his young, three old niece, Carla, my oldest daughter certain bawdy songs; which he delighted in her reciting at the family dinner table, sometimes and usually to the embarrassment of her parents. Being a proud and concerned uncle, he also took her to Sunday school and church every Sunday morning where he sang in the choir and her father was the church choir director, and the whole family participated in the service or regularly attended as members of the congregation.

On one such Sunday morning as he was in the ministers' receiving line with Carla beside him, waiting to shake hands with the preacher, Carla presented Jim and all the morning worshipers with a really fine rendition of his newest teachings, when as she shook the ministers hand,she asked him if he would like to hear her new song, and the preacher replied obligingly to the young girl," Yes". Jimmy was not concerned because for the past week he had spent considerable time teaching his protégé **"Jesus Loves Me"**, and was puffed up like a toad with this opportunity to showcase his efforts. Standing a bit back to allow all to hear, a big smile came on his face as he prepared to be serenaded with what he was sure would be Carla's' big debut. However, Carla had a different agenda and with God, the minister, and half the church members eagerly listening she gave out with a rousing rendition of "**Little Egypt**", with lyrics as some of which are: Little Egypt came a struttin' --- wearing nuttin' but a button and a bow ---with a diamond big as Texas on her toe! Etc—Etc ---Etc. That little episode ended my young daughter's career with her uncle as agent and song mentor. However it only made their relationship stronger, as I believe that secretly both she and Jim were proud of their little fiasco. The Judge is an accomplished writer and will probably take exception to my many transgressions on the Queen's

English, but for the most part he cannot deny the content.

While I was home for the summer between my freshmen and sophomore years at OSU, I worked as a swamper on a jinn truck for a local truck line moving oilrigs. This job allowed me to have time to coach the local American Legion baseball team and so I convinced the local chapter of American Legion to be a sponsor by purchasing uniforms and equipment. Jim, or Jimmy as we called our younger brother at that time, was about eight years old and quite young to be playing with the teams that I coached or with which these teams competed. However, he was really quite capable and the older kids, some as old as sixteen, respected his ability to play baseball, though he was small, many times when we were short on players or ahead in a game, he found himself in the lineup. It was just such a situation that resulted in this next story.

I scheduled a game with what was presented by phone to me, a junior American legion team in Sedan Kansas. Our oldest player was about sixteen, so when we arrived at the ball field and their players were seen driving up in their own vehicles, sporting mustaches and some with partial beards, and standing eight to ten inches taller than our guys, I tried to back out of playing the game, as I did not want to get any of our kids injured. The Sedan coach would not hear of us not playing, as he smelled a sure and sweet victory over the larger town in Oklahoma. I finally caved in to his argument for continuing the contest, deciding that since we had driven such a long distance to get to Sedan, we might as well use the time for a good practice; but I did not inform our team of how I felt, and they were naively looking forward to another victory. I always knew these kids were pretty talented, but I had no idea just how well they could play until that day. We played seven innings and those giants never got a whiff of a hit. Our little pitchers kept them off balance the whole game; and in addition, our guys batted around the very first inning and were sixteen runs ahead by the seventh inning. Jimmy began working on me to let him play early in the game, but I was really scared to put him into the fray against those much older and bigger fellows. However, by the fifth inning, he was really getting hot under the collar with my attitude, and when he thought I was not going to play him and time was fast running out for me to do so, he got serious about putting the heat on me to put him into the game. By this time I got tired of his bellyaching and jawing at me. So, with two out in the bottom of the seventh inning, I figured I could manage to keep him from getting hurt for the remaining out and this would keep him from yelling at me as we rode in the car all the way back to Pawhuska. I moved Philip from third base to the outfield, took out the right fielder and put Jimmy on third base where I figured he'd be safe, as no one had hit the ball very hard to this side previously due to our pitching and their lack of hitting. Boy, did I miscalculate as one of Sedan's biggest and oldest players was up to bat; and before I could call time to get Jimmy out of harm's way, this guy swung at the first pitch, as though he wanted to make up for all their team's grief in one brief swing.

He made contact with the ball, which became a head high screaming line drive right at my little brother's head. Jimmy instinctively snapped his glove hand up to protect himself and THUD! That blue darter stuck in his glove, lifting both the little guy's feet out from under him with such force that he came down to rest unceremoniously on the third base bag, his bottom squarely on the bag and his legs pointed straight toward home plate, but still holding the glove and its possession of the ball in the same upright position as he had caught it, years later his body position still reminds me of a stop traffic sign,. A great sigh of relief came from the field as we saw Jim was not killed by that monstrous hit, then a roar of approval as we all also realized he had tendered the games final third out.

# Some Sour Grapes

As I said earlier, working at the trucking company generated my income for this summer and what a summer it was. I was nearly killed twice while working with these truckers who were extremely careless pursuing their dangerous livelihood during this very hot dry season. The summer was going pretty good and I was getting along well with most of these good ole boys, when on one particular day I was assigned to a fairly new and inexperienced driver with whom I had had no previous assignments. We were sent by the dispatcher to the local pipe yard about noon one beautiful June day to pick up six drill stems. For those who do not know what oil field drill stems are, they are usually thirty feet long, weigh sixteen pounds to the square inch, and are solid steel with a collar on one end and the other end ringed to allow for the drill bit to be attached. To make this short, let's just say they weigh about 3500 lbs each and are really dangerous to maneuver, especially for an inexperienced person. When we arrived at the pipe yard, I jumped out of the tandem truck as I was supposed to do and went inside to find out where the load was located in the yard, but it was lunch- time. All the men at the yard were on lunch break, so I reported back to the young driver; this I had been taught to do by my former drivers as they made all final decisions, when we were on site. Surprisingly, my driver said not to worry he had located the drill stems in the pipe yard and was going to load them without any further help, as he was in a hurry to complete this assignment and call the dispatcher for another job, as we got paid by the task each day. I assured him there was no hurry as I had heard our dispatcher state she was not going to send any more work our way until she had covered the other guys in our company first. This appeared to anger the young fellow, and he took it as an affront to his authority by me, so I kept quiet as he positioned the flat bed beside what was obviously six drill stems in the yard. I again jumped out of the truck, went back to where the overhead wench was located, then dragged it by its long, loose-hanging chain to the middle of the drill stems. The wench had a smaller chain attached, which was used to wrap pipes then go through a D ring and attach the whole bundle to the overhead wench. This then allowed a person to lift the load to the height of the truck bed and standing on the ground, push the load into position on the truck bed. When the frustrated driver, who was watching in his rear view mirror, saw me loading only one at a time, he jumped out of the truck and hurriedly pushed me out of the way, grabbed the wrap chain, put it with some authority around all six stems; then standing up with disgust motioned for me to pull the load to the height of the truck bed. I looked him in the eye and knowing I was probably going to get my butt fired if his idea worked, but also knowing I would be dead if it did not said, " I'm going to step over here behind this 20 inch pipe that holds up the rail for the wench. If you are going to load all that at one time you'll have to do it. Now he was really pissed, so he started raising the six stems. Getting them level and a bit higher than the truck bed he began pushing them toward the truck, when suddenly the D ring gave way and the whole load came down on him. He was a mass of blood and guts with some of the stems resting below and some above on his body. Although I tried later and couldn't do it, I immediately lifted the top stem off of him and managed to pull his gasping dying frame from the mess and placed it on an old door which was lying about twenty feet away.

As I did so, two of the workers at the yard who had been eating near by and viewed the whole scene came to help, but it was too late. The driver, who had a large family of a wife and six children, died right there. What a nightmare, and it could have been prevented by simply not being in such haste to move those drill stems, and it would have been me if I had not refused to load those stems in that manner or had not stood my ground with the driver.

The above accident happened on a Thursday, the drivers family had his funeral on Saturday and I was back at work at the trucking firm on the following Monday when the Tandem driver I normally worked with came to me and said we had been assigned a job helping to move a rig located over by Grayhorse, which was about twenty miles from the office and shop where we were standing. I gathered up a five-gallon ice and water jug and my lunch which I knew, if things went as they usually did, the old devil I worked with would probably steal and eat before I could have time to enjoy, and he did. However, that would turn out to be the least of my problems in today's turn of events. When we arrived at the work site, my driver told me we were scheduled to first help tear down the A frame of the rig which we were only going to move about 1000 yards to where it was easy to see the new dirt pad that had been freshly prepared. I hopped down from the high seat of the tandem I usually worked on when moving such equipment. and went over to the jinn pole truck. Its driver was the son of the fellow I had ridden with to this location, and the guy I usually teamed with on most jobs. He told me to go climb the A frame, attach a line from our truck on one leg of it, and pull the pins out so that we could let it down. This was a very dangerous job, and I was just starting to climb up the stairs toward the main floor when the master driller let out a line of cuss words that any sailor would have been proud to utter. I looked over in the drillers' direction and noticed blood spewing everywhere from his hand; he had caught it between the cable and drill stem, and it had snapped his fingers off. Knowing he had help on deck from his deck hands, I continued to climb up on top to complete my assignment as instructed by my driver as I was really scarred by now and wanted to get this job completed. After the drilling crew got the injured Driller into a car and headed for the hospital in Pawhuska, they helped me get the A frame down, and my driver sent me to work as a swamper on his Dads tandem. I really didn't want to work with the old man, as he was very hard to work for or with and very careless; but since there was no one else to do it, I kept my mouth shut and obediently set out to help him move the 20 ton water pump to the new location.

After he had positioned the tandem about ten feet in front of the huge piece of equipment, I unrolled the cable from the wench on the truck and carefully tied it to the water pump with a Y, making it possible to lift the pump on to the tandem. Just as I was about to signal the old driver to load the pump, his son yelled for me to tie the jinn truck onto a small piece of the rig, so I left the old man's truck to do this. When I returned the old driver had already loaded the water pump by himself and motioned me to get in the truck with him, so that we could move the water pump to the new location. What he did not tell me was that he had used a six-foot cheater pipe to tighten the come along holding the lines together; and when he sent me underneath the truck to loosen it, the come along handle whacked me in the head so hard it knocked me out. Just what the old fellow expected; I'm sure. Not waiting to see where I was, he began to lower the water pump, which would have surely crushed me into a bloody mess had not his son seen the whole episode and ran to stop him just as he got about one inch from my head with the equipment. The guys on the rig rushed me to the hospital; and after one nights stay, I was back at work. These two instances made me pretty skittish though, and I was determined to get even and then get the hell out of that job, and I had just the plan to do so. If it worked; if not, I would really be up that well known tributary, without a visible means of escape!

The workers at the trucking business all had a revolving poker game which passed the time for them while they waited for an assignment from the company dispatcher, and I knew the old man would be playing in the game, as it was raining and he did not like to work in the rain. So I quietly sat down in the game; and after a few hands in which I had been really lucky, I bet on a real poor hand and ran a very convincing bluff, which I won. I made sure the guys behind me watching my hand were aware of just how much of a bluff it was, and a few hands later my chance came to nail the old man, and I was ready to take the risk. I drew four diamonds and the ace of hearts, keeping the ace upside down and in the middle of my diamonds so as to appear to have a pat hand flush, as by now I had most of the other guy's pay checks on my side of the table, those that were not in the pot. As a result, the old man figured to recoup all his loses in one hand and betting everything he had and even going into his pocket he called that pat hand. With a great deal of bravado I quickly, but carefully laid down my flush hand, making certain the outside cards protected the ace of hearts. After showing the hand, I then gently pushed every card into the large pile of spent deck that was on the table for all to see. Knowing I had better get the hell out of there before those Bubbas decided to take their money back, I calmly gathered all the money from the table and walked out to my old car, promptly leaving that job and those fellows to discuss how an 18 year old could be so lucky. Fortunately, the ace of diamonds had never been dealt or I would have been in deep dodo!

# The Grapes Begin to Ripen

There were a number of peculiar circumstances that had long lasting, although various degrees of character influencing effect on my personality, During the three years from 1950 to 1953, which when I try to recall, make me somewhat unhappy and somewhat thankful for their trials and heartbreak. Although they were really quite hard to contend with at the time, they truly formulated a better life for me in future years.

As earlier written, Crawford Norman was a demanding employer, but his demands were for the most part necessary for his employee's safety, or for his customer's welfare. He had many rules, which once imparted by him to an employee, he expected to be rigidly enforced by all affected. In his butcher shop, one such rule was to never leave a knife on the butcher block, and after using a knife it must be immediately returned to the holder along side the block. Such rules were followed with such rapidity as to be automatic for the employees, and therefore the following accident that occurred about two weeks before I was to leave for my first music camp at Gunnison Colorado, was a real shocker and one that my left hand still carries a reminder in today.

Bill Crawford, the head butcher; and I were very busy on this particular morning. In addition to preparing the meat case for the day's business, which was a very demanding job, we had customers lined up about five deep waiting to order their cuts of meat. One of these ladies was a very particular customer whom no matter what we prepared for her would always manage to find something wrong with it. Mr. Norman cow towed to her like she was the queen of

Sheba, probably due to the fact she purchased expensive cuts from him, so we made every effort to please her in spite of her insolent and overbearing attitude. This lady was third in line, so by the time we wrapped the orders of the folks in front of her she was obviously heated, and very impatient. Bill was a bit frustrated by her impatience, but was making small talk with her and trying to mellow her attitude, personally I was keeping my mouth shut, and working as fast as I could to get the woman out of the store before she managed to get my butt in trouble. As usual she ordered a cut of meat that we did not have prepared, and which would require breaking down a beef front quarter to wrap for her. As I mentioned, we were very busy and with the customers standing and watching every move we made, like gawkkers at a ten car pile-up, not only did we have to be careful to clean every item and equipment as we cut and wrapped each order, but we also had to keep the cheeses and fresh meats separated in a pleasing manner. Simultaneously, as she ordered her shoulder roast, Bill was cutting a moon of longhorn cheese from a new ten pound round. He cut it with one of our largest knives, and I finished wrapping some pork chops and placed them on the counter top telling my customer thanks for his order. Bill without looking up, as that was the number one rule when using a knife, told me to go get the front quarter out of the cooler so he could cut this ladies roast. Seeing he was wrapping the cheese, and knowing I'd need room on the block to place the front quarter, I hurriedly placed my left hand under the remaining big round of cheese intending to place it in the cooler as I went to get the beef. As I did my heart sank, in his haste to please the customer, Bill had broken the rule of leaving a knife sticking in that round of cheese, because along with the pain shooting up my arm, I noticed the big knife with its handle still sticking through the round of the cheese. I leaned over the cheese so as to be able to lift it with one arm, lifted the cheese with my free right hand so as not to cut the rest of my left hand into, and gently pulled straight down with the impaled left hand, blood, my blood! Went everywhere. Setting the cheese down with my right hand, I quickly grabbed one of the markets white cleaning towels tightly wrapped it around the gapping wound of my left hand and then placed my thumb of my right hand on the artery of my left wrist, all the time hoping against hope that I had not severed the tendon of the pinky finger of my left hand, if so my saxophone days were over, and if not they would surely be slowed down for a few weeks; and I was to leave for music camp in two weeks.

Luckily, the tendon was only nicked, and I attended the camp as planned, but with my hand bandaged, and very hard to operate.

Mr. Norman seemed only to be upset, not with my injury, but with me; for spewing my blood all over his butcher shop, in front of his pickiest customer, whom he told me, he was sure he would not see again! How considerate, and caring he was! He tried diligently to avoid paying the medical bills, incorrectly blaming me for being careless and negligent in my duties, and not once mentioning Bills careless behavior.

The knife episode at Servall Market, and Mr. Normans attitude about my well being, had reshaped my thinking somewhat as to what and how I might be treated by others down life's road. When I returned from music camp, I was determined to be able to protect myself physically from most bullies, so along with a friend, by the name of Paul Posetopah, who was two years older than me I started taking boxing lessons. These lessons came about, when Paul and I learned that the New York State boxing champ was in town visiting some friends and would be willing to teach anyone interested. This resulted in the kids at school, **in their kindness,** renaming me "Punchy".

*L to R—Walt Longstreet, his father Walt Sr., and Carroll E. Redwine stopped for lunch on way to Gunnison, Colo*

Simultaneously, during my Servall years and time spent learning to box I was into what I thought was my one great love affair. Thank God that girl recognized the silly times for what they really were and had enough gumption to throw me over, or I might never have had the lucky chance to meet Shirley and fulfill the true destiny of my life. However, as so often happens, at the time she impaled my tender young heart, she crushed me and my ten foot ego as though we were a small bug under her heel, and for me, I had surely been introduced by this vixen to my final chapter of revelations as stated in Gods holy word. All she needed was the sign, for she really was the beast, as I envisioned it. This rejection, plus my peer's new name for me, plus the next little fiasco forced upon me by almost everyone of my classmates whom at that time I respected, embittered me greatly. This embitterment would continue to form my attitude toward others for many years, as I took on a " TAKE NO PRISONERS, " attitude.

Earl Cook was the class bully. Earl was not a mental mammoth, and had enrolled at Pawhuska schools our freshman year, transferring in from a small country school I understand. He was a sandy haired, wiry bodied fellow who was much prouder of his muscular prowess than of any mental powers he lacked, and although our paths seldom crossed, as we moved in totally different circles; when they did, we had little to say to each other, generally avoiding one another with mutual disregard.

My junior year, our paths crossed in the thick of a real storm, as I refused to play football in favor of spending more time with my musical studies, and pissed off the coaches, and most of my ball-playing buddies. Earl was a really good football player, tough, uncompromising, and a leader on the field. However, listening to the coaches chiding me during team practice, as they sincerely could not afford any more defections from their already small number of players, he somehow got the idea, because I left the team, I was his special harassment project. He made my life miserable every chance he got, especially in front of my classmates, who for reasons unknown to me, but probably because they were afraid of him, appeared to side with his disparaging remarks to me.

Evading Earl seemed to grow harder and harder as the fall days grew shorter, and I took a lot of very ugly words from him and turned the other cheek, as I was somewhat leery of getting in a battle I could not win. About the first of November I heard through the grapevine that Earl had told a number of our classmates he was set to whip my butt. Whether I would fight or not made him no difference.

After hearing this from more than one person it was no surprise, when one beautiful fall day as I returned to school from lunch at home, there was a large group of kids gathered at the bridge over which I had to cross to get to the school yard, and Earl was at the front of the group, glaring at me as I approached what he was sure would be his day in the sun.

When I saw Earl and all those folks with whom for so many years I had been classmates, waiting with that obvious plan for my destruction; I really was hurt inside and it made me mad as hell, that these folks would force me into this position, so I determined if it was to be, then so be it, but since he planned to beat the devil out of me I damned sure was going to get in my licks while he tried, and I was not going to make it easy for him. Then remembering all I had been taught, I gave that hot rod, braggart, and son of the north range, all he wanted and all those guys he had gathered to watch his little show knew it. Those boxing lessons really paid off, I used every punch and combination of punches shown me at least five times, and it was the one and only time I ever used them. We were both a bloody mess, with no real winner after thirty or forty minutes when the bell rang calling all involved back to class.

That afternoon we both got called to the principals office, where the principal, Mr. Bean, gave us both three licks for fighting, I do believe to this day Mr. Bean hit Earl much harder than me. I know he winked as we left the office. I learned from Gordon Buck that Earl died from Cancer some years back; I must say I hope it did not hurt the cancer!

My last two years of high school fairly well set me on track to becoming a professional musician, as I competed in the regularly scheduled state sponsored music contests of vocal and instrumental music. I attended music camps at Gunnison, Colorado during the summers of my sophomore and junior years, studying jazz and concert music as a performer on saxophone. All this while I was singing in a very good quartet with three other young men by the names of Robert Moore, Bill Blankenship, and D.R. Johnson. We were also all very good friends. Our Quartet received a great deal of help both musically and organizationally from Boyd Whitworth, our highly talented choral teacher and friend, who through his efforts on our part kept us performing almost daily at some community function. I started my first band with the begrudging aid of George Bright, he preferred I spend my time studying symphonic literature, and three classmates who were really excellent brass players, Bob Pyle, Frank Ross and Walt Longstreet. My junior year at PHS, I continued to develop it and perform in it, as did my three aforementioned friends. We continued to work in this band during our early years at OSU. Fortunately for me a local Pawhuska florist, Jim Miller, who had previously managed and performed in his own highly successful group, but had since retired from performing, donated his entire library and some equipment such as jazz music stands to my group. As I mentioned earlier, I continued to develop and manage my band during my years at OSU utilizing this small group of close friends as a nucleus and adding many new instrumentalists to fill out the necessary instrumentation to complete the highly successful Blue Notes Band, Our music was to be heard through out the area Sunday afternoons each week, for thirty minutes on KSPI radio, danced to three nights a week at nearly every fraternity and sorority house and in all Stillwater night spots, the band became so popular with area fans that the University hired us regularly to entertain at the Student Union. More importantly, we performed the music at the 1955 and1956 OSU Junior-Senior Proms

following the great Les Brown's Band performance at the 1954 dance. The success of the Blue Note Band on the OSU campus is readily apparent when it is further

*<<Original Blue Notes Band performing at Oklahoma State Universities` Cordell Hall November 1954*

noted that when this band made its first appearance in the fall of 1954 there were three additional highly regarded bands regularly performing on campus, but by the fall of 1955 there were only two groups, Ashley" H "Alexander's` band and the Blue Notes.

Rehearsing, booking and performing with the Blue Notes Band in addition to keeping up all the business end of this venture was quite a challenge, especially since the owner, operator, and business manager did not own a vehicle and was simultaneously enrolled in eighteen hours of highly intensive music classes at the OSU School of Music; henceforth the 17 to 18 year old with an ego big as Texas, who was ignoring the time to devote to these academic subjects was warned by the college registrar's office, after receiving his first two semesters grade reports of 1.5 and 1.2 respectively, that he was on academic probation and would be expelled if a 2.0 or higher was not forthcoming in the fall of 1955. Attending classes at Oklahoma State University was sometimes very interesting, as no one on campus knew when Frank Eaton (the original cowboy) would show up in one of our classes and pull out his six guns and shoot them off right there in the classroom. The last time I had this happen was in a Humanities class in the main classroom building in the spring of 1955, after this last little show, the powers that be would not let him shoot his gun in the classrooms anymore, as it scared the professors to much. I can tell you that he looked almost exactly like the cowboy mascot of today, face and all, only his head was smaller, but it was shaped just like the mascot!

Although probation scared the hell out of me, as I have always been afraid of any type of failure, it did not corral my extreme passion for performing or running my band. It did result in my planning my time better, and achieving a 2.8 grade average during my next three semesters, during which time the Blue Notes Band continued to be considered THE group on the OSU campus and continued to travel extensively throughout northern Oklahoma and even into southern Kansas as far north as Arkansas City where we had our introduction to the dance hall (road house) scene.

About this time OSU tuition was becoming a real problem, as I had not made a great deal of money during the past summer, and what little I had was fast slipping through the holes in my spendthrift pockets. Buddy Gibble was chauffeuring me to most of my gigs, and he mentioned he would like to buy the band from me. I gave it some thought, and after some soul searching, and much discussion with Bud, as to who would make all the basic decisions, I approached him with a partnership proposition, so with the $1500.00 he paid me for his half of the future profits and ownership of one half the Bands book and equipment, I paid my fall semesters' room and board and my tuition.

This deal soured me on all future opportunities as to partners; I would not have a partner in business for any reason, ever! Buddy was a great guy until he started meddling in our business. The situation with the band transpired just as I thought it might, I lost a good friend and eventually had to either buy him out or sell to him, as we couldn't agree on one darn item that affected our band, so within two months Buddy was the proud owner of the Blue notes band. Unfortunately for him and the guys in the band, I had been signing all the contracts: THE CARROLL REDWINE BAND, SO-----he owned a band that was totally unemployed!!!! That's when I took one half of the money he paid me for the remaining half of the band, purchased a new book, cut personnel expense in half by only using the best five side men on campus, each of whom I guaranteed a monthly income of $350.00 and started the new and highly successful: WINE DOT BAND. Damn, there is that take no prisoners attitude again! I've got to work on that!

I booked the band into a very large dance hall just south of Arkansas City, Kansas in the fall of 1956. It was our first gig at such a place and I do not remember how I made the contact, but I do remember well arriving at the place to set up my band. The job was scheduled for a Saturday evening 9 pm downbeat, and we arrived at about four-thirty pm Saturday to set up. As we pulled into the large open parking lot that surrounded the long wide building, I ascertained it was likely that only the manager was inside as there was only one lonely old car in the lot in addition to the two, which we occupied. After spending some time knocking and pounding on the front door of this club, and getting no response, we walked the half a city block to the back door and begin to knock again. Suddenly a haggard little guy about fifty years old with a scowl glaring from ear to ear and a very sour attitude stepped from around the corner of the building we had not surveyed. He asked what the hell we wanted, and our evening appeared to be started on a down hill slide; however, I did not want to make an issue of his dour attitude and really get it moving in that direction, so I grinned disarmingly and told him we were the band for this evening and would like to gain entry to the building so we could set up. As fate would have it, this nut was the manager and said we should enter the door that was presently being pounded on, as he brushed past us and unlocked it. I usually tried to get a feel for any new areas we performed in before we sat up. So, I walked into the building with the manager where I realized, though it was pretty dark, I was standing on the stage. As my eyes became accustomed to the poor lighting, I noticed with some apprehension, that the stage was separated from the rest of the club area by a large chicken wire screen which was attached to the stage ceiling and stretched earthward reaching the floor about six feet in front of the stage. Not having a clue as to why the wire was there, I naively tried to get the manager to let us set up in front of it, so as to be available to our crowd as we enjoyed having them close and a part of our evening's entertainment. However, he would have none of my ideas and told me in no uncertain terms I was to set up on the stage behind the chicken wire, assuring me and my band, which was also upset by this arrangement, that before the evening was over, we would appreciate his cage. Besides, if we got too upset, we could leave out the back door that was readily available. After some discussion among ourselves, we decided since we were about one hundred miles from Stillwater and in need of tuition for next semester, we had better go ahead and perform as requested; so we pulled our vehicles closer and unloaded our equipment onto the club's stage as suggested.

We began on time as usual, playing to a smoked filled, packed house of the rowdiest, rudest, crudest, foul-mouthed beer guzzling crowd one could imagine. A crowd who spent their entire evening baptizing the band in a sea of harrowingly thrown, empty beer bottles, expertly aimed at that wonderfully stout chicken wire, while the band performed as though they were at a Sunday school picnic, totally oblivious to their patron's sadism. That was my first and last performance at beer bars; as a result I feel totally justified in saying I may have added many years to my life.

Buddy Gibble, who played jazz trumpet in the Blue Notes and would soon own half the band and eventually by fall of 1956 all of it; came running up and down the halls of our dorm one Thursday afternoon on the weekend of OSU homecoming in the fall of 1955. He was desperately seeking two male dates to fill in for some guys from OU, who had notified him they would not be able to keep their obligations for a triple date to view the OSU homecoming decorations. Buddy's girl friend and he, had arranged the triple date with two young ladies who along with Buddy's' girl, resided on the 4th floor at Willard Hall.

He was noisily begging every guy on our floor to fill in for the OU guys but was getting absolutely no positive responses from any of our men and creating quite a scene with his efforts, so when he got to my room I was pumped and ready with my big NO! Due to my rigorous schedule that included many other responsibilities besides eighteen hours of class work, (I never took less than eighteen hours and my last semester was a twenty-six hour marathon,) college choir,

The Blue Notes, marching band, concert band, ROTC commitments, and the college orchestra. I had only one or two hours to enjoy my snooker game, and I had reserved early Thursday evenings to satiate this appetite. When I delivered my answer to Bud, he nearly croaked, as he was depending on me for his last line of defense. Sure his good friend would bail him out, he came on with how good looking the girls were, and when that did not work fessed up to the fact that his girlfriend had threatened him with being totally cut off if he embarrassed her in front of her roommates by not being able to deliver them a blind date. Never

*Shirley J. Smith 1955*

mind, that I later found out that they had agreed to go on this fiasco, only to please her. Buddy had such a look of disappointment on his face that I could not totally abandon him, so I capitulated a bit and assured him that if he would diligently continue looking for someone else to accompany him, and should he fail to find anyone by six

*Shirley J. Smith June 1954*

thirty pm, (it now being three thirty pm;) I would bail him out. After I said this, you know how hard he looked!!! He left my room, and came back in about ten minutes accompanied by some poor guy who obviously was not any happier than I was to be going on a blind date. This was my one and only blind date in a young life filled with many fun dates, Buddy assured me again that he had made a real effort to find another person in addition to the guy with him, but no one was available. So reluctantly, as we crowded into Buddy's small car, I explained to him I would go, but should we arrive at Willard Hall and the girls were even slightly less than he had advertised, he was going to find me unceremoniously jumping ship, and he was going to lose one third of his escorts.

We drove the short distance to Willard Hall where we went inside and waited for the girls in their living room area, which was near the elevators. Our dates were freshmen students, so they were on the 4th floor; soon the elevator doors opened, and I caught a glimpse of a real dog coming out. I immediately headed for the outside doors with my head down so as to avoid any eye contact, I took, a route that forced me to walk closely by the elevators. I did not notice the gorgeous black- haired beauty who grabbed my arm, after which I alarmingly, looked to my left and downward, then gazed into those warm, smiling brown eyes, and my fear melted, as I drank in her milk-smooth, warmly tanned complexion, and she brightened the whole place for yours truly, when she said quite unassumingly, "Hi handsome," and gently pulled me toward her surprisingly warm body, as we glided through the large banging dorm doors and down the four wide stone steps into the misty parking lot. Now one would think after such a great beginning this evening was going to be unusually pleasurable, but the next step was to pack all six of us into Buddy's little car, a feat which required much discomfort both mentally and physically, as the girls had spent considerable time getting dressed and were wearing carefully prepared elegant fall attire, and we boys were wearing our best suits with white shirts and ties, so very shortly upon stacking us all together in a non- air -conditioned car with the windows rolled up due to the light rain that pelted continually on the fogged up windshield, all our efforts toward a genteel appearance had dissipated, and together with the physical discomfort and the frustration of being unable to view the house decorations through the cloudy windows, the evening quickly turned downhill.

Enduring about thirty minutes of this loathsome togetherness with my date, who told me as she banged around on my bony lap her name was Shirley Smith that she was a pre-vet major and she hailed from the Tulsa area. Both of us admitted we were coerced into participating in tonight's disaster. Blind dates were a first for either of us, and this experience would most likely be enough to last a lifetime. Therefore we mutually agreed, much to our companion's chagrin, to put this night behind us by going home. So, after convincing our illustrious driver everyone would be much more comfortable in his car without the two extra bodies, He drove us mercifully back to Willard Hall. After disembarking from Bud's torture chamber, I walked Ms. Shirley Smith to the large outside door, and after apologizing for ruining her evening, opened the dorm door and watched, as she gracefully disappeared inside, secure in my mind that this would be my one and final time to see that beautiful lady. I walked back to my dorm room in the light rain still begrudging the fact I missed my snooker game for such a bust of an evening.

The Blue Notes performed often in the Student Union Ballroom, many times to a packed house of OSU students, and Saturday night two weeks after the homecoming weekend found us on that stage. During the dance we usually took a short break about halfway through the evening, and when I stood up to announce to the crowd we were going on break, Bob Pyle, the first trumpet player and my good friend since junior high school, quickly grabbed my arm to get my attention before I could leave the stage. I could not hear him very well due to the large1500 person college crowd in the room and had to ask him twice what he was saying, but I finally understood him as he asked, " Did you notice that beautiful girl who kept winking at you behind her dancing partners back, as she was swirling around the dance floor immediately in front of the stage". I assured Bob I had not been aware of this, and asked him to point her out to me. Then as we left the stage together, he pointed out the same willowy, dark-haired beauty I had so casually left two weeks before at the door to Willard Hall. I was impressed, but as she was well escorted and appeared happily so, and I was really busy with my obligations on stage, I shrugged her advances off as a simple flirtation and quickly forgot about the whole situation.

Monday of the following week while changing classes in the classroom building, I was heading up the wide stairway which was extremely crowded with students, two abreast, hurriedly ascending and descending and excitingly holding conversations in every direction as they prepared to find their next class. Suddenly I was caught up in those smiling brown eyes, which at first glance I did not recognize; but I quickly became aware that they were, although busily engaged in a conversation with the guy beside her, truly focused on mine. As we quickly passed on the congested stairs, we acknowledged each other with a wry smile, and I made a mental note that fate must be interacting with us, as her lovely lips formed the silent words, "call me"! This was the third time our paths had crossed in the past two weeks, but I really did not know how to reach her, as Buddy had made all the arrangements for our previous date, so I hurried to the music building to find my good friend, who I was sure had Shirley's phone number. I called her and we visited amicably, as I requested a future date; however, her calendar was full for the coming weekend, and I was performing both nights, so we decided to meet for church Sunday morning and lunch afterward. How could either of us know that a blind date, that neither of us wanted or enjoyed would lead to a partnership filled with a great many years of wonderful adventures, enough to fill a few books!

We dated often for the rest of that fall semester, but Shirley had been pretty serious about a fellow from an earlier liaison and wasn't sure her feelings for him weren't genuine, so when we parted company for the Christmas break, with me obligated for a number of performances and her former beau home from the Navy we mutually decided to part company. This was just what the doctor ordered for our relationship; and when we returned to OSU for the spring semester, we did a lot of talking about what each of us wanted and expected out of life and each other. I credit these serious and sincere inquiries with helping to seal our bonds together in a truly fair and permanent manner.

The first weekend after we both returned to the campus, I asked Shirley to go steady, she said she would have to think it over, as she was not sure about our relationship. Not wanting to appear overly

*Left to Right: Shirley and Carroll then Shirley's two dorm-mates with their dates at the Okla. St. University Spring Dance (Cupid`s Fling) Feb., 1955*

aggressive I dropped the idea, but the following weekend I went to St. Louis to perform with the collegiate men's' chorale. We did not see each other due to our busy schedules for the next two weeks. However, while I was in St. Louis, I bought a large teddy bear for her (if she told me yes, and only if so!). I called her for a movie date the next week, and she agreed. Leaving the bear in my dorm room until after getting to hear the big decision, we walked to the movie in downtown Stillwater, as I still did not have a car. All through the movie I anxiously awaited her approaching the subject, all the while avoiding my doing so. As we came out of the movie she asked," Do you not want to know?" Coyly I asked, " know what?"

Shirley stopped walking and looked me in the eyes, she said," About going steady, you did ask me didn't you?" There was no going back, I was trapped and was going to hear the answer whether or not it was favorable. I looked into those inquiring, gorgeous brown eyes and melted as she said "Yes!" " My answer is yes I will go steady with you." I said, "great!" " Lets go to my room, I have something for you" We walked to my dorm, and that's how Shirley became the owner of the teddy bear that our oldest daughter, Carla: played with until she was six years old.

We eventually married on December 22nd, 1956. We probably would have married sooner, but I could not figure out a way to support a family and go to school, and Shirley was a very practical person in those days. Due to a lack of funds she didn't return to OSU in the fall of 1956, but took a job at a finance company in Tulsa, and continued to reside with her folks, Hollis and Ester Smith who owned their home Northeast of Tulsa very close to the town of Catoosa, Oklahoma. Shirleys' living in Tulsa and my attending classes in Stillwater couldn't keep us apart, as I kept the roads hot racing back and forth to be with her, usually driving most of what was left of Saturday night after performing with my band until after midnight, and arriving at her parents home early on Sunday morning, where we would spend one glorious day a week together. Our wedding became a possibility, due to my auditioning and being accepted as a performing sideman with the US Army Field Band of Washington D.C., which is a chapter in itself.

# The First Big Taste Test

The first week of December in1956 the aforementioned group was presented in concert at OSU by the allied arts series on campus, this was during my fall semester of my junior year, Chester A. Whiting a fine musician and army veteran of the second world war had developed this band and was still the director and commanding officer, the Major as I remember was from the old school and although very fair with his men, was a no nonsense military musician, and therefore his band was top notch in every respect. The Stillwater performance was held in Gallager/Iba Hall with about seven thousand concert listeners in attendance. It was a very impressive performance, and at its conclusion I happened to meet my woodwind instructor, Stanley Green, in the lobby while trying to make our way through the large crowd and out of the hall. We both remarked about how impressed we were with the band's performance, and I further told Mr. Green, that I would really enjoy performing with such a fine organization. To my surprise, he told me he thought I was ready to perform at that level and suggested I contact Major Whiting to see if the band had an opening for which I might audition. Stanley further explained, the whole organization was staying at a local hotel that evening and would not be leaving Stillwater until mid-morning the following day. As a result of our conversation, I contacted the Major early the next morning (he was quite cordial for such an early morning call) and referred me to Smith Sutley, the saxophone section leader, as any audition would necessarily be heard and adjudicated by Smity with final approval by Major Whiting. The Major also informed me that there was indeed an opening in the sax section, and that Sergeant

Sutley had been listening to over one hundred and thirty different performers from throughout the U.S. for the past three months trying to find a replacement for his solo alto position. Hearing this, I felt there was not much chance of my winning the job, but I thought taking the audition would be a great experience and who knows, (nothing ventured?) The director also told me I should call immediately if I was going to audition, as the band was departing the hotel at ten am, and it presently was eight- thirty. I told him I would be right down, hung up the phone, grabbed my instrument, and the seven major works for sax I had been preparing for my junior recital and hurried down to the hotel, which was only about twelve city blocks from my room in the dorm.

Arriving at the hotel lobby that was buzzing with band members preparing to load their bags and equipment, I immediately requested to see Smity, whom I addressed as Sergeant Sutley, not wanting to appear too informal. The Sergeant was waiting for me as the Major had informed him of my call, and after a hand shake and brief hello, he ushered me into a small side room off the main lobby where he listened to my rendition of the Ebert Concerto, and two pieces by Debussy, and then ask me to ad lib on some blues in the key of F with a young pianist who was traveling with the band. When I finished, he asked me to visit with a couple

*Ester, Shirley, and Hollis Smith in 1939*

of the band members who had quietly listened to my audition, but had said nothing up until this time, then he left the room. For what purpose, he did not explain, although I later found out it was to visit with the Major and if he concurred offer me the job.

Smity returned to the audition room shortly and told me the job was mine if I wanted it, but with some stipulations, and then he further explained, "Due to the fact that the Band will be leaving on an extended tour of Europe in April, and we would need you to perform with us on that tour, you must report for duty right away." I realized if I was to leave OSU immediately I would lose the past semester's class work, and that would be quite a financial loss, as well as a loss of the many hours I had expended completing these courses. So, I asked if it would be possible to report the fifteenth of February after this semesters work was completed, and Smity said he thought this would be a tight fit, but might work, and so we agreed on the spot that I would be accompanying the band to Europe in April. After writing a letter on Field Band stationery to the effect I was accepted into the band he told me I would receive a letter from the General of the 2nd Army's office within two weeks guaranteeing my position, and that I should keep it in my possession at all times in the future to assure that I would end up in Washington D.C. and not in some insignificant post band in the hinterlands. This turned out to be really sound advice, as many times over the next three months I needed to flash that sucker around to save myself from just such a fate, especially while taking basic training in Ft.Ord, California, as the officer in charge of the post band there, tried many times to secure the letter from me without me actually holding it in my possession, which I was sure would have resulted in the letter being misplaced, accidentally of course, and my permanent assignment to the local band. We said our goodbyes and without even going back to the dorm room, I headed for Tulsa to propose to that beautiful raven-haired lady, as I now had a way to support her, never mind I would seldom get to be with her due to my touring and performing throughout the globe for the next three years, a thought, that as of yet had not occurred to me.

# Licensing of All Future Vintages

I arrived at Shirley's house in Tulsa about eleven am, and as soon as I could get the family greetings over and get Shirley by herself, I

*Shirley in her wedding gown*
*December 22 1956*

*L to R best man; Quincy Smith,*
*Maid of honor; Betty Keim,*
*groom; Carroll and bride Shirley,*
*at wedding reception December*
*22,1956*

explained the morning's events that had transpired in Stillwater, and showed her the confirmation letter from Smity and the Major. Then I promptly asked her to marry me, and spend the rest of her days letting me try to make both of us happy. Fortunately for me she was willing to take the risk and said, "Yes!"

Knowing that I had to report in February, we decided to have the wedding during my Christmas break from OSU. It would be held at the First Christian Church in Pawhuska, as at that time, although Shirley was a member of the Baptist faith, she did not have a local affiliation with that faith, and it was logical to do so, because planning and executing the wedding was easier to accomplish with the aid of my parents at their church. (Goodbye Baptist, Hello Christian). It might appear that these life long decisions were made rather flippantly, but truly: they were made jointly, and were based on many past months of discussions as to what we both expected and wanted from our lives together.

The wedding was held at four pm on Saturday the 22nd of December 1956 at the first Christian Church of Pawhuska with the local minister officiating. Mary McCartney, a good friend and local vocalist, sang " Because", and some other song I can't remember; Shirley, dressed in a powder blue suit, walked radiantly down the aisle accompanied reluctantly by Hollis, her Dad, who showed up at the last minute to give her away as she had requested, after he had said," Absolutely not" three weeks earlier, and who after the wedding gave us $ 40.00 cash as a wedding gift. A gift that would turn out to be extremely important, as it was really needed at that time. My

*<<Papa and Mama Smith, with their baby Hollis Smith,*

best man was Quincy Smith, a boyhood friend, who was currently performing as the drummer in my newly organized band THE WINE DOTS. The reception was held in the over flow area in the back of the sanctuary with Champagne, the beautiful wedding cake, and other typical goodies provided by my ever-alert mother with Shirley's approval. We left the church to go change clothes at my parent's home there in Pawhuska on 805 E. 13th St .at about 5:30 pm, as a heavy snow began to fall.

Following a quick change of our wedding clothes, we piled into Shirley's 1949 Pontiac

*The First Christian Church, **Disciples of Christ** in Pawhuska, Oklahoma. Picture taken on our wedding day December 22,1956*

convertible and headed out in the blinding snowstorm for Wichita, Kansas. We drove as far as Sedan Kansas, most of the way with

**The Serving Table an** *unknown wedding guest. My Grandmother Berryhill, in the deep back left corner, my Mother Clarice Iva Berryhill, Redwine serving punch, Shirley's Mother, Esther Mae Smith, serving wedding cake, and standing far right, another female wedding guest December 22, 1956*

the emergency brake on as I was so excited I forgot to remove it and the snow was just to bad to go any farther. So after getting some snack foods at the local grocery, truly just a quick stop filling station, we took refuge in the local motel. It was really a shabby little ten-room affair. But, we were so in love and giddy with our newfound happiness, a cave in the side of a mountain would have sufficed. So, we spent that night and the next day in this motel; and since the snow was mostly melted by the next afternoon, we returned to my folks on the 24th for Christmas Eve and stayed with them until the afternoon of Christmas Day when we traveled to Shirley's parents home for Christmas Dinner.

# Two Bottles Survive Their First Crate

I had to perform on the 30th and 31st at Enid Oakwood Golf and Country Club and Seminole American Legion respectively, and we had to go to Stillwater to locate an apartment, so that we would be able to finish my fall semester's final exams, (back in those days the university always had fall finals after Christmas break, it was a great way to ruin a good holiday season) We found that available apartments in Stillwater were very scarce, and the only reason one was vacant was due to its dilapidated condition. When we did find one on the 28[th,] it was really a prime example of a shack, boy what a dog! It was truly the only place available, and we had to have something right away. The apartment was in an old run down house on a side street behind a Bar-B-Q joint and had two small rooms, an eight by ten living area with a pull out couch, that when we pulled it out, kept anyone from opening the front door or going into the four by five foot kitchenette. The very small kitchen was adorned with an oily, grimy, single sink and a two-burner hot plate, and with walls so thin, that we were serenaded every morning during breakfast by the couple in the adjoining apartment potty training their screeching child. The so-called bathroom was entered by traversing downward a flight of ten narrow, rickety, rotten wooden steps to a dirty, spider web infested, unpainted concrete floor, where when anyone finally arrived, he or she was greeted with an awesome sight. It included an old rusty iron bed that we were invited to sleep on, but wouldn't, and a filthily, brown stained, open commode and a shower head that protruded ever so obtrusively from its wire banded perch against an unpainted and water soaked couple of two by fours forced under the head- thumping floor joists, that shouted look-out from their place close above the basement ceiling. For this jewel, we had to pay one hundred fifty dollars per month; it was a good thing I was performing on this weekend.

I earlier mentioned, the Wine Dots performed the first two weekends in January, so financially we survived until

*above: Esther Smith Miller`s mother and father, and Shirley Smith Redwine`s maternal Grandparents: MaudieWeaverVanBerg, and Hal (Dutch) Van Berg*

*L. to R.; Maude"Nanny" Van Berg, Esther Mae Van berg Smith, who was "Nanny's" daughter, Shirley J. Smith, "Nanny's" Granddaughter, and standing: Hollis L. Smith, Son-in- Law, Husband and Father. Circa 1940AD*

semesters end. When although we had no way of knowing it, this would be one of the last visits we would be privileged to have with Shirley's maternal grandmother (Nanny). Shirley and Nanny had an extremely fond relationship. We drove to Tulsa from Stillwater to get Nanny and take her to spend a few days at Shirley's parents home over by Catoosa, however we did not know that during the weeks we had been gone, Hollis and Ester had moved to Pryor, and had not told anyone in the family, so after being surprised by the empty house in Catoosa and not knowing where her parents were, Shirley and I took Nanny back to her home in Tulsa, then called Hollis's sister Prentiss in Pryor to try and locate Shirley's parents.

Prent, Shirley's aunt in Pryor, assured her that her parents were well, and told her how to contact them, which we did, then we notified Nanny of where they were. Shirley moved in with my parents, while as a lowly army private with matching income, I marched off to Ft. Chaffee, Arkansas for a week, and from there to Ft. Ord, California for the following fifteen weeks to complete my army basic training, which was required before I received my automatic rank of Sp-5 and a substantial raise as a full-fledged PERFORMING member of the U S ARMY FIELD BAND.

# The Wine Drinks in California

Marched off was a metaphor, as I was sent to Chaffee from Tulsa on a government bus, which was loaded with new recruits. While visiting with Smity after my earlier audition, he had mentioned that although I would be required to take my first eight weeks of basic separated from my wife if I got married, it was common practice by the army at that

*Shirley and Carroll on leave in Oklahoma April 1957 just before European tour,*

time to allow a recruit and their spouse to cohabitate off post for the final eight weeks of their basic training. When I enlisted at the recruiting office in Tulsa, I was given further assurance that Shirley would be able to join me after the initial eight weeks, and therefore we were planning for her to do so. As a result of this assurance, I was not very concerned when I was transferred from Chaffee to Ft. Ord, as I figured California's' Monterey peninsula would be a nice place for us to spend a few weeks while working a few hours daily for Uncle Sam.

My naivety was rampant, as not only does the army have its practices differently to suit its local chain of command, but generally lies, or at the very least twists the truth to cover its tracks especially to new recruits. If an officer or non COM tells you something, one had

97

better get it in writing, or adopt a wait and see attitude, as generally the capacity of these fellows gastronomical systems have fully peaked! More often than not the fellow putting out the information, although he truly believes he is giving out the army's' standard line, has absolutely no control of the final actions or results. Having explained the afore mentioned details, the reader will be prepared for what transpired over the next several weeks as it placed unusual and unnecessary hardship on Shirley, a nineteen year old small town girl, pregnant with her first child, alone, and half a continent from any one she knew except for her husband, who was of little help due to his military responsibilities.

*Carroll E. Redwine during basic training at Ft. Ord, California February, 1957*

Unaware that the military establishment deliberately takes many cruel and unusual actions, especially effecting their new recruits mental well being, I fully expected the leadership above me to honor everything the recruiters had assured me would be forthcoming, and certainly not to renege on the statements affecting my wife, as she was not in the army, and was paying their salaries as a U.S. citizen. So I wrote her a letter confirming our being able to live off base after my eighth week, requested she travel west, which she did, but not until the tenth week, and sent her my first months pay of $ 120.00, less five dollars, I held out as instructed by my 1$^{st}$ Sergeant for purchasing tooth paste and other personal care items, as these were not provided, and were required by the army to be in my foot locker at all times. (Now these gentlemen with unknown fathers know she's coming to town!) I knew from a phone call made to Shirley about my second weekend at Ft. Ord, that she had very little funds, as she was forced to pay previous obligations of wedding expenses (including her rings on which I had only made a down payment) with most of what she had available. This check was needed to buy her bus ticket and for road expenses she would incur enroute, we planned to use the remainder to obtain an apartment, and her government subsistence allotment, granted monthly would sustain us for the rest of our time in California.

# The Master Vintner Comes to California

All these plans appeared fine to both Shirley and me; however, someone forgot to tell the government. Shirley rode the bus to Monterrey, California, which was the closest town and about seven miles from Ft. Ord  She arrived at the Monterrey bus depot about 2:30 Saturday afternoon on what was fortunately for both of us, my first duty free weekend in ten weeks. My whole outfit had been granted weekend passes. I had been in town for about three hours waiting for her bus to arrive, and was standing about ten feet from the door of her bus when the door opened and nearly twelve to fifteen persons disembarked before I saw her enquiring and somewhat frightened eyes looking in every direction, trying to locate me in the busy crowd of soldiers and their loved ones reuniting, as Shirley and I were meaning to do. She walked past me as I called her name, obviously she did not recognize me, and I was not aware of how different I must have appeared to her from her last memory of me. In spite of the fact the army had miscalculated its food rations when my outfit had been reassigned to Ft.Ord from Chaffee, and all we had to eat for two solid weeks was creamed turkey, which was served to us at breakfast, lunch and dinner, and which a guard was eventually assigned to each table to make sure we ate the disgusting stuff; these past ten weeks of three heavy meals daily, rigorous outdoor exercise and physical training, and very regular hours; had changed me from a one hundred fifty five pound, gently faced civilian musician, with a 28 inch waist to a hulk of a two hundred pound giant with a 32 inch waist 44 inch chest and a very harsh weather beaten sun burned face. As a result even though I called her name, Shirley did not immediately recognize me, and being in such unfamiliar surroundings, she was beginning to have a concerned look about her. As she somewhat pulled away when I gently took her hand, I again called her name looking directly into those beautiful, but still a bit frightened brown eyes.

Shirley finally acknowledged me and after a long hug and a very public quick kiss hello, I gathered her bags from the luggage rack under the bus, and we set out to walk the people crowded two or three blocks to a small hotel, where we figured she was to reside for a few days until we could move to an apartment, we certainly did not count on her spending many lonely days at this location. We checked her into the hotel, dropped her bags in her room, and after a bit of freshening up; went back out on the streets to acquaint ourselves with the immediate surroundings, as neither of us had been to Monterrey before, and we knew Shirley would have to negotiate this area by herself for a few days until I could help her find her way around

I stayed with her Saturday, then Sunday morning we got up about 9:am and went to breakfast at a local beanery and afterward, spent the day sight seeing together. The last bus for the post left the depot at eleven pm, and fortunately I found a seat on it, as the post gates closed to everyone at eleven thirty pm on Sunday. Monday morning, I asked my drill sergeant if I might meet with my company commander, my request was granted and while meeting with the lieutenant, I told him I had been assured by the recruiter in Tulsa, that after my first eight weeks of basic I could live off base with my wife, and she was in Monterrey waiting for me to help her find a place for us to live. He sat back ever so casually, and promptly told me to "forget it", this was never going to happen, as his recruits were going to each and everyone be living together on the base and for me, " to get my ass back to my outfit and get to work on today's' assignments."

I was really upset, as presently I had no way of communicating with Shirley to inform her of my dilemma, and I knew she would be expecting at the very least some kind of personal contact. As a recruit, I was not allowed to use a telephone unless at first gaining permission from the drill sergeant, and he would not grant me this, saying that I should tell him were Shirley was staying and he would make the call for me. I refused to do so, as I had heard many sordid stories during my last nine weeks stationed in California, about how the cadres in this camp had mistreated wives and girl friends of the recruits, and from my reception at the commander's office and suspicions of the drill sergeant, I was determined not to let this be Shirley's cup of tea.

I survived the rest of the week, by telling myself I would get to see Shirley on the next weekend and explain things at that time, she was a sharp kid, and I knew she would find a way to search for an apartment and make her time alone count in the best manner possible. Friday evening after dinner the whole company was called to muster and in front of the whole group of 240 troops weekend passes were handed to everyone, excepting me. The Black drill sergeant gave out with a great big laugh, as it became obvious to all the men in the formation, that I was the only one not to receive a pass, and dismissing the formation he turned to me and said, " keep you white ass on post baby, or you'll end up in Leavenworth, Kansas." No doubt meaning at the federal penitentiary, and I knew he meant what he said. The next morning I got up early and noticed there were very few people on the base, especially the men and cadre of my barracks. So after breakfast at the company chow hall, I moseyed aimlessly around, carefully checking to see if the sergeant or his buddys had spent the night on post, as they were often prone to do. I could not find even the faintest trace of the bastards, and really didn't expect to, as I figured and rightly so, that they had spent the night at home with their," Mommas" in town.

When I was first sent to basic I traveled to Chaffee in a nice business suit, and although the cadre at my first post had told me to mail those clothes home, as they issued my regulation army clothes and gear to me, I did not comply with their request, and had hidden them carefully away under my inside sheets of my bed. These civilian clothes turned out to be just what I needed to successfully commit my first and last federal felony against my old buddy Uncle Sam. I pressed the suit carefully on my bunk and donned the tie and white shirt, and walked out of the main gate like I owned the place! As I passed the young guard at the gate, I shot him a glower like "who the hell do you think (YOU) are to check me for a gate pass, " and kept walking without looking back. I was so caught up in my anxiety to visit with my lovely wife, that although I felt the absent drill sergeants eyes on my back all the way into town, this feeling past, as I jumped off the old truck bed on which I had hitched a ride, and continued on walking the last four or five blocks to the hotel where we had stayed last week, and I anxiously hoped she would be waiting.

Shirley was reading a paperback in her room when I arrived, and was expecting me, as she had no idea of the situation we were in or what had transpired between the army and me during the past week. After getting reacquainted we started telling each other the experiences of the past few days, and I explained the army's position as to our being able to have an apartment off base, she told me she had been searching for an apartment, and had met a girlfriend of one of my fellow recruits. The young lady was a native of the area and had a car, so Shirley, with the aid of her new friend, had been able to explore the city over the past week, and they had eaten lunch at the home of the young friends aunt. We spent that glorious night at her hotel and didn't get out of bed until about noon. When we did get up we dressed and spent the rest of the afternoon walking around the town and dreading our inevitable separation which came all to soon, as again I caught the last bus to the post, this time with a hell of a lot more stress involved, as I did not have a pass and the military police were checking every bus to catch just such felons as me.

My strategy was to board the bus at the last minute, after the police had checked the people for their passes, but when I got on the bus there was only one seat available and I was forced to take it if I was to ride back to the post. I took this seat, and just as I sat down two guys, one a shore patrol and one an army mp boarded the bus and began looking and asking to look at passes. I decided to run another big bluff, as I remembered I was wearing civilian clothes. The police checked the passes of the fellows in the seat in front of me, across the aisle from me, and behind me, but as I sat very still looking straight ahead and acting as though I was not a party to their actions, they skipped me. Phew!! No arrest yet. Next big problem, how do I get through the post gate, as I was aware the guards had checked every pass last week? When my bus unloaded at the main gate, there must have been 300 G Is lined up to show their passes, and the gate was closing in ten minutes, so I pulled out my billfold, put my selective service card, which was the same size as last weeks pass in the top window and got in line, as if I went through this gate everyday. The guards were really hurrying to get all the men through the gate before closing time, and I took advantage of this by holding my billfold with my right hand and flipping it open for only enough time for them to glance at the card, which in the poor light available did somewhat resemble the real thing. Without appearing hurried, I casually flipped the billfold back and put it in my pocket, as the guard motioned me through the gate. Wonderful! I sleep on my own sheets tonight and not in the brig! Fortunately for me, no one had checked to see if I was on base the whole weekend and I never tried this trick again.

Monday morning came to early, as by now I was really bored with the daily routine. The first words the drill sergeant uttered that Monday morning was to ask me how I enjoyed my weekend on post, as I pretty well had the place to myself and I just said, " fine Sir!" And looked straight ahead. Thinking he would have more fun out of me, he picked up a paint brush and threw it my direction, as I caught it, he told me to pick up the gallon of gray paint behind him, take it to the first latrine I came to and get some experience as the company artist! He added, " And if you know what's good for you, you will not spill a drop or fail to put that paint on the correct objects".

This little art lesson was imparted to me at about 8am and with a nice hour break for lunch, I made that gallon of paint last until 5 pm, that was when the drill sergeant sent one of the guys in my barracks to tell me to clean up my area and go to the chow hall for dinner. Our company was supposed to be a rifle and ground assault group, and from the very first day of our training it was obvious our cadre, except for the company commander, who was a professed west point graduate; didn't have a clue about ground troops or rifles, as they were all tankers and only knew what the lieutenant had time to impart to them immediately before they schooled the company recruits. This was really obvious Tuesday morning, the hilarious first time our drill sergeant attempted to explain how we were to break down and clean our weapons. After faking his knowledge of the rifle for about ten minutes, during which we knew better than to laugh, least we end up scrubbing toilets, he left our platoon to get one of the other two sergeants on duty that day to help take the weapon apart. Our drill sergeant casually returned about fifteen minutes later, accompanied by one of these fellows and the two of them, in front of us, spent the next thirty minutes figuring out and at the same time explaining to us, as though they were highly skilled in this area, how to take apart and clean our weapons. The weapons had been packed in heavy grease before they were issued to each of us. As a result we left the area, with the remnants of dirty grease all over us, four hours after enduring a class, that was supposed to take only one hour of that morning we preceded to the chow hall for lunch, where the rest of the company had a good laugh at our expense. Wednesday morning, as I stood unobtrusively as possible in the days first formation, my name was called loudly, and I quickly marched with all the dignity I could muster to front and center, fully expecting to spend another day, unsupervised; painting another latrine, as there are always plenty of latrines that could use another coat. But the drill sergeant was one step ahead of me as usual, and told me to pick up the box of brushes and cleanser behind him, along with the mops and brooms lying nearby and follow him. I obeyed meekly, as I could see by his stride he was on a very special mission and I was a central player in it. He lead me and three other recruits to the dirtiest, nastiest latrine that was available and pointing with a commanding gesture, said,

" Gentlemen I will spend the next two hours sitting on this stump, while you turn that eyesore into a temple fit for the commander and unless you intend to spend the rest of the day running around the perimeter of this post, you had better be finished in two hours!"

The rest of the week was pretty uneventful, I guess the sergeant was too busy to mess with my head or had decided that I wasn't going anywhere, and he could whack me anytime he wished. The weekend came and again I was the only recruit without a pass, but I really didn't care this time, as Shirley had called on Friday evening to say she and her new friend with the car would be driving out to the post and spending Sunday with us. Although Saturday was hell, not getting to be with her, and surely wasn't as good as spending the time at the hotel, I knew we would be together on Sunday, and I realized I was quite fortunate last weekend slipping out of the post and not ending up in jail.

Shirley arrived with her friend at my barracks about ten am on Sunday morning. She hopped out of the car and her friend after agreeing to return to pick her up after dinner, which we would eat in the chow hall as the guests of our old Uncle, drove off to locate my buddy, whom had been given a pass and so, would be spending the night in her bed. We fiddled around the post sight seeing, with me boring her to death with explanations of what transpired during the week in each area she was observing. We walked and visited until the chow hall opened, and we took advantage of the free lunch, which was as I remember cold cuts and salads.

After lunch we again walked around the post stopping to rest, as often as possible, as there were not many places to sit, in this working environment. Since we were not allowed to enter my barracks, (no civilians) inside, we eventually ended up at the USO building, and went inside; here the local town ladies had thoughtfully prepared cookies and punch for the troops and their guests. There were quite a few folks milling around, and when we went through the serving line I was really embarrassed, as I watched Shirley, who was normally very discreet and proper, stuffing cookies into every available pocket. I showed my displeasure with her actions with a disbelieving look, but she didn't seem to care what I thought, and continued her plundering of the cookie trays. I did not understand why she would do this since I knew we had been served a satisfying lunch and were going to be enjoying dinner within the next three hours. I must stop here to recount the fact that I have never been very good, to pick up on other's heavy loads. Shirley's' singular burden at this time should have registered with me, but standing there, over weight; and well feed by the army, it never occurred to me she might be in serious financial straits and I passed the cookie incident off as bad manners, what a jackass I was, even to think, she might be so inclined. After some more visiting and playing some cards at the USO, we had dinner and Shirleys's friend came as agreed to take her back to her room at the hotel (cookies and all).

The next weekend I finally got a pass, I guess the guys in charge of my life finally realized their efforts to ruin it were not justified, or they just screwed up, and some underling unwittingly issued a pass in my name, which is what most likely transpired.

Saturday I hurried into town as early as the Sergeant would allow the recruits to leave the barracks. This weekend I would discover to my real consternation that Shirley was living on the cookies she had taken from the post and little else.

Since she believed I had no way to help her, she had been surviving on some day old bread from the bakery below her room, and had used her last five dollars which consisted of two, two dollar bills, and a silver dollar her dad had given her for luck before she left Oklahoma. With these meager funds she had purchased a package of sliced cheese, a small jar of mayonnaise, and the bread mentioned above. I would still not have been aware of her plight, as she was still trying to protect me from this knowledge, but I asked her if she would fix me a sandwich, about an hour after I got to her room. Shirley went to the only window in the room, reached out on the window ledge and retrieved a small jar of mayonnaise and two Kraft singles, then she went back to the small lamp table beside her bed and sitting down on her bed, twisted open the partial loaf of bread and begin to prepare the sandwich. We visited about what had happened to each of us during the past week, Shirley related to me, that although she had been renting books from the small hotel library downstairs, the librarian (desk clerk) had been generously allowing her to read them freely for the past week, and this really helped her to while away the time. As I ate the snack, and as I took a drink of water and used my handkerchief as a napkin, I ask her if she had anything else to eat, (anything, meaning chips or possibly nuts), and she begin to cry, as she understood me to indicate by this request that she was not doing well as a new wife, or taking care of herself while I was away. She also knew that piece of cheese was all she had left to give. When I saw the tears swelling up in her eyes, I ask her what was the matter, as I still had not figured out the situation. (I was so perceptive!) She continued to silently cry, as she tried to explain she had nothing else for me to eat, and my heart sunk into that deep pit of my stomach, as

I begin to realize she was telling me she had been living so meagerly for the past week, and was still only thinking about my welfare.

I was so miserable when I finally got the whole picture that holding her closely; we both had a good cry.

What she did not know was that I had won $ 20.00 in a poker game the night before, and so we immediately got dressed and left the hotel to get her a decent meal. Since I knew she was quite hungry I suggested we go to the little café directly across the street, but she would not go there, as the far eastern people who owned and operated the place used curry spice in almost every dish they prepared, and the smell permeated the air for blocks. This aroma constantly nauseated Shirley, who was pregnant, and as a result; our fifty years together has never seen the use of curry in any dish prepared in her kitchen, and never will!

We both survived the remaining week that climaxed with my graduation drill ceremony that she attended holding her suitcase. After which we immediately picked up my monthly check, my bags of gear, and headed to the bus station to catch a ride to Oklahoma. This was a bumpy ride on a bus that literally stopped at every small town and even some desert outposts, between Monterrey and Tulsa. A trip taking two full days to get us to Pryor, where we would pick up Shirley's car, and spend most of the thirteen- day leave I was granted before reporting to Ft. Meade Maryland for duty with the U S Army Field Band.

While driving through Tulsa on our way to visit my parents in Pawhuska, we past a maternity shop at the corner of Yale and 11th. Knowing that Shirley was in need of some dresses, as she was in the last days of her fourth month of carrying our first child,

I suggested we stop and see what was available. She agreed, and we went shopping. Now shopping with Shirley is no small or short time affair and about one hour later, Shirley selected three maternity outfits from the many that she had carefully looked over, then tried on and now she proudly placed on the payout counter. The clerk checked the prices on each item, and told us we owed the store $80.00. Since this was the same figure we had calculated before bringing the goods to the front of the store, I placed a $100.00 bill on the counter for the clerk to make change. In a huff, due to the time we had been there and as it was nearly 5pm closing time; the clerk handed me back $120.00 as change, then rudely and quickly stuffed the clothing we had purchased in a shopping bag, handing the bag to Shirley. I thought she had made an error, and told her so, but she was adamantly stanch in her determination of the price and making change, and ushered us to the door, as she pulled the shade down and placed the closing sign in the window, then opened the door for Shirley to exit the shop. I tried once more to speak to her about the change, but to no avail, so we left and drove to Pawhuska with our gifts, which I must say on Shirley; looked quite nice.

Our thirteen day vacation from the rigors of military duty ended all to soon, but had some interesting twists, as we tried to get Shirley settled in Oklahoma for the long three months we would have to be apart, while I spent the summer touring Europe performing concerts for Mr. Eisenhower and his Republican administration.

# Letting the Vintage Rest

When we arrived in Oklahoma and picked up our car at my parents home, we went immediately to Shirley's' parents new home in Pryor, Oklahoma amid some concern as to why they had not

*Shirley and Carroll on leave in Pawhuska spring 1957*

contacted us about their move. When we finally found them, they said they had been forced to move quite suddenly when Hollis got a chance to sell the other place and purchase this one, and that in their haste and trauma of moving had simply failed to realize we were coming home so soon. Along with our days of enjoying being together, we tried to see as many relatives as possible, as we had been apart from them, as well as each other for some weeks. These events had taken their toll on Shirley, who found them to be really traumatic, especially in conjunction with her pregnancy, which together with the fact that I was preparing to leave for a long stretch and her Nanny being old and by herself, caused her to nearly lose our first child, due the physician told us, to stress.

The in-laws new house was at the edge of Pryor and had two stories, so they had rented the top story to a couple, and Shirleys' parents were living on the ground floor of the drafty old home. When they realized Shirley would need help, as she would be alone for the next few months, they immediately commandeered the top story for her residence, so we spent the next few days before I left sprucing up the place. Reluctantly, on the next to last day of my leave, Shirley drove me to the airport in Tulsa, where we said our very melancholy goodbyes, and I boarded a plane for what was apprehensively to become one of my life's great adventures.

# Redwine in the Vineyards of Europe

I arrived at the air terminal in Washington D.C. on Sunday afternoon about 2pm, and took a shuttle to Ft. Meade, Maryland as instructed by my orders, that I had received the day I graduated from basic. When I arrived at the BOQ where the band was stationed, there was only an office sergeant present, and he had not been notified of my coming, so as a result he had no idea where to put me for the night. After a few phone calls and reading my orders two or three times, he assigned me to the enlisted men's' barracks for that night with the idea that I would be moved if necessary the next day. The few men present when I walked into the barracks were cordial, but certainly not friendly, as one of them, I can't remember whom, showed me to an empty bunk, and told me I would need to go to the office to obtain bedding for the night, or plan on sleeping on the springs. Not wanting to spend the cold early spring night in misery I took his advice and went immediately to obtain the necessary sheets, towels, and etc. One thing I had learned some time previously was when you are the new guy on the block, be cordial, but keep to yourself until invited to participate in the residents happenings, so when I returned, I fixed my berth, hung up my extra clothes, put my gear as neatly as I could out of sight, and casually walked to the first open door down the hall, and asked which way I would need to go to find the chow hall for dinner, as it was now five-thirty pm and my experience with the army had been that chow on Sunday was generally served and the chow hall closed by six-thirty pm. This schedule allows the men in charge of this operation to escape from duty by seven-thirty pm. Also, I just wanted to get out of the barracks and see what the area looked like on this part of the post. The fellow who had his door open was good at giving directions and after an enjoyable short walk of about four city blocks, I found myself at the mess hall, where as I suspected, I had been dead on target about the army's' Sunday evening mess routine. Chow was pretty meager, but I wasn't very hungry anyway and managed to find a baloney and cheese sandwich, with some really bad French fries and a glass of tap water, that as I expected being east of the Mississippi, tasted like sewer water. Since the troops working Sunday mess made it obvious to all of the dinner guests they were not happy to be spending their evening serving and working this detail, I ate as quickly as I could, without appearing harassed, and got the hell out of there. By the time I walked back to the barracks, darkness had fallen on this fine spring day, and after the hassle of my trip and subsequent arrival at a destination where no one was expecting me, both my mind and body were ready for bed. Surprise! Surprise! When I walked into the barracks all three men who had been there before and nearly ignored me said, " Hi," and asked, If I wished to come in their rooms. I told them I truly appreciated their invitations, but due to the days events would need my rest before I was to meet the surprises to be presented me on the morrow, and saying good night I went to bed, and immediately to sleep.

When I awoke Monday morning at seven am no one was up, so I went to the latrine at the north end of the barracks, showered, shaved and washed out the underwear, I had worn yesterday. Then dressing in freshly starched and ironed fatigues, I went to the commander's office to report for duty as directed by my orders. Major Whiting wasn't in yet, but was expected shortly so I was taken, to the Quartermasters barracks by a young Sp-5 to obtain the required clothing and equipment issued to a member of my unit. The quartermaster's office asked for a copy of my orders, and having them with me, as I had just shown them to the Band office, made life easier than I expected. Not expecting me to have them, the clerk in charge told me to go to my barracks and pick up a copy, and looked a bit peeved, when I pulled them out of my folder, as now he would have to go to work and measure me for my uniforms and equipment, then issue same, as he had no excuses for not doing so. It took nearly two hours to complete my responsibilities with the quartermaster and by the time I got back to the Majors' office, he had gone for the day, but the duty officer had told him of my arrival, and he had left instructions for me to spend the rest of that day at the medical facility getting the necessary shots and medical tests and clearances to obtain my passport for my coming tour of Europe with his band. Tuesday and Wednesday mornings were a copy of Mondays' latrine activity, and after breakfast at the mess hall, I hurried to the office, where I hoped to finally meet the elusive Major Whiting, to no avail. However on Thursday, as I walked in, I realized there was quite a stir in this office, and at the far end of the room, behind a huge desk sat the extremely charismatic Major with his tousled white mane, and giving orders breathlessly to every one in sight. Every time he spoke, there would be silence except for his voice, and at the end of his every command utter chaos, as those persons putting his words into action hastened to complete his bidding. Looking up from his list of tasks, he casually acknowledged his recognition of me, as though I was a fly on his breakfast roll, and he was about to flick me into oblivion. Then grinning that most disarming and warm mannered way of his, he welcomed me to the band as though he had nothing in the world on his mind, but me! He ask about Shirley, my health, my trip to his post, and then suddenly, as though making a 90 degree turn in his agenda, said," take this man to the Pentagon to secure his passport, he has an appointment in two hours." Waving wildly to the office help, but at no one in particular, he again wished me well, and I knew further conversation was definitely, finished, as I was ushered hurriedly to a Company Car, where Sp-5 Joey Greco a very nice fellow, who was one of the motor pool men, drove me to the Pentagon. At the Pentagon, the passport division had truly been waiting for my arrival. Their wait proven by their readiness to take my picture when

*Me, in the infamous wash and wear brown suit*

we arrived and within an hour I had a passport and was back in the car headed toward Ft. Meade. Even Greco was surprised with the speed the folks at the passport office had worked. When I got back to the post I noticed the band had just finished a rehearsal. Although all the faces smiled and were friendly, I did not recognize anyone, until I saw a warmly smiling Smity come out of the rehearsal area with his right hand extended toward me, we greeted each other and I ask him when I would be rehearsing with the band, as I was concerned about my preparation for performance with the band. Smity assured me I would not have any trouble with the music, and told me not to worry about this portion of my responsibilities, but to concentrate on getting all the Ts crossed on my paper work, and securing the gear, that would be necessary for me to make the tour, as we were leaving tomorrow, May 7th, 1957. What a surprise, we were leaving two days earlier than I thought. He said this, as he handed me a list of equipment and clothing I would be using on this tour. To meet this schedule I would need to pack right away, and place these items on the bands' truck that would be transported tonight to the Brooklyn Naval Yard. Tomorrow I would take my bags off the truck and carry it with me as I boarded the ship. I scurried around and completed the assignments as ordered.

The list of required uniforms included two uniforms that the quarter masters office had recently issued, a set of army dress blues and a set of dress gabardines and a note **not to** forget my saxophone. In addition to these items, I toured fourteen countries of Europe for the next two and one half months, with a small drop kit containing some band-aids, a toothbrush, a tube of toothpaste, six safety razors, two deodorant sticks, a small bar of soap, and a wash cloth, and the following designer clothing, two white dress shirts, two ties, one yellow and one brown, a black bow tie, a pair of black military issue shoes, and one of the worlds finest (dull brown), wash and wear suits. Although I'm sure the other band members must have found my fashion statement of the wash and wear suit amusing, since I wore it daily, they were kind and never once mentioned the tired looked of my persona.

The next morning I awakened early, donned the dress gabardine uniform as ordered in the note from Smity, and along with the rest of the band boarded the bands busses for my first trip as a member of this illustrious and famed musical organization. As we traveled to New York the bus was pretty quiet, most of the band members were old hands and were a bit despondent to be leaving their families for what they realized would be many weeks, a realization that had not yet made it's presence felt on the writer, for which the excitement of just being with all these great musicians was over shadowing any anxiety of any type, I tried to visit with Smity, but in addition to his being two seats in front of me and his obvious shortness of conversation, yours truly quickly gave up on that idea and spent the remaining bus ride enjoying the new sights, and trying to figure how much hay those big buildings along the interstate would hold.

The bands busses were not allowed due to security and congestion to unload close to the ship, and could only take us within about a mile of the gangplank. I have always thought that making the men walk and carry their gear was just the navy's method of getting even with the army for having to transport the army's finest band on a navy ship. We unloaded men and equipment, as previously mentioned, and began the long tedious walk carrying all our gear to the ship, It seemed as though we would never get there and it must have really been hard for some of the older men. I had just finished my basic training less than three weeks previously, and it was sure hard for me. This was one time I was glad I had spent the past three years moving my own band all over the country, as knowing how hard it is to get equipment from one place to another, I had really packed light and only had my horn and one light suit case to manipulate, and I noticed as I struggled to the ship, the older guys had done likewise.

When we finally arrived at the ship, out of breath and ready to unhand our gear, the navy guys chided all of us for being so out of shape. Then they took our biggest trunks and instruments aboard, leaving all the small stuff for each of us to carry. So, since I only had the two cases, I kept them with me for the next eight days on the voyage to the Old World Continent.

For some unknown reason I had pictured the voyage to Europe aboard this navy ship different entirely from that of reality. My vision was of standing on the deck feeding the gulls, and listening to the gently breaking waves, as they past the giant hull. Of beautiful star filled nights with moon beams glinting on the mast, as we glided ever so silently over a peaceful and tranquil ocean. The navy's' idea, and the one we would both be inflicted with, was for me to spend the next eight days eating the worst excuse for food ever imagined, being restricted from deck privileges, and existing five floors below decks, with absolutely no ventilation. Then, as if the navy could not inflict enough grief on this land loving son of the plains, on the third day out of port and for the next three days, the ship was tossed around like a cork in one of grandma Bs' butter churns, while we road out a major storm, it was a sickenly, ever on-going, nightmare, and one still vividly in my head. The tour was not starting out so good! I have included some of the pertinent army paperwork on these next few pages to verify my writing about this grand experience. These documents include news articles,letters written to the Secretary of the Army by various enmities commending the performances and Band's general conduct as it influenced the people of Europe, travel orders for the tour and financial documents verifying the army's payment for the tour, as well as the schedule of performances and the reported crowd participation in each performance and crowd totals as reported by the forward liaison and mailed to me by The U. S. Army Field Band archivist, Sgt Kathy Miller. Since leaving the Band in 1960 I have only been fortunate enough to get to hear them three times. Once in Texarkanna,Texas while my friend Sammy Fricano was the conductor, and in Muskogee, in the 70's and just this past year in Stillwater 2005, where they very graciously acknowledged both Bill Thompson and myself as former members and performers.

One of the most important aspects of any troop movement is morale, and to say that the bands' morale was not real good by the seventh day of being tossed about by the storm in that unventilated ship, truly was an understatement at best. Dante must have survived one of these United States Navy ocean voyages, because his seven levels of Hell was somewhat reminisent of our five levels below deck. So the Major, needing to get his men above decks, and also needing a rehearsal, scheduled a performance of the band for the ships personnel. I thought that this was a great idea when I first heard we were going to do it, but was not so sure how good it was, as I banged my way five circular flights of steps carrying my horn, and music stand with my music folio to the area on the deck, where we performed. At least we found that fresh air and sunshine still existed. Hooray for the Major!

| | Day/Mo/Year | Location (City & Country) | Hour | Mode of Travel |
|---|---|---|---|---|
| DEP | 7 May 57 | Ft Gg. Meade, Md. | 0930 | G/MV |
| ARR | 7 May 57 | New York City, N.Y. | 1600 | |
| DEP | 8 May 57 | New York City N. Y. | 1400 | G/B |
| ARR | 16 May 57 | Bremerhaven, Germany | 1400 | |
| DEP | 16 May 57 | Bremerhaven, Germany | 14300 | G/MV |
| ARR | 16 May 57 | The Hague, Netherlands | 2330 | |
| DEP | 20 May 57 | The Hague, Netherlands | 0800 | G/MV |
| ARR | 20 May 57 | Luxemburg City, Lux. | 1730 | |
| DEP | 22 May 57 | Luxemburg City, Lux. | 0800 | G/MV |
| ARR | 22 May 57 | Antwerp., Belgium | 1530 | |
| DEP | 23 May 57 | Antwerp., Belgium | 0800 | G/MV |
| ARR | 23 May 57 | Paris, France | 1500 | |
| DEP | 25 May 57 | Paris, France | 0800 | G/MV |
| ARR | 25 May 57 | Blois, France | 1500 | |
| DEP | 26 May 57 | Blois, France | 0900 | G/MV |
| ARR | 26 May 57 | Poitiers, France | 1200 | |
| DEP | 27 May 57 | Poitiers, France | 0900 | G/MV |
| ARR | 27 May 57 | Angoulême, France | 1100 | |
| DEP | 28 May 57 | Angoulême, France | 0800 | G/MV |
| ARR | 28 May 57 | San Sebastian, Spain | 1830 | |
| DEP | 29 May 57 | San Sebastian, Spain | 2240 | T/R |
| ARR | 30 May 57 | Lisbon, Portugal | 1900 | |
| DEP | 1 Jun 57 | Lisbon, Portugal | 0800 | G/MV |
| ARR | 1 Jun 57 | Sevilla, Spain | 1700 | |
| DEP | 3 Jun 57 | Sevilla, Spain | 0800 | G/MV |
| ARR | 3 Jun 57 | Granada, Spain | 1600 | |
| DEP | 4 Jun 57 | Granada, Spain | 0800 | G/MV |
| ARR | 4 Jun 57 | Madrid, Spain | 1700 | |

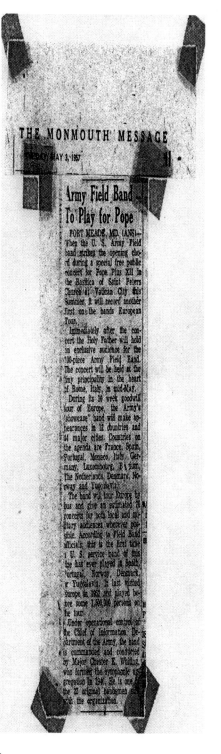

THE MONMOUTH MESSAGE

FRIDAY, MAY 3, 1957

**Army Field Band To Play for Pope**

FORT MEADE, MD. (ANF)—When the U. S. Army Field band strikes the opening chord during a special free public concert for Pope Pius XII in the Basilica of Saint Peters Church in Vatican City this Summer, it will record another first on the bands European Tour.

Immediately after the concert the Holy Father will hold an exclusive audience for the 100-piece Army Field Band. The concert will be held at the tiny principality in the heart of Rome, Italy, in mid-May.

During its 10 week goodwill tour of Europe, the Army's "showcase" band will make appearances in 12 countries and 44 major cities. Countries on the agenda are France, Spain, Portugal, Monaco, Italy, Germany, Luxembourg, Belgium, The Netherlands, Denmark, Norway and Yugoslavia.

The band will tour Europe by bus and give an estimated 70 concerts for both local and military audiences wherever possible. According to Field Band officials, this is the first time a U. S. service band of this type has ever played in Spain, Portugal, Norway, Denmark, or Yugoslavia. It last visited Europe in 1952 and played before some 1,500,000 persons on the tour.

Under operational control of the Chief of Information, Department of the Army, the band is commanded and conducted by Major Chester E. Whiting, who formed the symphonic congregation in 1946. He is one of the 20 original bandsmen with the organization.

| | Day/Mo/Year | Location (City & Country) | Hour |
|---|---|---|---|
| DEP | 6 Jun 57 | Madrid, Spain | 0800 |
| ARR | 6 Jun 57 | Zaragoza, Spain | 1700 |
| DEP | 7 Jun 57 | Zaragoza, Spain | 0800 |
| ARR | 7 Jun 57 | Barcelona, Spain | 1600 |
| DEP | 9 Jun 57 | Barcelona, Spain | 0700 |
| ARR | 9 Jun 57 | Marseille, France | 2200 |
| DEP | 10 Jun 57 | Marseille, France | 0900 |
| ARR | 10 Jun 57 | Nice, France | 1400 |
| DEP | 13 Jun 57 | Nice, France | 0900 |
| ARR | 13 Jun 57 | Genoa, Italy | 1600 |
| DEP | 14 Jun 57 | Genoa, Italy | 0700 |
| ARR | 14 Jun 57 | Rome, Italy | 2200 |
| DEP | 16 Jun 57 | Rome, Italy | 0900 |
| ARR | 16 Jun 57 | Naples, Italy | 1400 |
| DEP | 17 Jun 57 | Naples, Italy | 0900 |
| ARR | 17 Jun 57 | Rome, Italy | 1400 |
| DEP | 18 Jun 57 | Rome, Italy | 1100 |
| ARR | 18 Jun 57 | Florence, Italy | 1600 |
| DEP | 20 Jun 57 | Florence, Italy | 1200 |
| ARR | 20 Jun 57 | Verona, Italy | 1530 |

| | Day/Mo/Year | Location (City & Country) | Hour | Mode of Travel |
|---|---|---|---|---|
| DEP | 27 Jun 57 | Belgrade, Yugoslavia | 0100 | T/R |
| ARR | 27 Jun 57 | Zagreb, Yugoslavia | 0600 | |
| DEP | 28 Jun 57 | Zagreb, Yugoslavia | 1030 | T/R |
| ARR | 28 Jun 57 | Salzburg, Austria | 2100 | |
| DEP | 28 Jun 57 | Salzburg, Austria | 2115 | G/MV |
| ARR | 28 Jun 57 | Berchtesgaden, Germany | 2215 | |
| DEP | 30 Jun 57 | Berchtesgaden, Germany | 0800 | G/MV |
| ARR | 30 Jun 57 | Munich, Germany | 1700 | |
| DEP | 1 Jul 57 | Munich, Germany | 1100 | G/MV |
| ARR | 1 Jul 57 | Nuernberg, Germany | 1500 | |
| DEP | 2 Jul 57 | Nuernberg, Germany | 0900 | T/R |
| ARR | 2 Jul 57 | Stuttgart, Germany | 1300 | |
| DEP | 3 Jul 57 | Stuttgart, Germany | 1130 | G/MV |
| ARR | 3 Jul 57 | Frankfurt, Germany | 1500 | |
| DEP | 6 Jul 57 | Frankfurt, Germany | 2100 | T/R |
| ARR | 7 Jul 57 | Berlin, Germany | 0800 | |
| DEP | 8 Jul 57 | Berlin, Germany | 2200 | T/R |
| ARR | 10 Jul 57 | Oslo, Norway | 1200 | |
| DEP | 11 Jul 57 | Oslo, Norway | 0700 | T/R |
| ARR | 11 Jul 57 | Copenhagen, Denmark | 1800 | |
| DEP | 14 Jul 57 | Copenhagen, Denmark | 0600 | T/R |
| ARR | 14 Jul 57 | Hamburg, Germany | 1600 | |
| DEP | 16 Jul 57 | Hamburg, Germany | 0700 | T/R |
| ARR | 16 Jul 57 | Frankfurt, Germany | 1800 | |

| | | | Flight #1 | | Flight #2 | | |
|---|---|---|---|---|---|---|---|
| Dep 17 Jul 57 | Frankfurt, Germany | | 1330 | | 2200 | | G/A |
| Arr 18 Jul 57 | McGuire AFB, N. J. | " | 0500 | " | 1200 | | |
| Dep 18 Jul 57 | McGuire AFB, N. J. | " | 0630 | " | 1300 | | G/MV |
| Arr 18 Jul 57 | Fort G. G. Meade, Md. | " | 1000 | " | 1755 | | |

I was really concerned about being able to perform at this level without a rehearsal, and when I remarked to Smity about this he answered, "PLAY SOFTLY", and I did! This concert went over so well that the Major used the same ploy that afternoon with the stage and jazz band. The next day we got off that torture chamber after she docked in Breimerhaven Germany, and shortly

*The Pleyel in Paris was a beautiful venue and what a wonderful crowd to entertain*

Regenerated our land legs, boy! What a relief to be back on solid terra firmma.

*Cards mailed home from this tour were received and saved by my parents in case I might some day wish to write about the tour.*

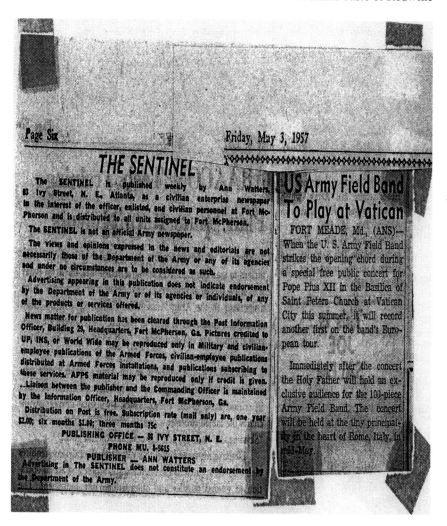

Page Six                              Friday, May 3, 1957

## THE SENTINEL

The SENTINEL is published weekly by Ann Watters, 83 Ivy Street, N. E., Atlanta, as a civilian enterprise newspaper in the interest of the officer, enlisted, and civilian personnel at Fort McPherson and is distributed to all units assigned to Fort McPherson.

The SENTINEL is not an official Army newspaper.

The views and opinions expressed in the news and editorials are not necessarily those of the Department of the Army or any of its agencies and under no circumstances are to be considered as such.

Advertising appearing in this publication does not indicate endorsement by the Department of the Army or of its agencies or individuals, of any of the products or services offered.

News matter for publication has been cleared through the Post Information Officer, Building 25, Headquarters, Fort McPherson, Ga. Pictures credited to UP, INS, or World Wide may be reproduced only in Military and civilian-employee publications of the Armed Forces, civilian-employee publications distributed at Armed Forces installations, and publications subscribing to these services. AFPS material may be reproduced only if credit is given. Liaison between the publisher and the Commanding Officer is maintained by the Information Officer, Headquarters, Fort McPherson, Ga.

Distribution on Post is free. Subscription rate (mail only) are, one year $2.00; six months $1.00; three months 75c.

PUBLISHING OFFICE — 83 IVY STREET, N. E.
PHONE MU. 8-5615
PUBLISHER — ANN WATTERS
Advertising in The SENTINEL does not constitute an endorsement by the Department of the Army.

## US Army Field Band To Play at Vatican

FORT MEADE, Md., (ANS)— When the U. S. Army Field Band strikes the opening chord during a special free public concert for Pope Pius XII in the Basilica of Saint Peters Church at Vatican City this summer, it will record another first on the band's European tour.

Immediately after the concert the Holy Father will hold an exclusive audience for the 100-piece Army Field Band. The concert will be held at the tiny principality in the heart of Rome, Italy, in mid-May.

We disembarked the navy's portable chip and paint project about 2:30 pm on the afternoon of May 16th and immediately boarded military shuttle busses with our colors painted on them. These buses took our equipment and us to The Hague, Netherlands. We were to stay in The Hague for the evening of the 16th and for the next three days, where we would meet the Burgomaster, and the U. S. Ambassador to the Netherlands who were our hosts for these performances. Afterward we would perform two concerts at Kurzaal

Hall on Sunday the 19th of May, and, although our days were not without free time to sight see, we did spend quite a bit of each day meeting the dignitaries of each city and country in formal settings with much Champaign toasting of each others countries As a young man I was extremely impressed with the miniature city replicating The Hague and spent some hours enjoying it.

Monday the 20th of May we motored to Diekerch, Luxembourg for a performance, outdoors in the town square. Totally unscheduled, we were invited to dinner afterwards at the Luxembourg army barracks, and then requested to perform in concert, (which we did!) a concert that did not start until after 10pm! The next day we performed in the Municipal Stadium of the city to a live audience of over 3000 souls and a TV audience estimated by our sponsor, the US embassy, to exceed 10,000.

Wednesday, the 22nd of May we traveled by bus to Antwerp, Belgium, and performed for over two thousand listeners in the Feestzaal. The Feestzaal, is one of Europe's' most beautiful concert halls, and I took the liberty of mailing a picture of me performing on that stage with the 2000 person audience in the background, to my fifth grade music teacher, Mrs. Harris, who in a letter of reproach had written my parents during the 1947 school year that they should take me out of music, due to my lack of talent. I then resolved to never make that mistake with anyone of my future students, no matter how their abilities struck me, and I've been pleasantly surprised many times by the sucesses of some of those students.

Thursday was a travel day, so after a bit of sightseeing we boarded the busses to go to Paris, where we would perform at the Salle Pleyel, another in a long line of magnificent concert halls, which were to

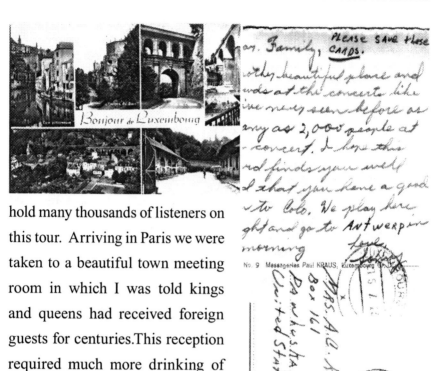

hold many thousands of listeners on this tour. Arriving in Paris we were taken to a beautiful town meeting room in which I was told kings and queens had received foreign guests for centuries.This reception required much more drinking of wine and much conversation by our hosts, one of whom was Charles DeGalle, who welcomed the band to his great country. Since I did not speak French, my personal remarks to the many dignitaries who so kindly came to visit with us were short and to the point, I smiled and nodded my head occasionally, as I hoped not to appear too stupid in front of all these illustrious folks. We performed in Paris on Friday evening, and ate dinner after the performance together at one of Paris's finest hotels; this was my first introduction to a seven-course meal, and to Guyier and Camebert cheeses. The meal was really great, and even the (escargot) snails were a delight, as I plucked them from their home in the special serving dish. The wine was pretty good until the Major decided we had experienced enough and told the Matre De to hold off on serving any more, as the natives were getting a bit restless. I do remember thinking these French chefs need a lesson on how to prepare a decent steak, as the main course was pretty lame.

The Field Band played four concerts over the next three days. Saturday the 25th of May we performed in both the afternoon and evening at Orleans, and Blois, France: Then on Sunday morning we traveled to Poitiers, France for an outdoor concert in the Municipal Park Band Shell, and traveled to Angouleme, France on Monday morning for an evening performance. At our last stop we spent

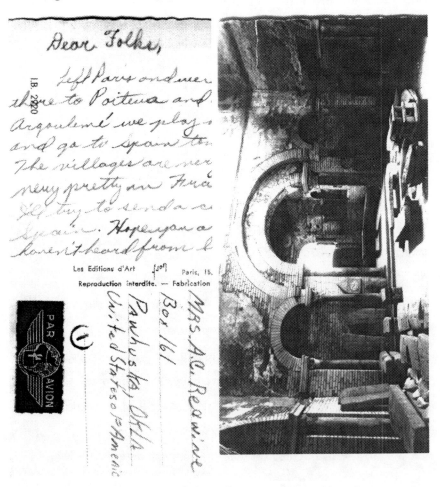

the night in three or four small hotels, as the town did not have accommodations for the whole band to stay in the same location. I was assigned a room on the third floor of a very small garret, which seemed to be less than ostentatious from the moment I entered the place, and proved to be a real sleaze bag, as I woke up the next morning itching in a number of places. I showed the blisters to Everett Short, our trumpet section leader, who was my seatmate on the bus. Sarge, as Everett was known, had been assigned by higher powers to baby-sit me on this tour, due to my obvious naivety. From Everett I learned the spots were my first encounter with **bed bugs!** Fortunately for me, it was also my only encounter with these little beasts, and I sure have not missed their bites.

We traveled to San Sebastian, Spain on military shuttles Tuesday, and I scratched my bug bites all the way there and through the evenings concert. The fact that I sat on the outside of my section and could in no way hide my dilemma from the crowd of 10,000 outdoor listeners was a real problem, especially in those hot dress blues. Fortunately, the bites only lasted about 24 hours and we performed indoors on the 29th in the Victoria Theater for about 1400 concert goers, and then caught a train at 2240 hours on the 29th that was to take us to Lisbon, Portugal for an indoor concert for 4500 people inside the Coliseu dos Reereios Friday the 31st.

The train ride through Spain on what I was told was the Orient Express was a real eye opener, I saw my first cork trees, and could visually perceive how the cork bark was harvested. In addition the villas along the miles, or kilometers: as the continent refers to their approximate same distance of track, were a delight to see with their red tile roofs and stucco walls, and when we finally arrived at Lisbon, the night life that did not start until 11 or12 pm was a revelation unto itself, as dinner was not served until about 10 pm or later, and the streets were devoid of anyone in the afternoon, and full of people from around 9: 00pm until 2 or 3 am. The jet lag of changing hours so often, quickly took its toll on my physical well being, and so I was forced to give up trying to see for myself if the town was still alive at the early morning time, and I retired to bed at what was considered early evening by Lisboners at 11:00pm.

From Sunday June 2nd through Saturday June 8th we continued to perform in the following Spanish cities: Seville, Granada, Madrid, Zaragoza, and Barcelona enjoying each day visiting with the gorgeous populace of this Old World civilization, watching their flamenco dancers, and being continually surprised that they appeared to truly enjoy our concerts, as we performed in front of larger crowds in each new venue. The crowds grew in numbers thusly, 10,000 in Seville, 16,000 in Granada, and 27,000 on Wednesday June 5th when after being introduced by the U. S. Ambassador, John Davis Lodge, we performed in the middle of the bull ring at the Plaza de Toro's in Madrid, where on the last note of **Stars and Stripes Forever** without prompting, the entire crowd of 27,000 in unison shouted Ole', and raised the hair on the back of my neck and on the necks of everyone else in the band. What an experience, certainly one I'll never forget! In Barcelona 7,000people jammed the Palacio Nacional de Montjuich to listen for two and a half hours to our concert and gave us five ovations still requesting more music after all five encores, as we left the stage to a standing ovation, the Major had to return to acknowledge the crowd one last time. Although the crowd of 2,000 in the Theater Principal of Zaragoza was considerably smaller it was no less enthusiastic, with many encores and standing ovations, a wonder to observe and a delight in which to take part.

Monday June 10th, found us performing in Cannes, France where we were originally scheduled for an outdoor show, but it rained and the performance was held inside the Palais des Festival that only accommodated 1500 persons, a real disappointment for many who could not get inside.

Tuesday June 11th the US Army Field Band with yours truly tagging along to perform as usual on the alto saxophone, set up on the palace square of the Royal Palace in Monaco, with Prince Rainier, and princess Grace (the former movie star Grace Kelly) and their young daughter seated on the third story balcony above, while our concert they appeared to enjoy was broadcast by both Tele Monte Carlo and Radio Monte Carlo. After the concert the Prince personally presented a hand engraved metal box of his own private cigarettes to each of the bands instrumentalists and conductors, then received the band and its personnel at a private reception in the

palace, **Very Impressive**, to a 19 year old kid from Pawhuska, Oklahoma! The news release given out the next day stated there were 3,000 people present for this concert, but I honestly was so taken by the Prince and his entourage that I could not confirm that figure.

When we arrived in Monaco the Harbor was filled to capacity with beautiful yachts, and the most impressive of these magnificent crafts was tied to the center pier, dwarfing all others, I of course asked to whom it belonged, and

Carroll E. Redwine

# HALL HERALD

Arlington Hall Station, Virginia                    May 31, 1957

## Band Performs For Monaco Royalty

The US Army Field Band will give a Command Performance for the Prince and Princess of Monaco on the Palace grounds overlooking the Mediterranean Sea during its 10 week good will tour of Europe this summer.

Prince Rainer has invited the citizenry of his tiny principality to attend the concert to be given by the world-famed Army "showcase" band on June 15. Following the concert band members will be special guests of the Prince and Princess at a buffet and reception in the palace.

### Postponed Cruise

According to an official spokesman of the band, Rainer and the Princess (former Hollywood movie Star Grace Kelly) have postponed their scheduled summer cruise to hear this unprecedented concert by the Army's only traveling band.

The spokesman said, "The international goodwill created by the band's foreign appearances helps pave the way for a closer friendship between servicemen overseas and the people of countries where US Army personnel are stationed."

### 70 Appearances

Presently touring Europe by bus, the band is scheduled to give an estimated 70 concerts in 12 countries and 44 major cities for both local and military audiences wherever possible.

During its last visit to Europe in 1953, the band played before more than 1,500,000 persons.

134

was told by one of the local dock workers, that its owner was gambling at the casino, and his name was Aristotle Onassis, Greek shipping magnate, who was at that time said to be the world's wealthiest individual. Unfortunately, I was not allowed to meet him, as the band was forbidden to enter the casino, by order of our officers. This was a darn shame, as I know he would have liked to shake my steady hand, and shot a little craps with the luckiest Okie in Monaco. I thought the Major was a bit selfish in not sharing me and my fine gambling abilities with the Prince, but quickly forgot about it, as we had to hurriedly travel to Nice, France for an outdoor concert in the plaza across from our hotel. Only about 4500 people came to the afternoon concert, and we had a great time after this show, sight seeing in Nice, and trying to make a few bucks by cashing one or two $20.00 travelers checks on the exchange rate at the local banks. Sometimes the rate in the next country made it necessary, before we left the present one.

Thursday the 13th of June we traveled to Genoa, Italy, where

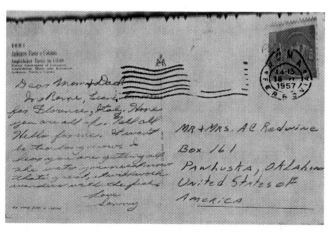

we performed outdoors for about 8,000 folks, and I had my first taste of Pistachio ice which I purchased from a street vendor much to the chagrin of the old guys in the band, who were sure I was going to get a serious case of diarrhea. Friday was a travel day that quickly found us in Rome, Where, as we disembarked our busses in the hot mid morning sun, the royal Italian cabinnery band performing badly many great Italian composers serenaded us. The clarinets were extremely harsh and the brass was weak and immature. However, the day quickly became a real winner after this group finally succumbed to the heat and we got checked into our hotel, which as I remember was a really nice place, and allowed us to walk to some of Rome's greatest ancient sites. I spent many hours inside St.Peters Basilica, amid awe and great wonderment at this most holy and grandiose architecture, and magnificent holdings, which through the ages, God has divinely inspired men to artfully, create.

Saturday, June 15th we performed at the Basilica di Massenzio in Rome. The Basilica was the site of some ancient ruins very close to the Roman Forum and Coliseum, and virtually all members of the United States diplomatic corp. including our Italian Ambassador was present with Ambassador Zellerbach introducing the performance. The crowds grew in attendance as we performed in each new Italian city and by Sunday June 16th, when we performed in Naples at the Piazza Plebiscito for an outdoor audience of nearly 60, 000 the audiences had become unwieldy, as we did not use amplification, except for the bands announcer. This lack of projection plus the crowd's normal noise caused about 10,000 persons to leave somewhat before the end of the concert due to the fact they could not hear us in the back of the crowd.

The Band had a couple days to enjoy the sights before our next performance in Florence, where I purchased some beautiful leather goods to present to my family as gifts. These included a pair of white kid elbow length gloves for Shirley, who I was missing terribly.

Master Sergeant, Kathy Miller, Librarian of the U. S. Army Field Band; has been very kind to sift thru the Bands archives, and mail the writer much needed information, which when reviewed brought back many familiar faces and memories. One such document was a complete summary, written for the Chief of Information's' Office in

*Official report given to Chief of Informations office by the U S Army Field Band`s liason officer and. Copied from Bands archieves.*

### 1957 EUROPEAN TOUR SCHEDULE AND CROWD TOTALS

| | DATE | PLACE | ESTIMATED AUDIENCE |
|---|---|---|---|
| 1. | Sunday, May 19 | Kurzaal Hall (inside), Scheveningen (The Hague) The Netherlands (Sponsored Jointly by Burgomaster of The Hague and the U.S. Ambassedor) | 1,000 |
| 2. | Monday, May 20 | Town Square,     (outdoors) Diekireh, Luxembourg (totally unscheduled – band invited to dinner at Luxembourg Army barracks, then asked to play afterward in concert that didn't begin until after 10 p.m.) | 3,000 |
| 3. | Tuesday, May 21 | Municipal Stadium,  (outdoors) City of Luxembourg (Also televised live for 45 minutes  –  Program sponsored by American Luxembourg Society under auspices of U. S. Embassy) | 15,000 |
| 4. | Wednesday, May 22 | Feestzaal  (inside), Antwerp, Belgium | 2,000 |
| 5. | Friday, May 24 | Salle Pleyel (inside), Paris, France (Sponsored Jointly by Seine Area Command, U.S. Army,  and L'Association France-Etats-Unis) | 4,000 |
| 6. | Saturday, May 25 (afternoon) | Post Gymnasium,  (inside) U. S. Army base, Orleans, France | 500 |
| 7. | Saturday, May 25 (Evening) | Public Market Place, (inside) Blois, France | 3,000 |
| 8. | Sunday, May 26 | Municipal Park Bandshell, (outdoors) Poitiers, France | 2,500 |
| 9. | Monday, May 27 | Municipal Theater (inside) Angouleme, France | 1,300 |
| 10. | Tuesday, May 28 | Public Park, in front of City Hall (outdoors) San Sebastian, Spain | 10,000 |

(more)

Washington D. C. of this tour by the bands Liaison Officer. Another was the travel voucher and mode of transportation used on each date of the tour showing which cities and countries were involved. This document will be included here to authenticate and verify the writers veracity as to crowd numbers and performances, in addition to aiding the readers knowledge of scantily provided dates and cities on this tour by the writer, and his recalling of same, 40 years after they took place. With this in mind, it should be sufficient to mention that we also performed in the following Italian cities: Verona,

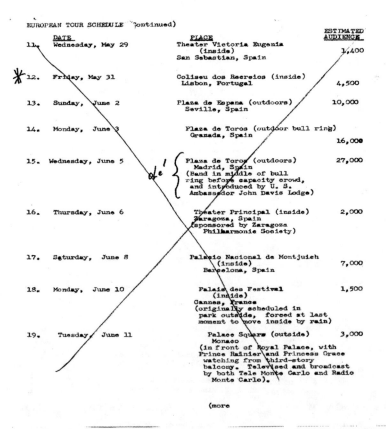

EUROPEAN TOUR SCHEDULE (continued)

| | DATE | PLACE | ESTIMATED AUDIENCE |
|---|---|---|---|
| 11. | Wednesday, May 29 | Theater Victoria Eugenia (inside) San Sebastian, Spain | 1,400 |
| 12. | Friday, May 31 | Coliseu dos Recreios (inside) Lisbon, Portugal | 4,500 |
| 13. | Sunday, June 2 | Plaza de Espana (outdoors) Seville, Spain | 10,000 |
| 14. | Monday, June 3 | Plaza de Toros (outdoor bull ring) Granada, Spain | 16,000 |
| 15. | Wednesday, June 5 | Plaza de Toros (outdoors) Madrid, Spain (Band in middle of bull ring before capacity crowd, and introduced by U. S. Ambassador John Davis Lodge) | 27,000 |
| 16. | Thursday, June 6 | Theater Principal (inside) Zaragoza, Spain (sponsored by Zaragoza Philharmonic Society) | 2,000 |
| 17. | Saturday, June 8 | Palacio Nacional de Montjuich (inside) Barcelona, Spain | 7,000 |
| 18. | Monday, June 10 | Palais des Festival (inside) Cannes, France (originally scheduled in park outside, forced at last moment to move inside by rain) | 1,500 |
| 19. | Tuesday, June 11 | Palace Square (outside) Monaco (in front of Royal Palace, with Prince Rainier and Princess Grace watching from third-story balcony. Televised and broadcast by both Tele Monte Carlo and Radio Monte Carlo). | 3,000 |

(more

*The author made the large x in pencil or ink, when he was keeping a record of which pages he had included and this mark has no effect on the information presented herein.*

EUROPEAN TOUR SCHEDULE (Continued)

| | DATE | PLACE | ESTIMATED AUDIENCE |
|---|---|---|---|
| 20. | Wednesday, June 12 | Theater de Verdure, Jardin Albert 1 (outdoors) Nice, France (plaza opposite Hotel Plaza) | 4,500 |
| 21. | Thursday, June 13 | Piazza Della Vittoria (outside) Genoa, Italy | 8,000 |
| 22. | Saturday, June 15 | Basilica di Massenzio Rome, Italy (old Roman ruins within stone's throw of Roman Forum and Coliseum. Virtually all members of diplomatic corps including U.S. Ambassador Zellerbach attended) | 4,000 |
| 23. | Sunday, June 16 | Piazza Plebiscito (outdoors) Naples, Italy (large crowd at first tended to leave early because of difficulties in hearing - too much outside noise) | 40,000-60,000 |
| 24. | Wednesday, June 19 | Piazzale degli Uffizi, Florence, Italy (outdoors) | 8,000-10,000 |
| 25. | Thursday, June 20 | Teatro Romano, (outdoors) Verona, Italy (2,000-year-old ruins of Roman Theater - taped for broadcast on AFN Verona and also for NBC Monitor in U.S.) | 8,000-10,000 |
| 26. | Friday, June 21 | Civic Theater, Pavia, Italy (near Milan) | 2,000 |
| 27. | Sunday, June 23 | Piazza San Marco (outdoors) Venice, Italy | 15,000-20,000 |
| 28. | ~~Monday~~ Monday, June 24 | Castillo de San Giusto, Trieste, Italy (almost rained out, but completely filled by time rains let up and concert started...beautiful setting atop hill overlooking city) (more) | 10,000-12,000 |

Carroll E. Redwine

| DATE | PLACE | ESTIMATED AUDIENCE |
|---|---|---|
| 29. Wednesday, June 26 (afternoon) | Municipal Stadium (outdoors) Belgrade, Yugoslavia (All-soldier audience of Yugoslav officers and troops) | 20,000 |
| 30. Wednesday, June 26 (Night) | Tajmadan Stadium, (Outdoors) Belgrade, Yugoslavia (Sponsored by Yugo Concert Bureau; admission charged for benefit of Ambassedors' Charity Relief Fund) | 4,000 |
| 31. Thursday, June 27 | Dynamo Stadium (Outdoors) Zagreb, Yugoslavia (Paid Admission, Also for Yugoslav Charity - Troops Admitted Free) | 20,000 |
| 32. Saturday, June 29 | Skyline Room, (Outdoors) Gen. Walton Walker Hotel, Berchtesgaten, Germany | 1,200 |
| 33. Sunday, June 30 (afternoon) | Parade Ground (Outdoors) U.S. Army Camp, Augsburg, Germany (11th Airborne Division) | 2,000 |
| 34. Sunday, June 30 (Night) | Kongress Hall, Deutches Museum, (inside) Munich, Germany | 3,000 |
| 35. Monday, July 1 | Soldiers' Field Stadium Nurnberg, Germany (Presented by 3rd Armored Cavalry Regiment) | 5,000 |
| 36. Tuesday, July 2 | Killesberg Park (Outdoors) Stuttgart, Germany | 5,000 |
| 37. Wednesday, July 3 | Eintrecht Stadium, (Outdoors) Frankfurt, Germany (10-minute portion - drum act, etc) televised live over all-European TV network) | 19,000 |
| 38. Thursday, July 4 | Amphitheater, Heidelberg, Germany (Hqs. USAREUR - Gen. Hodes, C.G., among those attending) (more) | 6,000 |

140

EUROPEAN TOUR SCHEDULE (continued)

| | DATE | PLACE | ESTIMATED AUDIENCE |
|---|---|---|---|
| 39. | Friday, July 5 | Stadthalle, Bad Godesberg (near Bonn) Germany | 6,500 |
| 40. | Sunday, July 7 | Olympic Stadium Berlin, West Germany (over 100,000 expected for program to include mammoth fireworks display and singing by German boys' choir) | RAINED OUT |
| 41. | Wednesday, July 10 | Jordall Amphitheater (outdoors) Oslo, Norway (U.S. Ambassedor Frances E. Wilson, making her first appearance in public in Oslo since her reassignment from Switzerland, in audience) | 5,500 |
| 42. | Friday, July 12 | Tivoli Park (Outdoors) Copenhagen, Denmark (in outdoor concert center of beautiful amusement park) | 15,000 |
| 43. | Saturday, July 13 | Tivoli Park (Inside) Copenhagen, Denmark (In music hall inside amusement park) | 3,000 |
| 44. | Monday, July 15 | Ernst-Merck Halle, (Inside) Hamburg, Germany (So many people tried to get in, minor rioting broke out and several people lightly injured). | 8,000 |

Tour Data:  43 Concerts Played; one Rained Out.

Estimated 350,000 total in Audience, over 72,000 in Spain alone and 115,000 in Italy.
Radio and Television Conservatively Estimated at one and half million.

Traveled 12 Countries; over 12,000 miles in Europe; mostly by bus and car; sometimes train. Touched on Austria, Sweden, Scotland and Newfoundland during trip.

Pavia (near Milan) Venice, which was a real delight. We were required by theYugoslaves to travel in cilvilian clothes on the next portion of the tour, as we were the first U. S. group to perform behind the iron curtain. However, we performed in dress blues.

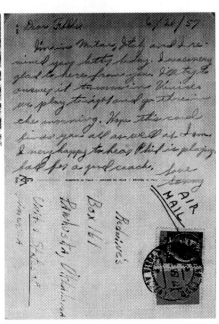

*Milan opera house in which I performed and from where I sent Ms. Harris her note*

*Below is a letter of commendation from the American ambassador to Italy to the secretary of the U. S. Army mailed after our performance in Rome.*

THE FOREIGN SERVICE
OF THE
UNITED STATES OF AMERICA

American Embassy
Rome, Italy
June 20, 1957

Dear Mr. Secretary:

The other evening I had the pleasure of hearing the Army Field Band on the occasion of its concert in Rome. I was pleased both by the music and by the warm reception the Italian audience accorded it.

A love of music is one of the tastes Americans share with Italians. A successful performance of this kind is a valuable manifestation of America's friendship for Italy. The band's tour of this country has been, I am sure, viewed by the Italian people in that spirit.

Please accept my appreciation, both as music lover and as diplomat, and convey my congratulations to Maj. Chester E. Whiting and the members of the band.

Sincerely yours,

James David Zellerbach
American Ambassador

Hon. Wilber M. Brucker
Secretary of the Army
The Pentagon
Washington 25, D. C.

JUN 2 6 1957

APPEARED ON SUMMARY

We took a train from Trieste and entered the country of Yugoslavia for performances in Zagreb and Belgrade two of its most important cities.

26 June 1957

Major General Guy S. Meloy
Department of the Army
Office of the Chief of Information
Washington 25, D. C.

Dear General Meloy:

On the 20th of June the United States Army Field Band playing in the 2000-year old open air Roman Theater presented a free public concert to over five thousand Italians from the city of Verona and its vicinity. The concert was a huge success and received enthusiastically by an appreciative and discriminating audience. The approving applause was intensive throughout the program but reached its peak in the presentation of the William Tell Overture by Rossini, one of Italy's great operatic composers. Major Chester E. Whiting, the conductor, demonstrated very clearly a fine sense of showmanship and technical excellence.

I place the understanding between nationalities that is achieved by a successful community relations program second in importance only to preparation for our combat mission.

The Band's contribution in bringing together Italians and Americans in their appreciation of good music has helped greatly in forwarding the cultural aspects of our program. Newspaper publicity following the concert has been highly complimentary and has frequently expressed the desire to have the Band play again in Verona.

The concert performance of the band members as well as their conduct while visiting "our" city has strengthened our friendly and cordial relations with the local population.

I extend for myself and my command our thanks and appreciation for having the United States Army Field Band present one of the concerts of its European tour in Verona.

E. E. FISCHER
Major General, USA
Commanding

Капетан РОБЕРТО Л. БАЈРН
баритон солиста

СИМФОНИЈСКИ ОРКЕСТАР АМЕРИЧКЕ ВОЈСКЕ

БЕОГРАД, 26 јуна. — Приликом своје друге гостовања у Европи Симфонијски оркестар америчке ваздухопловне посетиће и Београд...

Мајор ЧЕСТЕР Е. ЗАЛТИНГ
диригент и аранжер

Концерти ове САД приказаће се тако и у тријумфалним турнејама по Европи. У Копенхагену фестивалски директор ...

## КОНЦЕРТНИ ПРОГРАМ

Национална химна Југославије и Сједињених Америчких Држава

| Марш војника из Вашингтона | C. S. Grafulla |
| Висока химна | Harry Zimmerman |
| Фанфаре и Allegro | Clifton Williams |
| Darms | Kay Samuel LaSonde |
| La Fonda | Paul Yoder |
| Увертира — „Фигарова женидба" | Mozart |
| „Забуњен сам" | Richard Rodgers |

### О Д М О Р

| Марш циркуса Барнум и Бејли | Karl L. King |
| Tuba | Don Gillis |
| Тико — Тико | Zequinia Abreu |
| Увертира — Euryanthe | Carl Maria von Weber |
| Лепе узбудљиве мелодије | Richard Rodgers |
| Тргом насељеника | Ferde Grofe |
| Давно пре него што сам те упознао | arr. James Smith |
| Ти ме не познајеш | arr. Lon Norman |

(вокални солиста — George Norman)

| Цвркутибим | Pesciozza |
| Majur Stars and Stripes Forever | John P. Sousa |

26 ЈУНИ 1957    У 20 ЧАСОВА

The whole time we were in Yugoslavia it felt like we were being watched by some evil force and our officers reminded us not to go anywhere alone, and to be very careful what we talked about in public, or visited about in our rooms, which they were sure had been bugged. I wanted to see for myself what the populace was being forced, to tolerate, so I immediately checked into the grand new 10 story hotel where the band was to be billeted, as a show of prosperity by the Yugoslavian government, and then I went out on the mostly deserted city streets, to see what the shops were like and maybe talk to some of the locals. What a surprise awaited me, at four o'clock in the afternoon the shops were closed, and the streets mostly deserted of citizenry. What really opened my eyes was that although the shops appeared to be in business, none of them had anything to speak of in their windows. For instance, in a building that purported to be a shoe shop, only one pair of shoes would be shown for sale in the window, and upon further investigation of the place by cupping my hands against the window and peering inside; there did not seem to be any others available. This lack of goods was prevalent in every store; it was as if the city was a ghost town, and the few people on the street were obviously avoiding any contact with me, even to the extent of eye contact or greetings of any type. I felt like a woman in the boardroom of a1950's fortune 500 company. However, our three outdoor concerts in this country, as you can verify in the Liaisons' report were attended by a total of nearly 45,000 highly receptive persons, a great number of which were Yugoslavian government troops.

The following Saturday June 29th we traveled to what I have always considered the most beautiful place on earth, Berchtesgarten,

Germany. Here we went by cable car to Hitler's private retreat, Eagles Nest, 13,000 feet up the mountain which shadows the most beautiful of valleys with a rushing stream roaring through it, icy cold and pure enough to drink. After spending about an hour at Eagles Nest, we traveled back down the mountain and performed outdoors in the Skyline room of the General Walton Walker Hotel for about 1,200 concert listeners.

With the exception of two concerts in the lovely Tivoli amusement park located in the city of Copenhagen, Denmark, and one in Oslo, Norway, cities which I found to be extremely friendly to the U. S. and to our band, and two of the most beautiful, clean, and interesting cities in which we performed; the rest of our performances were in the following West German communities: Augsburg, Munich, (where I visited the great beer hall, and spent the afternoon listening to the wonderful German band, and downing a glass military boot of the best beer I ever drank ), Nurnburg, Stuttgart, Frankfurt, Heidelberg, Bad-Godasberg (near Bonn):and Including the two concerts performed on the ship, we played 45 performances on this 72-day tour that began on The 7th of May 1957 and ended on The 18th of July. There were an estimated 350,000 Europeans who heard our music, of which 72,000 were in Spain and 115,000 in Italy, with radio and television coverage to another conservatively estimated one and a half million folks. We performed in 12 countries, and visited 4 others Austria, Sweden, Scotland, and Newfoundland; while traveling over 12,000 miles in Europe, and returning to the good old U.S.A. by commercial air transportation on the 18th of July.

When the band arrived at Ft. Meade, Md. On the 18th I gathered my horn and suitcase from the bus, put the horn in the rehearsal room; repacked the suitcase, and after making sure I had 10 days leave, caught the first plane out of Friendship airport in Baltimore for Tulsa, and a reunion with that raven haired beauty I had been missing so badly for the past three months. She met me in Tulsa, and we spent the next ten days making up for all that time we had been apart, and getting packed, so we could move our home to Maryland in Shirley's 49 Pontiac Coupe convertible her father, Hollis had given her the summer before our wedding, and which we planned to drive to our new home on the East

*Left is a card mailed to our folks on our first move to Ft. Meade, Md. as we went through St. Louis Mo.*

Coast.

Hamburg.

CONDUCTOR - MAJOR CHESTER E. WHITING (Dirigent)    ASSISTANT CONDUCTOR - CAPTAIN ROBERT L. BIERLY (Hilfsdirigent)

PROGRAM - PROGRAMM

NATIONAL ANTHEM - NATIONALHYMNE

| | |
|---|---|
| MARCH - WASHINGTON GRAYS - MARSCH | C. S. GRAFULLA |
| FANFARE AND ALLEGRO | CLIFTON WILLIAMS |
| D H A R M A | SAMUEL LOBODA |
| L A F O N D A | PAUL YODER |
| OVERTURE - MARRIAGE OF FIGARO - OUVERTUERE - DIE HOCHZEIT DES FIGARO | MOZART |
| SO IN LOVE - "SO VERLIEBT" | RICHARD RODGERS |
| PIANO SOLO - KLAVIER SOLO. - RHAPSODIE ON A THEME OF PAGANINI - RHAPSODIE UEBER EIN THEMA VON PAGANINI | RACHMANINOFF |
| (Soloist - Valentino Marconi - Solist) | |

I N T E R M I S S I O N - P A U S E

| | |
|---|---|
| MARCH - BARNUM AND BAILEY'S FAVORITE - MARSCH | KARL KING |
| TULSA | DON GILLIS |
| TICO TICO | ZEQUINNA ABREU |
| OVERTURE - EURYANTHE - OUVERTUERE | CARL MARIA VON WEBER |
| SOME ENCHANTED EVENING - EIN BEZAUBERNDER ABEND | RICHARD RODGERS |
| ON THE TRAIL - AUF DER FAEHRTE | FERDE CROFE |
| LONG BEFORE I KNEW YOU - LANGE BEVOR ICH DICH KENNEN LERNTE | ARR. JAMES SMITH |
| YOU DON'T KNOW ME - DU KENNST MICH NICHT | ARR. LON NORMAN |
| (Vocal Soloist - Sänger - George Norman) | |
| DRUM NOVELTY - CIRIBIRIBIN - TROMMEL NEUHEITEN | FESTALOZZA |
| MARCH - STARS AND STRIPES FOREVER - MARSCH | JOHN P. SOUSA |

PROGRAM SUBJECT TO CHANGE
AENDERUNGEN VORBEHALTEN

148

We arrived in Severn, Maryland shortly after the first of August, with all our worldly possessions piled in the Coupe, and began to search for an apartment. As usual we were very fortunate to find a great one, which was totally furnished, on the whole second floor of a lovely old farm home, in a rural setting. The first floor occupants were young newly weds with a very young baby, and the husband was stationed at Ft. Meade very close to where I would be each day. All this for $125.00 per month, which Shirley considered a lot and I thought was cheap.

The month of August was somewhat uneventful, but did have a few interesting wrinkles. Shirley and I purchased some needed furniture, especially a crib for the baby who was obviously coming in a couple of months, and two lamp tables and a coffee table to spruce up the living room of our very nice apartment During the shopping trip to

*Getting in a few licks before rehearsal*

Baltimore to obtain these items we experienced our first serious case of discrimination, when one of the furniture store clerks called me aside to tell me the store would not allow Shirley to enter due to the color of her skin. They only served white people! Needless to say we bought from another store. Then after we made our purchases, and were driving back to Severn we got lost in a Baltimore Neighborhood and some black kids tried to stop our vehicle and attack us by forming a human chain across the street in front of our car. I had been driving pretty slowly looking for street names, but when I saw what was coming down, I was really frightened that they were going to hurt Shirley in her condition, so I politely floor boarded the car, and although they waited until I was sure some would be struck by our car, at the very last instant the chain broke, and amid much cursing and rock throwing we speed away to safety.

My job with the Band during the months of August and most of

*L to R-- William O. (Bill) Riser on tenor sax-trombone section leader & fine trombonist Elwood H. Edwards giving advice, and C. E. Redwine enjoying a little practice time with the alto sax during a break in band rehearsal at Ft. Meade, Md. 1958*

September was spent rehearsing, with a short tour of New England during the last two weeks of August and first week of September. This was my first time to experience New England in the fall, and in addition to the area being dressed in its most beautiful foliage, the entire band was invited to the beach for a real East coast clam bake. We were guests for a seven course meal with Maine lobsters as the main course two days after the clam bake, and while we were in Boston I was privileged to get to "set in" during a jam session with some of Bill Holman's and Stan Kenton's side men. What a treat! As I mentioned earlier the Field Band was on post often during this fall, and I really enjoyed it, the band was really good, even though the assistant conductors, who the Major saddled us with, were not very capable. When the Major would handle the rehearsals, or when on a rare occasion he would assign Tony Salatti to conduct us; the Band would always play with a great deal of enthusiasm, and artistic feeling. Tony was the second chair solo clarinetist, a fine

*U.S. Army Field Band performing a concert at one of the many military installations around Ft. George G. Meade, Maryland in fall of 1957*

family man with a houseful of childern and a very accomplished amateur photographer. We performed about three times a week in the Washington D. C. area, and I really was a happy camper being close to home where I built a dog house for our new puppy, in which he would not stay. And helped Shirley get the nest ready to care for Carla Rene' Redwine, the world's most beautiful baby; who would be greeting us with her always happy face and delightfully inquisitive attitude on the 4th of October, 1957.

The Army is always experimenting, it seems and although most of the time Army medicine is outstanding, now and then these experiments are really wacky. Shirley happened to be using their facilities, for pre-natal care and childbirth at one of their most wacky times. The pre-natal care consisted of no vitamins, minerals or pamphlets of any kind, each patient had to take their own urine sample at home and bring it unceremoniously with them to a rigidly scheduled appointment. A different physician examined her each visit. No fathers were allowed in the hospital even to view the newborns, and certainly not during their births, which immediately afterward the mothers and their babies were rolled into a large open ward to care for their own children without aid of nurses or additional physicians. Then with strict compliance as to time, the father was allowed to visit this ward for five minutes once a day, for two days: when the patients were released weather or no! Since Esther had traveled to our home from Pryor, Oklahoma to help care for Shirley, for a few days after her dismissal from the ward, I let her take my place on the second day of Shirley's incarceration, as both Ester and Shirley needed to see each other on this very auspicious, though trying occasion. The reader might be wondering as we did, WHY? Why would the medical people treat anyone in this manner? Simply put, they wanted to see what would happen psychologically to the mothers, and the troops involved! (To hell with good sense!) Who ever was planning the bands itinerary was really doing a great job of it. Carla was born, I got to rehearse most of the library used by the current conductors, our family had some time with Esther, who was a big help for about ten days before she went home to Pryor and we performed very few times before I had to leave on the 1957

153

Southeast Tour.

This allowed us to get our lives fairly well adjusted with Carla, and even though I had to leave for these performances on the 3rd of November, Shirley was very fortunate to have the wonderful help of Gene and Zila Smith, the parents of our best man Quincy. The Smiths were long time friends of my family,who had lived for some years in Pawhuska. Presently the Smiths lived in D. C., and they came to Severn and took both Shirley and Carla to enjoy the Thanksgiving Holidays, then stay in the Smith's home with them for over two weeks, while I was performing in the months of November

*I Carried these "2" pages with me on this tour!! C.E.R. -2005*   1 October 1957

SOUTHEAST TOUR    ===    November = December 1957

THE U. S. ARMY FIELD BAND

| LOCATION | TRAVEL DATE | CONCERT DATE |
|---|---|---|
| Roanoke, Virginia | 3 November 1957 | 4 November 1957 |
| Knoxville, Tennessee | 5 November 1957 | 6 November 1957 |
| Chattanooga, Tennessee | 7 November 1957 | 7 November 1957 |
| Corinth, Mississippi | 8 November 1957 | 9 November 1957 |
| Birmingham, Alabama | 10 November 1957 | 10 - 11 November 1957 |
| Tallahassee, Florida | 12 November 1957 | 13 November 1957 |
| Tampa, Florida | 14 November 1957 | 15 November 1957 |
| Wauchala, Florida | 16 November 1957 | 16 November 1957 |
| Miami, Florida | 17 November 1957 | 18 November 1957 |
| Hollywood, Florida | 19 November 1957 | 19 November 1957 |
| Miami Beach, Florida | 20 November 1957 | 20 November 1957 |
| West Palm Beach, Florida | 21 November 1957 | 21 November 1957 |
| Orlando, Florida | 22 November 1957 | 22 November 1957 |
| Daytona Beach, Florida | 23 November 1957 | 23 November 1957 |
| Savannah, Georgia | 24 November 1957 | 24 November 1957 |
| Charleston, South Carolina | 25 November 1957 | 26 November 1957 |
| Due West, South Carolina (Erskine College) | 27 November 1957 | 28 November 1957 |
| Wilmington, South Carolina | 29 November 1957 | 30 November 1957 |
| Elizabeth, North Carolina | 1 December 1957 | 1 December 1957 |
| Fort Monroe, Virginia | 2 December 1957 | 2 December 1957 |
| Fort George G. Meade, Maryland | 3 December 1957 | END OF TOUR |

and early December.

There were also quite a few of my classmates working or stationed with the military in Washington during this period and Gene and Zila made sure all were welcomed at their home.

Two of these former classmates who had Thanksgiving Dinner with the Smiths and Shirley were Wesley Yates, (deceased) who was a guard at the tomb of the Unknown Soldier, and Barbara Millsap (now married and living in Ponca City, Oklahoma) both good friends of mine in high school.

Sergeant Miller, kindly provided a copy of this tour's schedule from the U. S. Army Field Bands archives,in addition to the one I had

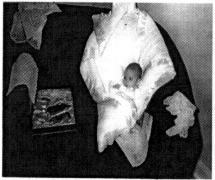

*Carla Rene Redwine at her home in Severn Maryland Dec 1957*

*Our oldest daughter Carla R. Redwine at her first Christmas in Severn Maryland, December 1957*

in my files which is shown previously on page above.

Carla, Shirley, and I had many great days together over the next three months, as the band stayed fairly close to home performing in the area and rehearsing on those days when we did not perform. This allowed me to spend some quality time with our little family, even going out to dinner once in a while and to church on the weekends, with a bit of shopping in between.

The first time we visited the Post Px, we were both impressed with the wide variety of goods available, and especially surprised to find this store provided fresh top grades of vegetables and fruits, many of which we could not find in the local stores. My income as a member of the band in addition to the military prices on these goods, put us in the unusual and enjoyable position for the first time in our marriage to purchase what ever we wished for our table, so like kids in a candy store, we were both picking up many items we really did not need.

We had not been together long enough to know a great deal about what each other truly liked, so it wasn't long before Shirley mentioned she would like to have some pork liver, and in my most undiplomatic manner; I told her I would not eat liver of any kind, and did not want it on the table. (This was a real mistake!)

Shirley just nodded ok, and I took this quiet answer completely out of its intended context, for about five minutes later, when we were in the vegetable section, I observed the PX was stocking a very nice basket of fresh Black-eyed Peas, and mentioned exuberantly how much I liked them, Shirley flashed me a real scowl, and shot back she could not stand the smell of them, and hated black-eyed peas. I figured, what the heck with all the other foods we obviously agreed on, why create a problem. As a result of this incident for the next 15 years of our marriage, although Shirley would order liver on some occasions, when we were dinning out, she never prepared it for our table, and likewise she never prepared black-eyed peas, which I simply did without. The reader should keep in mind; this shopping trip took place in early December of 1957.

One very cold gray evening in 1972, I came home from a trying day of rehearsals at Clarksville High School, and with all the family sitting around the dinner table, Shirley came out of the kitchen with a big bowl of black-eyed peas and a beautiful pan of cornbread, I could not believe my eyes, the aroma was magnificent, and I spoke out in wonder as to the fact she did not like black-eyed peas, Shirley looked me straight in the eyes and said," I was just mad about the liver! I really like the peas!" That's what I call holding a grudge, fifteen years, over a piece of liver!

We spent our first Christmas away from either side of the family, and although we missed them greatly we became more of a family

*Left to right; Shirley J Smith Redwine, Carroll E. Redwine holding their oldest daughter Carla Rene` Redwine This picture taken while on leave in Oklahoma in Grandma and Grandpa Berryhill`s front yard, just prior to going on the 1958 tour.*

unit because of it, as we learned too more and more to depend on each other for all our needs.

The U.S. Army Field Band with C.E. Redwine playing saxophone left for a late winter tour on February 5th, 1958. The day we left the post it was chilly, but for this area of the East Coast a fairly clear day, that is; it was overcast skies, but without precipitation. A copy of the tour schedule is included on the next page to save time and verify where and when we performed.

By the time we arrived in Moorhead, Minnesota where the band was to premiere the **Land of Wheat** a new composition by Don Gillis with the composer conducting, a huge snowstorm had hit the Baltimore and D.C. area. This was one of the worst storms to strike this area in many years and when I called Shirley, she told me that it was a good thing we had a second story apartment as the cars parked out side of the house were totally covered in snow and the drifts were even higher.

Due to the deep drifts, the soldier Ray Helmer; could not drive to the post. Ray lived in the first floor apartment below us with his wife, Helga, a lovely young German National, and their very physically handicapped baby;. Therefore he shoveled his way to the main road, where the snowplows had been able; after the first couple of days to work their way through, and then he walked the three miles distance to the post, performed his army obligations, and purchased two cans of baby formula, which he placed in his pockets and carried back to his wife, and Shirley. If not for Ray's efforts the babies would not have been able to survive, as traffic was not able to flow normally for over six days. The large piles of snow were still somewhat prevalent when we returned to the post on the 22nd of February.

As the reader can see by the insert of the schedule, the tour performances included a few in March, which were closer to the post. The band, left the second week of April 1958 on an extensive tour of the Far East, where over a seven week period they performed concerts in Honolulu, Hawaii, staying in the Kaiser Hotel for nearly a week, where along with Everett Short and others, I daily enjoyed a ripe pineapple for breakfast with Rita Hayworth and her large entourage around the hotel's private saltwater lagoon and after about three weeks in Hawaii flew to Guam, and Midway, stopping only to refuel the planes, and eat a good meal then continuing to Okinawa,

U

THE U. S. ARMY FIELD BAND

February - March 1958 Tour

| CONCERT SITE | TRAVEL DATE | CONCERT DATE |
|---|---|---|
| Ottumwa, Iowa | 5 - 6 February 1958 | 7 February 1958 |
| Des Moines, Iowa | 9 February 1958 | 10-11 February 1958 |
| Moorehead, Minnesota | 12-13 February 1958 | 14-15 February 1958 |
| Colorado Springs, Colorado | 16-17 February 1958 | 18-19-20 February 1958 |
| Fort George G. Meade, Maryland | 21-22 February 1958 | End of tour |
| Fort Monroe, Virginia | 17 March 1958 | 18 March 1958 |
| Norfolk, Virginia | | 19 March 1958 |
| Fort Eustis, Virginia | | 19 March 1958 |
| Fort George G. Meade Maryland | End of tour | |

where we performed two concerts before flying on to Japan.

In Japan we performed in Shapiro, Hiroshima, Tokyo, Niko,

アメリカ陸軍交響楽団の特別演奏会

**THE UNITED STATES ARMY FIELD BAND**
13 MAY 1958, CAMP ZAMA, JAPAN

and a number of U. S. military installations.

Digressing here seems appropriate, and amid some concern about memory of these events, I would like to relate some of the most vivid and to me most interesting occurrences of this trip to this point.

While in Tokyo, we were favored to perform a privately attended concert for Crown Prince Akihito, and his intended bride, a performance that was broadcast nationally throughout Japan. This was a most honored opportunity, as in Japan, the Emperor is a sacred personage, and is rarely seen by anyone. Additionally, this was the first time in Japan's history that the Emperor had taken a commoner as his wife. At the conclusion of the concert, The Emperor graciously congratulated the Field Band on its brilliant performance, thanking every band member personally with a gift of a silver cigarette lighter, which was adorned with a picture of Mt. Fuji, and an inscription, as to the gifts' significance. The Band stayed in Tokyo for nearly a week, performing in the immediate area, then boarded a military plane for Seoul, Korea, which was another harrowing experience.

Although most of the Field Band members were true war veterans, there were a number of (Johnnie Come Latelys) such as myself present. Therefore, when the band boarded the plane for Seoul, it came as no surprise that the Air Force pilot came back to issue some basic instructions in case of an emergency on board. His assistant, a young Captain, who was obviously enjoying his position, as he laughed and cut up from the minute he introduced himself and his commander, accompanied the pilot. After his basic introduction, he welcomed us aboard, and pointing to a colored bulb above the cockpit door which separated the forward controls and our passenger area proceeded to explain, if that red light comes on; you, as he jestered to all of us, must open that door to the right, as he further pointed to the small door on our left, put on that parachute, which you are now using for a seat cushion, quickly jump out that open door, and count slowly to ten; then pull that Big D ring. If the chute does not open, start praying, and pull that smaller ring below the Big D ring. He then pointed to the door to his immediate right and said," Do not go out that door, because you will get chopped to pieces by the propellers  By this time, he truly has everyone's attention, and one of the young guys in the band asked," If that light comes on, can we call you?" The pilot answered, " Son, if that red light comes on I will already be gone!"

There was a roar of very nervous laughter from the guys in the band, after which the pilot continued;" See that huge overhead door you just marched through to get inside this cargo area"? He pointed behind us, and we all turned to look at the door, which was big enough to drive a tank through, our guardian then admonished us, "DO NOT LEAN ON THAT DOOR"! Those doors have been known to fall off! Now the fellows in the Field Band are notorious for being the worlds number one observers of natural phenomenon, and since there was only one window available to view and take pictures of Fuji, and that 14 x 16 inch window just happened to be in the center of the huge overhead door, it was not the least bit unusual that nearly everyone of us leaned on that door and huddled against it, as we filmed Fugi's image while flying 10,000 feet above the sacred Japanese mountain. Besides we thought, the pilot was probably just making sure we would stay in our seats, with his scare tactics. The joke was on us, when with all of us seated as instructed for touch down, and as our plane's wheels first bumped terra firma at the air field in Seoul; that big ole door came off and we watched it bounce uncontrollably down the runway behind us. There was not a man among us that did not acknowledge the others eyes and shake his head with the realization we could have had that happen at 10,000 feet, and been sucked out of that plane without our parachutes, which not one of us had bothered to wear.

While in Seoul we performed a very unusual concert for Sigmund Rhee, the leader of Korea and Mrs. Rhee, Sigmund's wife. The concert was held in a brick wall enclosed soccer field, and the band's busses and our equipment trucks entered the field though two great wooden doors that were each approximately 20 feet high and ten feet wide, centered in a wall about four feet thick and 20 feet tall, which totally enclosed the soccer field on which had been placed a concert stage, which was partially covered with a concert shell. After our trucks and personnel entered, the gates were quickly closed; we set up our equipment, warmed up, and upon command of our Sergeant Major, Bill Calendar; we took our seats on the stage. Where upon the great wooden gates opened once again, and a truckload of Korean Soldiers, each with a machine gun, came roaring through, followed immediately by a black stretch limousine, which pulled up about 75 feet in front of the stage, and stopped. Four of the soldiers jumped from their truck and positioned themselves between the band and the limo, about 10 feet apart, and facing outward toward the wall, where suddenly every 20 feet, completely surrounding the field, soldiers with their weapons drawn popped up like sentinels. Then without apparent command, the other four soldiers in the truck unloaded a large roll of red velvet carpet, placed it next to the doors of the limousine, and unrolled it until it was about 20 feet in front and center of the stage. They then went to the back of the truck and unloaded two large plush chairs, placed them at the end of the red carpet closest to the stage, covered them with clean white sheets, and went to open the limo doors for Mr. and Mrs. Rhee; Whom they escorted to the chairs. Then upon a nod of his head by the Korean President to Major Whiting we performed a two-hour private concert.

At the conclusion of Stars and Stripes Forever, The Major mouthed the words to the band," I'm going to go meet that son of a bitch!" and he turned around on the podium to step toward the Rhees, but as he did so, the four guards immediately stepped in front of him, and blocked his way with their weapons across their bodies. The Major stopped abruptly, but Mr. Rhee gave a big nod of approval and the guards lowered their guns, so he went out to the chairs and shook hands with both Mr. and Mrs. Rhee conversing with them for about five minutes and wishing them well as they reentered their car and left. We began to pack up our equipment on stage, and as the limo went through the gate, the guards just appeared to melt away as suddenly as they had first appeared. We spent the next two days performing for the troops in Korea, and then returned to Japan, for additional performances in major cities and garrisons, this time seated as instructed all the way.

The Band returned to Ft. Meade by way of Hawaii where it rested for a week before completing the flight to the mainland and home base, getting home in the first week of June.

Then in the summer we went to New York City for concerts at Radio City Music Hall, and Carnegie Hall, and to a recording studio, where we spent most of July producing TV and Radio background music adds for the military. We played many military posts in the immediate vicinity, and for this I was really thankful, as we were paid an additional stipend for each performance of $20.00. However, I did not get to be with Shirley and Carla much as

We were on the road a lot and on August 18th, 1958. We left Ft.

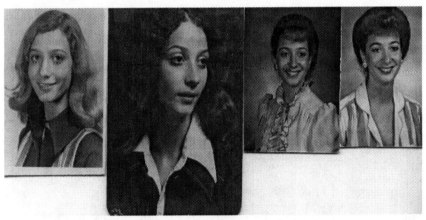

*Carla Rene Redwine-Reasoner pictured here at four different ages L to R age 12-17-27and38*

Meade on a major fall tour, a copy of which appears here in.

This tour included one of the most beautiful rail trips one could imagine, with our boarding a train in St. Paul, Minnesota after performing in this area for seven days from the 27th of August to the

NORTHWEST TOUR SCHEDULE - THE U. S. ARMY FIELD BAND - AUGUST - OCTOBER 1958

| LOCATION | TRAVEL DATE | CONCERT DATE |
|---|---|---|
| Erie, Pennsylvania | 18 August 1958 | 19 August 1958 |
| Cleveland, Ohio | 20 August 1958 | 20 August 1958 |
| Toledo, Ohio | 21 August 1958 | 21 August 1958 |
| Madison, Wisconsin | 24 August 1958 | 24 August 1958 |
| St. Paul, Minnesota | 25 August 1958 | 27-28-29-30-31 August-1 September |

(Depart St. Paul on Great Northern Empire Builder on 1 September, arrive Seattle, Washington on 3 September 1958)

| LOCATION | TRAVEL DATE | CONCERT DATE |
|---|---|---|
| Seattle, Washington | 1-2-3 September 1958 | 3 September 1958 |
| Bellingham, Washington | 4 September 1958 | 4 September 1958 |
| Yakima, Washington | 5 September 1958 | 6 September 1958 |
| Spokane, Washington | 7 September 1958 | 8 September 1958 |
| Lewistown, Montana | 9-10 September 1958 | 11 September 1958 |
| Helena, Montana | 12 September 1958 | 13 September 1958 |
| Miles City, Montana | 14-15 September 1958 | 15 September 1958 |
| Glendive, Montana | 16 September 1958 | 16 September 1958 |
| North Platte, Nebraska | 17-18-19 September 1958 | 20 September 1958 |
| Omaha, Nebraska | 21 September 1958 | - - - - - - - - - |
| Clinton, Iowa | 22 September 1958 | 23 September 1958 |
| Elkhart, Indiana | 24 September 1958 | 25 September 1958 |
| Greensburg, Pennsylvania | 26 September 1958 | - - - - - - - - - |
| Ligonier, Pennsylvania | 26 September 1958 | 27 September 1958 |
| Cumberland, Maryland | 28 September 1958 | 28-29 September 1958 |
| Clarksburg, West Virginia | 30 September 1958 | 1 October 1958 |
| Elkins, West Virginia | 2 October 1958 | 2-3 October 1958 |
| Fort George G. Meade, Maryland | 4 October 1958 | |

1st of September We then rode two days with some stops in between for picking up passengers, to Seattle, Washington where our tour busses met us. One particular aspect of this trip was getting to see the amazing peach orchards in Washington, and sampling their huge luscious fruits that were so large it was necessary to hold them cupped in both hands; so sweet and juicy, that one had to bend over forward to bite into them , as they spewed their nectar in every direction, and covered one's whole face with a wet smile.

The crowds were not as large as those in Europe, but the food was a lot better, and we did perform for some really enthusiastic Americans. We got home on October fourth after a fine tour that made me really proud to be a part of this band

Most of the next two months were uneventful except for band rehearsals on the post,performances in the area, honing my ping pong game learning new shots, with solo F-Horn performer and section leader Roderick Harrington, who consistently poured it on me, until I finally learned to hit his back hand.

Much more importantly, Carla and I would watch the Baltimore Colts on TV each week, and all three of us got to spend some great days riding through the countryside of Ann Arundel County, Maryland.

Performances with the band were somewhat sparse from the end of October "58

*Above left; our family 1956-- to the right- our family 1959- taken in old school house apartment, C.E., Carla, Shirley and twins-David and Dennis*

"Until June "59", and this was a good thing for our family as it was growing in size.

We knew Shirley was into her second pregnancy when I came home from the fall "58" tour. She had been to the post hospital a couple of times for prenatal exams, but other than telling her what she already knew, the physicians thumped and measured her and little else. In early December, she had scheduled another appointment with the clinic, but I had to be in

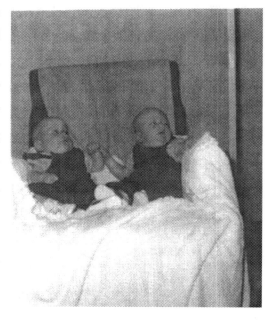

*Dennis L. & David L. Redwine at age four months*

rehearsal that morning to prepare for a ten day tour beginning May 14th. Knowing the hospital's feelings as to fathers accompanying their expectant wives; I drove Shirley to the Field Band's rehearsal building, and got out of the car, so that she could use it to meet her appointment. This was about 8:00 am, and about 10:00am while the band was rehearsing, one of the motor pool people who was outside the band hall, interrupted the rehearsal by coming onto the stage and speaking to me. At first I could not believe he was talking to me, as I certainly did not know him. And I did not want to embarrass the Major by stopping his rehearsal for this interruption. Then I understood the fellow to say," Your wife is outside crying." When I realized this was what he said, I got a terrible feeling in my stomach, for so many thoughts quickly dawned on me of the many quite serious possibilities that can affect a pregnancy, including the death of the mother and I remembered Shirley was seeing the doctor only minutes before. I hurriedly excused myself to the Major and headed outside to find out from Shirley what was wrong. She was standing by her car and still sobbing, so I rushed up to her and holding her tightly; truly afraid to receive the answer, I asked what was the matter? She said," I just came from the clinic and the doctor said "I'm going to have twins and possibly triplets." A great feeling of relief overtook me, and I joyously said, "That's great news", as I thought she was trying to make me feel good about the multiple births. Then she said, "You don't have to have them!"

Dennis Lynn Redwine and David Lee Redwine were born at ten minutes after midnight the 11th of May 1959 in the Ft. Meade army hospital. The tenth of May was Mothers' Day and the boys were the best things that ever happened to us, besides the births of our two girls. Shirley had even less help from the military medical staff than she did at the birth of Carla, eighteen months earlier.

Within eight hours of having a spinal block to aid the boy's birth, she was up fixing formula, and caring for the twins with absolutely no aid from the medical staff. The post infirmary, where this horror story took place, was found to have a staff infection and had lost the last two sets of twins born within its confines. . Shirley was really in poor condition to care for herself, much less the two new babies; which the physicians assured her might bleed to death if she left them alone, as they had just been circumcised She was forced to remain awake all night even though she had just given birth. Then on the first day after their birth, she walked the length of the ward many times, as she prepared their bottles, fed and changed the twins.

*Sergeant Miller sent the notice posted on this page to me in Oct. 2003*

CINFO-CL 353.8                                        31 December 1958

MEMORANDUM FOR: SECRETARY OF THE ARMY

SUBJECT: Scheduled Activities of the United States Army Field Band, First Half of 1959

1. Reference your request for the band schedule, the following information is furnished:

January 8    - Patterson Park High School, Baltimore, Md.
        13   - Arundel High School, Arundel, Md.
        16-18 - Premiere of the Big Picture, Philadelphia, Pa.
        20   - Booker T. Washington High School, Baltimore, Md.
        25-27 - Dedication of Civic Auditorium, Charleston, W. Va.

February 3-10 - 10th Annual Band Clinic, Moorehead, Minn.
        17   - Marley Junior High, Glen Burnie, Md.
        26   - Howard County High School, Ellicott City, Md.

Mar. 23 - May 1-Proposed Tour of Fourth Army Area

May 7-10    - Armed Forces Observances, Pittsburgh, Pa.
        11   - Two concerts, Senior High School, Phillipsburg, Pa.
        12-14 - Two concerts, Senior High, Junior High,
                Parochial High - Clearfield, Pa.

June 8-13    - Philadelphia (and environs) Traffic Safety
                Rallies
        18   - Graduation Exercises, Army War College,
                Carlisle, Pa.

2. These are the band activities presently scheduled. As additional requests are received they will be added to this list.

SIGNED

K. P. STORKE
Major General, GS
Chief of Public Information

SUMMARY: Abv complies with SA's request for Band Schedule
COORDINATION: NONE
SUSDTE: NONE
DUPL FILES: NA
CYS FURNISHED: NONE

RECORD TEMPORARY        CINFO-CL Col Melody/75716/olya

*Band Instrument Headquarters of the Northwest*

Finally about 8:00pm a young female nurse observed her anguish, and although she had finished her day of work, and was supposed to leave the hospital, she spent the night helping take care of the twins, so that Shirley could get a bit of rest.

On the next day, as the doctor made his rounds, Shirley begged him to release her and the twins, as she had her mother at home to help and knew she could not bear another day of this terrible torture, and we knew I was leaving on a ten day tour in two days to Michigan and Indiana, and since her mother did not drive, there would be no one to help get her and the babies home. After much pleading and due to the staff infection prevalent in the hospital, about 3:00pm that afternoon; when it appeared the doctor might never do so, he signed

10 February 1959

| CITY | TRAVEL DATE | CONCERT DATE |
|------|-------------|--------------|
| Detroit, Michigan | 14 May 1959 | 15 - 16 May 1959 |
| Ann Arbor, Michigan | 17 May 1959 | 17 May 1959 |
| Saginaw, Michigan | 18 May 1959 | 18 May 1959 |
| Lansing, Michigan | 19 May 1959 | 19 May 1959 |
| Grand Rapids, Michigan | 20 May 1959 | 20 May 1959 |
| Kalamazoo, Michigan | 21 May 1959 | 21 May 1959 |
| Dowagiac, Michigan | 22 May 1959 | 22 May 1959 |
| Fort Benjamin Harrison, Indiana | 23 May 1959 | 23 May 1959 |
| Fort George G. Meade, Maryland | 24 May 1959 | (End of tour) |

This Page Supplied by Sgt. Miller of US Army Field Bd
Per My 2003 Request.

Sept 12th, 2005
C. E. Redwine

the release, and within twenty minutes I wheeled her and the twins out of the side door, and into our car for the trip home. One would think most of the bad part of this episode was over, however it was just really getting started, as upon arriving at home, Shirley became very ill and it seriously scared both her mother and me.

I remembered seeing a physicians' sign on a house about a mile from our apartment and leaving Ester to care for Shirley; I jumped in the car, and drove to this place to try and get some help for Shirley, as I knew the post hospital, and its medical staff would in all probability be unavailable and this was obviously an emergency situation. The sign was a God send, as it had been posted by a retired physician, who really knew medicine, after knocking on his door for about two minutes, which seemed to me an eternity, a little old man with white hair and dressed in a pinstriped dark gray suit, complete with old fashioned bow tie, appeared at the door. He was at first very reluctant to assist me, but somehow; he must have heard the desperation in my voice and manner, for as I explained our situation and Shirley's harrowing last few days, he began to be quite concerned, and told me to drive my car, and he would follow me to our home in his.

This kindly old gentleman saved Shirley's life I'm certain. When he examined her, he appeared to know at once what was wrong and what to do about it. He told us due to the birth and her exhausting extenuating circumstances surrounding it; she was in shock and must immediately be medicated, he then told her to lie very still for the next eight hours. This was a real problem mentally for Shirley, as she knew I was leaving on tour in about twelve hours and Ester would be alone to handle eighteen-month-old Carla and the twins plus care for Shirley until she went home the first of June.

Since I was scheduled to make a four month tour starting the 28th of June, we determined it would be best if Shirley's folks came to Maryland as soon as the twins and she could travel. They would take the kids and Shirley back to Pryor, Oklahoma until I could finish the tour and pick them all up and we become a family again at the end of September. Hollis and Ester drove to Maryland and on June 20th, generously took Shirley, Carla and the baby boys, who would shortly become very ill with a life threatening skin disease back to Oklahoma. That must have been a story in itself, impatient Hollis driving 1,500 miles with two newborns and an eighteen month old granddaughter and their mother and grandmother in a car without air conditioning in the hot month of June, glad I did not get to experience that!

*L. to R.; Shirley J. Smith Redwine, and Spc-5 Carroll E. Redwine, and their young daughter Carla Rene` Redwine. This picture taken on San Antonio River walk while the U. S. Army Field Band toured this area in 1959*

I've placed a copy of some of our shows here to give the reader an idea of where we performed, until we left on the four month Alaskan Odyssey departing June 28th 1959 and not returning until September 23rd, 1959. This one was really something; we performed in darn near every large city and many small ones west of the Mississippi, and enjoyed the better part of three weeks in rugged, but magnificent Alaska. The

Bands' archives have also made it possible to verify this tour, so a copy of the tour schedule is included, and I'll just comment on this adventure thusly; this one tour could easily have a book written about it, and the wonderful musicians who performed its concerts and traveled to its cities. The best part of this tour for me was when on the 4th of July the band with me performing and the Major conducting, presented a concert in Tulsa's Mohawk Park and my whole family was able to attend; due to it's relative close proximity to my home town and tradition of the family holiday. Then following this treat, Shirley and Carla, traveling with a pregnant Kathy Thompson, whose husband Bill, sang lead Tenor in the Four Hits on shows accompanied by the band, met Bill and me on the 28th of July in San Antonio to accompany us for the next few days on the tour. We traveled in Bill and Kathy's car together meeting the band in each city for performances until August 4th, when Shirley received word by phone, that she was needed at her folks home in Pryor to care for our extremely ill twins, they both had taken a turn for the worse under the care of her parents. In addition to the twin's serious illness, two major things happened on this tour that certainly made a lasting impression on the young lad from the Osage. Very early in the tour's itinerary Yours' truly was invited to join the bands floating poker game, which was held in one of the poker player's rooms, and never spoken about to anyone outside of that room. Figuring to have a bit of fun, as my evenings were sometimes quite dull after we performed, and also figuring to make a quick buck or two, I agreed to check it out for a night or two, until I could be sure I wished to become a regular at the table.

Within two nights I was hooked, and was really looking forward to the game on each evening that we could find time to play. I told

*L to R; Shirley J. Redwine, Kathy Thompson, Carroll E. Redwine, and Bill Thompson—Picture taken in San Antonio while Band was on 1959 tour*

myself, that no matter wither I won or lost, I would take $20.00 to the game, and if I won I would continue to play until the game was over, but if I lost the twenty; I would quit and go to my room. This method worked fine, and I won a good deal of the time, until about three fourths way through the tour, when on a very unlucky night in Great Falls, Montana the band was late getting to the hotel after a very long performance, and the guys were milling around the room getting a drink, and preparing to start the game. One of the fellows, I will not name anyone; ask me if I would like to play a hand or two head up with him? Normally, I would have refused, as I really did not like to play heads up poker, but in a moment of stupidity I said, ok! The players in the poker game, really did not like for anyone to lose big, as we were all afraid it would cause a real hardship on each other, and could be bad for the band as a group, and until this particular night, although some fellows had lost a couple hundred dollars, no one had really lost a great deal of money. This was about to drastically change. In three hands I lost $1,200.00! On the first hand I drew four jacks and my opponent beat me with four kings.

The second hand I drew a small straight, and he had a small flush, and on the next hand, I drew three aces, and he had four nines. Unbelievable! I had to borrow money from one of the guys to finish the tour, and much worse, I was forced to call home to tell Shirley of my stupidity, and get her to take money from our savings to repay my benefactor. That was my last gambling episode for many years!

The loss was very hard to endure, especially four days later, when after riding almost five hours on the bus from Malta to Glasgow, I

HEADQUARTERS
DEPARTMENT OF THE ARMY
Office of The Adjutant General
Washington 25, D. C.

AGPA-O 200.4 (22 Jun 59)                                    24 June 1959

SUBJECT:  Orders

TO:        Mil Pers Concerned
           US Army Fld Band
           Ft George G. Meade, Md

     Fol named mil pers WP OA 28 Jun 1959 to various Posts, Camps, Stations and/or communities in Pa, Ohio, Ind, Mo, Okla, Texas, Ark, La, NMex, Colo, Alaska, Mont, NDak, SDak, Iowa and Ill on TDY aprx 90 days in conec W actv of OCINFO. Cipap. Ucmr proper sta.

| Name | Name |
|---|---|
| MAJ CHESTER E. WHITING 0936552 | SP6 PAUL V. HENRY RA 13 235 590 |
| CAPT ROBERT L. BIERLY 0958371 | SP6 GEORGE F. KORAN RA 13 235 628 |
| E-8 WILLARD S. CALLANDER RA 20 750 695 | SP6 JOSEPH J. LOPRESTI RA 42 223 441 |
| E-8 DEROLD L. SIMMONS RA 6 552 135 | SP6 ORRIN H. MILLER RA 13 293 812 |
| E-7 JESSE P. CAMPBELL RA 6 369 933 | SP6 PAUL E. MILLER RA 13 293 778 |
| E-7 ELWOOD H. EDWARDS RA 14 018 087 | SP6 JAMES C. O'LEARY RA 11 148 656 |
| E-7 EDWARD B. HENRY, Jr. RA 20 122 824 | SP6 GARNET M. PARKS, Jr. RA 13 235 616 |
| E-7 EVERETT N. SHORT RA 13 235 634 | SP6 VINCENT J. PEDANO RA 20 307 537 |
| E-6 ROBERT F. BOYER RA 37 109 073 | SP6 RICHARD J. RAUL RA 13 235 633 |
| E-6 WILLIAM E. BROWN RA 13 048 571 | SP6 JOHN F. RENZI RA 12 211 270 |
| E-6 DORAN E. DETWILER RA 20 304 386 | SP6 EDWARD P. ROSTEK RA 20 347 265 |
| E-6 PAUL O. HARTGE RA 17 129 556 | SP6 JOSEPH P. SCIMONELLI RA 20 129 233 |
| E-6 ROWLAND G. RITTE RA 13 293 804 | SP6 RICHARD B. STEVENS RA 13 235 613 |
| E-6 VINCENT F. ROMEO RA 31 326 674 | SP6 LAWRENCE O. UNDERKOFFLER RA 13235622 |
| E-6 WILLIAM A. VALDES RA 20 458 410 | SP6 JOSEPH J. VENTO RA 20 320 729 |
| SP7 ROBERT E. BUCKLEW RA 18 200 309 | SP6 NICHOLAS D. ZANGARI RA 31 269 878 |
| SP7 EUGENE W. COUGHLIN RA 39 721 263 | SP6 NICHOLAS C. ZEKOPOULOS RA 13 233 599 |
| SP7 GLENN F. FELDSTED RA 6 552 098 | SP5 JESSE F. AGONEY RA 12 244 379 |
| SP7 SAVERIO A. FIORE RA 6 717 394 | E-5 ROBERT B. ANDSTROM RA 27 378 664 |
| SP7 FRANK GRANOFSKY RA 13 293 810 | E-5 TERRENCE H. BARTHOLOMEW RA 13 557 13! |
| SP7 ANTONIO SALATTI RA 20 227 171 | E-5 DONALD BENEDETTI RA 12 549 016 |
| SP7 SMITH H. SUTLEY RA 18 199 580 | E-5 ROBERT L. BERTON RA 52 080 059 |
| SP7 FRANK B. WHITING RA 20 122 822 | E-5 THEODORE L. BLUMENTHAL US 52 456 596 |
| SP6 HAROLD C. COWDEN RA 6 660 850 | E-5 BURT K. CLARK RA 20 323 063 |
| SP6 LOUIS DiLAVORE RA 20 104 565 | E-5 MICHAEL E. COYLE RA 16 557 868 |
| SP6 MERLE W. GAUMER RA 37 141 545 | E-5 HARRY M. DAVIS, Jr. RA 11 353 716 |
| SP6 JACK F. GILBERT RA 22 886 240 | E-5 WALTER B. DUKE, Jr. RA 18 530 425 |

WEM/ptd/ers

AGPA-O 200.4 (22 Jun 59)                                   24 June 1959
SUBJECT: Orders

E-5 JAMES J. ERTTER RA 43 029 824          E-5 JOHN R. MYERS RA 33 611 139
E-5 JAMES A. FARNSWORTH RA 28 194 772      E-5 HAROLD T. NAKAO RA 13 274 972
E-5 SAMUEL J. FRICANO RA 12 525 838        E-5 JOSEF A. OROSZ, Jr. RA 12 470 551
E-5 ALBERT G. FALLUCCI RA 11 356 083       E-5 SOLOMON F. PETERS, Jr US53287436
E-5 KENNETH A. GARLOW RA 13 604 515        E-5 GLEN E. PHIBBS RA 18 530 428
E-5 JOHN T. GARVEY, III RA 13 625 152      E-5 RICHARD H. PITTMAN RA 13 625 086
E-5 JOSEPH H. GAUDIO RA 13 642 539         E-5 JOHN G. POTOCHNEY RA 13 463 484
E-5 EVERETT M. GILMORE, Jr. RA 26 396 374  E-5 CARROLL E. REDWINE RA 18 523 078
E-5 ALLEN D. GRAY, Jr. RA 11 351 563       E-5 MICHAEL P. RICCOBENE RA 13 488 741
E-5 JOSEPH A. GRECO RA 13 463 712          E-5 WILLIAM O. RISER RA 35 400 995
E-5 LEROY K. GUTHRIE RA 13 598 090         E-5 KENNETH E. ROSS RA 33 209 708
E-5 JOE M. HAAS RA 14 663 392              SP5 DAVID H. SHEETZ RA 13 582 530
E-5 RICHARD N. HAIL RA 12 550 843          SP5 WYCKLIFFE R. SULLIVAN RA 13386636
E-5 BURTON E. HARDIN RA 18 547 523         SP5 JOHN R. TENNEY RA 18 522 981
E-5 ROBERT F. HILL RA 18 530 427           SP5 WILLIAM L. THOMPSON RA 18 530.426
E-5 LAWRENCE D. HINER RA 15 603 350        SP5 BERNARD P.O. VANDERBERG RA13583051
E-5 BERNARD HOFFER RA 12 565 274           SP5 ARTHUR R. WAXMAN RA 12553308
E-5 JAMES D. HUBARD, Jr. RA 13 628 022     SP5 NORMAN B. YEARICK, Jr RA 13 640 136
E-5 GUNNAR A. H. JOHANSSON RA 13 464 089   SP4 BONNIE L. BYARS, Jr RA 33 545 111
E-5 JAMES H. JUDGE RA 13 028 607           SP4 DONALD J. McKINTOSH (M) RA19266153
E-5 ROBERT P. KESSLER ER 16 567 519        SP4 GLENN W. SALTER (M) RA 53 215 428
E-5 DAVID H. KNIGHTON RA 13 525 578        SP4 VIRGEL L. WINNINGHAM RA 54 093 256
E-5 JOHN O. KROMER RA 17 524 211           RCT JOHN M. JANNITTO (M) RA 11 355 898
E-5 KENNETH LESIGHT RA 13 588 002          E-3 EDWARD A. LIVINGSTON RA 16 624 457
E-5 HARRY C. LONG (M) RA 34 086 081        E-3 GILBERT M. FERNANDES RA 11 355 251
E-5 JAY MAGIDMAN RA 13 595 146             E-5 JAMES D. MATTHEWS RA 13 636 834
E-5 DAVID C. MORSE RA 15 577 356

TDN: 2192020 52-1101 P2500-02-03-04-05-06-07-08 S18-102 CDA 2540 13000 (USAFB-41-
59). FY 60, 2102020 36-1017 T2500-02-05-07-08 S18-043. OCONUS tvl by rail, bus,
mil and/or coml acft, mil and/or coml sur auth. Bag alw of 65 lbs, personal eff,
is auth ea while tvl by acft.

SP INSTR: Capt Bierly appointed Act TO UP par 13, Sec IV, AR 55-53. UP Chapter 15
Sec III, AR 37-103, Capt Bierly dsg Cl "A" Agent Off to Disb Off, Fin Off, Ft George
G. Meade, Md fpur disb funds in an amt not to exceed $108,600.00 ($107,100.00) for
tvl and $1,500.00 for emerg purposes and supply) in coneo W this man. The cond
under which this WB perf are such that the util at all times of aval Govt qtr
and mess fac is deemed impracticable in that such util will adversely affect the
perf of asg dy (JTR par 4451).

109,000.00

    By Order of Wilber M. Brucker, Secretary of the Army:

2600 to '59

                                              Adjutant General

DISTR:
    Indiv thru contact (10 ea)
    Contact, OCINFO, Attn: Maj Finigan x54743 WILL CALL
    CG, Second USA
    CG, USARAL

THE U........ND
FOURTH AND FI........ 1959 TOUR

| LOCATION | TRAVEL DATE | CONCERT DATE |
| --- | --- | --- |
| Gettysburg, Pennsylvania | 28 June 1959 | 28 June 1959 |
| Zanesville, Ohio | 29 June 1959 | - - - - - - - |
| Indianapolis, Indiana | 30 June 1959 | - - - - - - - |
| St. Louis, Missouri | 1 July 1959 | - - - - - - - |
| Springfield, Missouri | 2 July 1959 | - - - - - - - |
| Tulsa, Oklahoma | 3 July 1959 | 4 July 1959 |
| Oklahoma City, Oklahoma | 5 July 1959 | 5 July 1959 |
| Fort Sill, Oklahoma | 6 July 1959 | 6 July 1959 |
| Camp Wolters, Texas | 7 July 1959 | 7 July 1959 |
| Fort Worth, Texas | 8 July 1959 | 8 July 1959 |
| Dallas, Texas | 9 July 1959 | 9 July 1959 |
| Fort Hood, Texas | 10 July 1959 | 10 July 1959 |
| Tyler, Texas | 11 July 1959 | 12 July 1959 |
| Texarkana, Texas | 13 July 1959 | 13 July 1959 |
| Shreveport, Louisiana | 14 July 1959 | 15 July 1959 |
| Alexandria, Louisiana | 16 July 1959 | 16 July 1959 |
| New Orleans, Louisiana | 17 July 1959 | 18 July 1959 |
| Baton Rouge, Louisiana | 19 July 1959 | 20 July 1959 |
| Beaumont, Texas | 21 July 1959 | 22 July 1959 |
| Houston, Texas | 23 July 1959 | 24 July 1959 |
| Corpus Christi, Texas | 25 July 1959 | 26 July 1959 |
| Harlingen, Texas | 27 July 1959 | 27 July 1959 |
| San Antonio, Texas (Fort Sam Houston) | 28 July 1959 | 29 July 1959 |
| Austin, Texas | 30 July 1959 | 30 July 1959 |

Fourth and Fifth Army – Alaska 1959 Tour – The U. S. Army Field Band (Cont'd)

| LOCATION | TRAVEL DATE | CONCERT DATE |
|---|---|---|
| San Antonio, Texas (Clinic Local Bands) | 31 July 1959 | 1 August 1959 |
| San Angelo, Texas | 2 August 1959 | 3 August 1959 |
| Abilene, Texas *Shirley Went Home* | 4 August 1959 | 4 August 1959 |
| Lubbock, Texas *from Hexe Twins Very Sick* | 5 August 1959 | 6 August 1959 |
| Roswell, New Mexico | 7 August 1959 | 8 August 1959 |
| El Paso, Texas (Fort Bliss, Texas) | 9 August 1959 | 10 August 1959 |
| Albuquerque, New Mexico | 11 August 1959 | 12 August 1959 |
| Santa Fe, New Mexico | 13 August 1959 | 13 August 1959 |
| La Junta, Colorado | 14 August 1959 | 15 August 1959 |
| Fort Carson, Colorado | 16 August 1959 | 16 August 1959 |
| Colorado Springs, Colorado | 16 August 1959 | 16 August 1959 |
| Colorado Springs, Colorado | 17 August 1959 | 17 August 1959 |
| Denver, Colorado | 18 August 1959 | 18 August 1959 |
| Glenwood Springs, Colorado | 19 August 1959 | 20 August 1959 |
| Denver, Colorado | 21 August 1959 | Depart for Alaska *See insert!* |
| Great Falls, Montana | 3-4 September 1959 | Return from Alaska |
| Great Falls, Montana | 5 September 1959 | 5 September 1959 |
| Shelby, Montana | 6 September 1959 | 6 September 1959 |
| Harve, Montana | 7 September 1959 | 7 September 1959 |
| Malta, Montana | 8 September 1959 | 8 September 1959 |
| Glasgow, Montana | 9 September 1959 | 9 September 1959 |
| Williston, North Dakota | 10 September 1959 | 10 September 1959 |
| Belle Fourche, South Dakota | 11 September 1959 | 12 September 1959 |
| Rapid City, South Dakota | 13 September 1959 | 13 September 1959 |

2

Fourth and Fifth Army Alaska 1959 Tour - The U. S. Ar Field Band (Cont'd)

| LOCATION | TRAVEL DATE | CONCERT DATE |
|----------|-------------|--------------|
| Martin, South Dakota | 14 September 1959 | 14 September 1959 |
| Pierre, South Dakota | 15 September 1959 | 15 September 1959 |
| Madison, South Dakota | 16 September 1959 | 17 September 1959 |
| Vermillion, South Dakota | 18 September 1959 | 18 September 1959 |
| Des Moines, Iowa | 19 September 1959 | - - - - - - - - - |
| Peoria, Illinois | 20 September 1959 | - - - - - - - - - |
| South Bend, Indiana | 21 September 1959 | - - - - - - - - - |
| Youngstown, Ohio | 22 September 1959 | - - - - - - - - - |

Fort George G. Meade, Maryland - END OF TOUR - 23 September 1959

15 April 1959

3

Carroll E. Redwine

THE U. S. ARMY FIELD BAND

ALASKA TOUR - 1959

*INSERT!*

| LOCATION | | CONCERT DATE |
|---|---|---|
| Lowry Air Force Base, Denver | | DEPART FOR ALASKA |
| Ladd Air Force Base, Alaska | 23 August (ETA 1000) | |
| Ladd Air Force Base | | 24 August 1959 |
| Fairbanks | | 24 August 1959 |
| Eielson Air Force Base | | 25 August 1959 |
| Fort Greely | | 26 August 1959 |
| Fort Richardson | | 28 August 1959 |
| Elmendorf Air Force Base | | 29 August 1959 |
| Anchorage | | 30 August 1959 |
| Port of Whittier | | 31 August 1959 |
| Kodiak Naval Station | | 2 September 1959 |
| Kodiak Naval Station | 3 September (ETD 0900) | DEPART FOR MONTANA |
| Great Falls, Montana | 3 September (ETA 1800) | |

exited the bus to discover I had left my saxophone in the hotel in Malta. This was grounds for dismissal, and I knew it. So without letting anyone know what was going on, I quietly and quickly called the hotel in Malta, and after making certain my sax was still in the room, told the innkeeper to hold it for me, as I was flying there to retrieve it. I then called the local airport, scheduled a private plane to take me to Malta and return, and hurried to the plane, because it was now 2pm and we performed at 7:30pm that same. evening. I flew to Malta, caught a cab to the hotel, grabbed my horn, and admonished the cab driver to race back to the airport; where I made the return flight to Glasgow, arriving just in time to change into my concert uniform and catch a cab to the performance. The Field Band had already left the hotel, and Smity was mad as hell when ten minutes before the downbeat, I finally showed up back stage. He had been looking everywhere for me and was quite shook-up. I gave him some song and dance about not checking the performance schedule, and missing the bus due to my eating at a restaurant across town. I don't think he believed it, but he was kind enough not to press me any farther on my story, as I'm sure he knew something would have to be done about it. That was nearly a complete disaster, but it taught me a great lesson, and I checked, and rechecked from that day on to make certain I had all my bags, and equipment necessary to my performing and personal well being.

The Field Band returned to Ft. Meade on the 23rd of September, 1959 from their Alaskan tour, and I immediately set out for Oklahoma to spend about three weeks at home with my family, before returning to the post with Shirley and the babies; where, due to the fact we had let our apartment go while in Oklahoma, it was necessary to search for and rent another home for the family while I was embarking on a short two-week tour through Ohio and Pennsylvania. On this tour we played in Centerville Ohio as in years past for the pumpkin festival. This festival was always interesting and colorful and we had lots of fans in the area. In Pennsylvania we performed in famous venues such as Philadelphia's outdoor concert stage, Robin hood Dell and Pittsburg's beautiful indoor concert hall. It was really enjoyable to perform for so many friendly faces, and we always were treated with the utmost respect, as we were billeted in the finest hotels of each city.

When we returned to Ft. Meade, I was expecting to get to spend a good deal of time with Shirley and the kids, and was quite surprised to be confronted by Bill Callander the Sergeant Major who told me to get my house in order for a long tour, as the Band was to leave in a week for South America, where we would be spending about three months on tour. Bill said this as we were unloading the busses and it obviously came as a surprise to everyone.

I called Shirley to come pick me up at the post, and in my mind tried to figure a way to break this news to her, as I knew she was a bit tired of raising three kids by herself, especially now that she was living in the very unsavory conditions of our latest rental housing that was an old abandoned school house, and the only rental property available in the area that we could afford. This housing was also in a very bad area of Laurel, Maryland close to the racetrack, all in all a very poor place to live for the children or Shirley. The old school house still had windows everywhere, these were necessary due to it's lack of air conditioning, and was heated, using the word loosely, by an oil burning floor furnace that was truly a big square metal vat with an automatic spigot in it's wall that allowed oil to pour into it's floor where one would toss a lighted match through it's iron grated top and the resulting explosion would quickly become a live fire. One would feed the fire more fuel oil by turning a crank attached to the end of a long iron shaft which controlled the flow of oil into the vat. This resulted in the grate, atop of the furnace and level with the hard wood flooring; becoming a red-hot bar- b- q grill in the middle of a hallway that the family had to negotiate carefully past to get to the bathroom. In addition to these wonderful amenities, the house was alive with mice, and bopping these mice became my number one game during the next month, as I would sit watching television and with a shoe in both hands would delight in throwing the shoes at the mice (QUITE ACCURATELY I MIGHT ADD).

Shirley bundled the kids up and drove into the post to pick me up and we returned to the old school house, where she told me the landlord, who was a real looser of a guy named Mickey, had been hitting on her continuously while I was away and she was frightened of his intentions.

Mickey was married to a very frail woman who had Spinal Bifida and spent most of her time in a wheel chair, although Mickey had managed to impregnate her at least seven times, as they had seven small children. Mickey proudly told us that his wife was originally planning to be a nun at the local convent, but he had saved her from all that. Mickey and his lovely family lived in the small house that adjoined the old school, as his parents had purchased this property for them, so their grand children would have a roof over their heads, as they knew Mickey could not or would not hold a job.

When we arrived at the house, it was a cool fall evening and

Mickey was waiting outside to greet us, so we said hello and quickly went inside where we got reacquainted, then put my bags away. During the course of the evening, I continually tried to find a time to break the bad news of the coming South American tour to Shirley, but the time never came that seemed to be favorable, as if there would ever be a good time for it? So finally, we sat down to dinner, and while we were eating, I decided that I must get this terrible news out in the open, and I said, without looking up to make eye contact, "I've got to go to South America next week." Without looking up, Shirley replied, "If you go, don't come back! And that was when I decided to get out of the Field Band!

We had a good week end together, and on Monday thinking the band would need to make arrangements to fill my position I made a very difficult trip in to visit with Major Whiting and resign. At that time it was really with mixed emotions that I did so, but I have never regretted that decision in any manner. It was the best decision of my life, as my family has become everything I could have hoped for and more than I dreamed possible. This decision made possible my being in a position in the coming years to closely hold, cherish, teach, and respond to them in a manner that would have never been possible had I continued to tour with the Band.

Resigning from the Band was not as easy as one might think, as the Major was not happy with anyone who would turn their back on his illustrious organization which he had spent a lifetime building. Although he accepted my resignation cordially, he immediately set out to make it clear to those others who might be thinking of leaving their positions with the Band that if they did so, they would pay a high price for their efforts. I was naïve enough to think that because the

Major smiled and wished me well in the future that we would part as friends. This was certainly not the case, although he allowed me to continue playing in his band for about three weeks, he immediately found a replacement for my chair, and I was sent into the clarinet section as a 4$^{th}$ part performer. Then about two weeks later I was sent into exile totally, when he gave orders for me to begin working with hammer and saw as a common laborer redecorating his offices. That was the end of my performing with the band, and the beginning of my financial woes as the extra monies I had been receiving from performing were cut off. This led to my getting a moon lighting job at the local hardware store in Laurel, and made it necessary for me to work eight to five on the post and six to mid-night at the hardware store. The difficulties relating to this strenuous schedule continued for the next three months until I was released from the military.

This period of exile included the Christmas Holidays during which my military pay was so meager that for a short time just before my January check came; we were totally broke. I remember well during this dark financial abyss Shirley washing clothes at the wash-a-teria two doors from the hardware store on a very bleak and cold winter night. I had a few minutes break from the hardware store, so I went to the washateria and ask her if she had any money that we could use to get a coke, explaining I was totally broke. What I did not know was she had saved a quarter for us to get a coke together, and she dug it out of her pocket, and handed it to me with the words, " just this quarter", Big shot that I was, I stepped to the door and while saying " That won't buy anything ", I threw the quarter as far as I could. I did not know until years later that she had saved that lonely quarter for us, and I sure felt like a heel when I discovered it.

Fortunately the Eagle screamed loudly the next day. And although the military checks were small they were steady and along with the moonlighting job sustained our little family until we could get back to Oklahoma and the bosom of greater family.

We loaded our old 52 Chevy with the few personal belongings we still had on hand after shipping the majority of our goods by mail, piled the three kids on top of the bedding and headed back to Oklahoma the first day of March 1960, encountering one of the worst blizzards to hit the eastern states in years, mainly Pennsylvania and through which we nearly perished. Our trip nearly ended in disaster as we were following a huge eighteen- wheeler through the Pocono Mountains on the Pennsylvania Turnpike. We were being guided by the truck's tail lights, as we could not see the road due to the blinding snow, when fortunately for us our car threw a rod in the motor and the car came to a stop ina drift on the side of a mountain. I knew we didn't have much time to get the babies to some kind of shelter, as the temperature was below twenty degrees outside and the warmth of the car would be quickly falling as the motor was no longer working.

Worried that someone might crash into the car on the snow packed highway, I quickly determined that my best course of action would be to get my family out of that car and away from the scene. So I told Shirley to keep the doors closed, and I jumped out to try and find some local folks to help me relocate my family. Standing there on that lonely patch of four lanes our position seemed really hopeless, but as I surveyed the surrounding storm, I noticed off in the distance, about a mile from me, a faint light. Thinking I must get some help immediately and seeing nothing else available, I headed toward this distant light, wading snow sometimes to my waist, I finally came upon a farm house with the light on in only one window, and began knocking frantically on the door. It seemed like an eternity before the door finally opened and a young man about twenty stood framed in the light. He said he was just getting ready to retire for the night and had been undressed when my persistent knocking had beckoned him to the door. He explained, normally he would have turned the light off much earlier, but for some unknown reason tonight he had been neglectful and left it on. He might not have known why, but by now my praying wife and I were sure a higher power had led us to his light, as he loaded us all into his four wheel vehicle and took us the three miles back down the turnpike to a motel and safety.

The next day I walked about one hundred fifty yards from the motel to a car dealership and traded our busted Chevy for an old Dodge giving the owner my last one hundred twenty five dollars. When he found it was all the money we had, he gave me back twenty five to help get us back to Oklahoma, as the babies would need food and then the angel assured me the old Dodge would make it to our destination. Remember I said earlier we were fortunate that the car's motor blew out, well-l-l –l- l—l---

We reloaded the Dodge and headed west, and about a mile west from where we had broken down in the Chevy, we found the eighteen wheeler we were following before our car trouble occurred. The truck had piled up and was hanging off the side of the mountain, surely we were saved a similar fate by the motor of our car playing out, as we would have followed that truck over the side of that ravine due to the bad visibility and our blindly following him. Some might call this luck; I call it divine intervention, and have benefited from such action many times before and since, as I have tried to show in these writings

The rest of the trip was pretty uneventful until we reached the Oklahoma border and I noticed that the front end of the Dodge was really beginning to shimmy. This was soon to cause the tire on the right front to blow out and I had to get out and change the flat, but after the tire change, we made it to Shirley's folks home in Pryor where a new chapter in our lives would soon begin.

# Getting Rich in the Insurance Business

When we arrived in Oklahoma from Maryland and had visited a few days with each set of parents, it became apparent my talents as a musician were no longer of sufficient monetary value to support a family of five in a state that listed cattle, oil, and agriculture as it's primary economic stocks. If we were to eat regularly I would have to put the horn in the closet, and find another means of earning a living. At least for a while, until I could incorporate music somehow into a profitable and regular paycheck, either together with another avocation, or as a primary source, making money would of necessity take precedence over making music in my life. As usual I had not planned very far in advance for this very real economic dilemma, and after about a week of vainly searching the newspapers for a position as president of some fortunate local company or corporation to offer my valued services, I gallantly succumbed to the obvious fact that

*Left to Right* **THE FIVE GENERATIONS** *Carroll E. Redwine, Carroll's Mother, Clarice Iva Berryhill Redwine, holding Carroll's son David Lee Redwine, Carroll's Maternal Great Grandmother, Agnes Vulgamore; with Carroll's oldest daughter, Caria Rene Redwine standing in front of her, and Nellie Berryhill, Carroll's maternal Grandmother holding Dennis Lynn Redwine Carroll's other twin son. Picture taken spring 1960 in Pawhuska, Oklahoma at mother Clarice's home*

though highly educated, I was highly unqualified to earn a living for my family. Totally ignoring this, I brasingly ask my father, who had twenty two years of success selling insurance to intercede on my behalf with his firm, the Metropolitan Life Insurance Company. No sense going small might as well go with the biggest and best. Dad checked with his immediate superiors and they made it clear to him they would give me the opportunity to take the company's employee exams, but that no favoritism would be shown to me, and should I be fortunate enough to pass the rigorous testing, I would still need to complete the companies insurance school in New York and pass the state of Oklahoma's' licensing exams. At this time it appeared very unlikely that selling life insurance would be in my future. During the next thirty days I was tested, retested and finally given approval to attend the insurance company's three-week course in New York City, after which I sat for the Oklahoma Insurance Boards and passed, receiving my license to sell life insurance in our illustrious state. For this I was assigned a debit in West Tulsa, one of the worst places to sell insurance in the Tulsa dstrict, but I did not know this and through hard work and perseverance, I excelled as one of the districts' outstanding salespersons.

The Tulsa job required our family move to west Tulsa, where we rented a furnished house, then spent very little time together in it, as the insurance sales job required many hours driving around the area making and keeping my appointments. However, Shirley was a big help as she spent many hours each day caring for, and playing with, our three children as well as keeping the house and doing all the things that were concerned with our financial responsibilities, which allowed me to be free to spend the many hours necessary to be a successful salesman

During the brief time we resided in West Tulsa less than six months expired, as we moved there in March of 1960 and moved from there to Pawhuska, Oklahoma in early September of the same year. This move was requested by the manager of the north Tulsa Metropolitan Insurance Company office that had contacted my father, and suggested dad allow the manager to promote him from regular debit agent to an insurance consultant's position. This position required no debit collections, but also carried no salary and was purely a sales position. This opened the debit position to me if I wanted to move from Tulsa . I visited with my father extensively about whether or not he felt comfortable with this new situation, and since he appeared to truly want to be free of the collections, and we could work together as a team I agreed to the move.

My dad and mother were very generous people especially with their kids and since they had recently purchased a new home one block north and east of the old home place in which I had grown up at 805 E. 13th,they suggested we move into the old house. Then being the type of parents they were, they said the money we paid them for rent would be held in escrow for us to use in the purchase of our first house. A friend of the family had a small rental house of two rooms that she rented to us for about one month, while mom and dad were getting their new home completed.

We moved into the old home place the first of October and this move was really exciting, as the move its- self included a hilarious adventure. Mom and Dad had moved out the day before we moved in and I had to work at my job as insurance agent until about 4pm the day of our move. So, we didn't get our furniture and other belongings into the old home until about 6:30pm. As we were carrying in the washing machine I noticed the screen door on the back porch was open, but I couldn't get past the kitchen stove and washer to close it, without hopping over the kitchen table, which was still in the middle of the room. I yelled to my brother James to close it , but he was in the front of the house working and didn't hear me. As I turned to go back to the front room to get his help with the washer, I saw a rat the size of a Chihuahua dog come bouncing in that open screen door. Knowing I couldn't get past the furniture to run him out of the kitchen, I yelled loudly to try scarring the monster back out the way he had come in. No such luck! That big ole rat climbed inside the case of the washer and disappeared. I couldn't get to his hide-a-way, so I just went on back to the front of the house and began working on moving our smaller belongings into the house. All this while laughing and explaining the rat to the helping family that by now didn't believe my story, as it was so bizarre. We got all the stuff off the truck and into the house by about 9:30pm, placing the large chairs, divans, and such; pretty much where they were usable, but there were boxes and cases and baskets stacked everywhere, as we hadn't had adequate time to put away the small stuff, of which there was plenty and about 11:00pm my brother, father, and mom left to rest at their home and we jumped into bed, as I knew I had to work the next day. It was nearly 12:30am when I awoke to the sound of something very much like the grinding of teeth that appeared to be coming from the dinning room next to my bedroom. I lay very quietly for a few seconds, which seemed to me a long time, as I tried to focus on where the sound was originating. While doing so, my eyes adjusted well to the darkness and to my surprise, I saw that doggoned rat sitting big as life in the dinning room window, chow'in down on a cracker he had stolen from the box he had mutilated on the dinning room table. I gently nudged sleeping Shirley, who was lying next to me in bed, told her in a whispering voice about biggy rat and slowly and very quietly slipped to my feet and headed toward the next room where I intended to bash ole rat with the first thing available. However the beast was way ahead of me and had disappeared by the time I arrived at his dinning area. I was sorely disappointed and although I looked for him all through the house,after about ten minutes I returned to a wide-awake wife and crawled back into my side of the bed. I lay very still for some time, but the rat was crafty and did not make an appearance until I had drifted off into dreamland.

About thirty minutes later, when in my foggy state of mind, I again was awakened by his crunching, I had a good view of the brazen sucker. He was sitting in the window perfectly outlined by the moonlight outside; helping himself to another of our crackers. We threw caution to the wind jumped out of bed and ran fast to his position, I hit him with the twins baseball bat, but this did not seem to faze the monster. He ran toward us and we both jumped back, as he headed to the living room and all the many boxes, bags, and junk we had not been able to put in it's rightful place. We quickly gathered our composure and followed the rat, arriving in the living room just in time to see its tail disappear through the nearly closed hall closet door. The house utilities had been left on for us but there were no light bulbs in any of the fixtures, this resulted in Shirley and me falling over each other, falling over the piles of our belongings, and bumping into every sort of furniture. We had brought a table lamp from the previous residence, and fortunately it had a bulb in it, so I grabbed it and after tearing though about four boxes found a number of short extension cords which I quickly plugged together then plugged these into the wall and the table lamp. Now we would get that dastardly little rat. Holding the table lamp in one hand and the cords in the other, I resembled the stature of liberty crashing from room to room, as we would alternately poke the rat from his hiding places, or shake the boxes onto the floor, which we quickly threw down as he jumped out, then we would take a swing at him usually missing, but once in a while bashing him good, then continue our chase to the rat's next hiding place, all the while me holding high the lamp, both of us yelling there it goes,! Or, bash him! Or; Shirley yelling,"Hold up that lamp!" or me yelling;"I got him this time, empty that box and I'll bash him". Running from one end of the house to the other, falling over stuff and generally creating havoc in our new abode for nearly two hours, we finally cornered the snaggle tooth rascal on the top of the large armoire I had built in my bed room as a boy. Upon cornering him this time, the rat was tired of running and decided to bare his ugly teeth. He would make a stand and fight. (Big mistake mister rat.) I grabbed my trusty baseball bat and dispatched that booger and with him hissing and wiggling on the floor I finished him with one more blow of the bat.

Then I climbed over spilled boxes, turned over tables, chairs, and piles of our belongings and carried him to the back door then threw the rat outside. As I returned through to the kitchen, Shirley met me in the dinning room doorway where the episode had began, we took one look at each other, and then as she was now holding the lamp, we surveyed the total destruction of the house, then we both began to laugh and continued to do so for nearly five minutes, as we sat down in the middle of the mess we had made. What an inauguration of our new home, one I would never hope to duplicate.

The1960-1961 school year began shortly before we moved to Pawhuska and my brother Philip, who received a scholarship award from the local Disciple's of Christ Church, had already enrolled at Phillips University in Enid, Oklahoma. Phil intended to pursue a degree in the area of divinity and eventually he would enter the Ministry. My youngest brother was completing his senior year at the local High School and I was fortunate to be able to see him play football and baseball on some of the best teams our school had ever fielded. Every weekend was filled with truly exciting games and the basketball team won the state championship that year. Shortly after arriving in town the First Christian Church Board Members asked me to serve as church choir director. I accepted, and brother Jim became my best church bass voice. We had a great time singing portions of the Messiah each Sunday during the Christmas Season and attending basketball games and other events in between getting to see Phil on holidays.

Christmas that year was very enjoyable, for the first time in many years we celebrated Christmas eve with a major number of relatives at the legion hut in Dewey. About ten pm Shirley and I loaded our little ones in our car and headed the car back to Pawhuska. We were to experience a really unusual phenomenon about four miles west of Bartlesville, as we climbed the first long winding hill that takes you from the Caney River Valley floor into the Osage hills, we noticed what appeared to be a glowing light off the right shoulder of the highway, it appeared to also be maintaining our speed and holding its height of five or six feet above the ground. No one said any thing about it for about three or four minutes, then we both spoke at once, remarking that each of us could see it and describing to each other pretty much the same sight. We all watched it for about three more minutes trying to ascertain if it was a reflection in the cars windows, when all of a sudden the glowing light which again appeared to be about the size of a large pie pan jumped to the other side of the road and took up a position about fifty feet in front of our vehicle. This scared the hell out of us and we rolled the windows up that we had just rolled down to verify whether or not it was a reflection and we also locked the doors. I do not know how we thought that locking the doors would help, but we did and it made us feel more secure. As the light jumped back across the road and took up a new position closer to the car, the thing, what ever it was, stayed with us all the way to within a half mile of the old Katy Under Pass located six miles North of Pawhuska. Then about one mile before we got to this location I said to Shirley, " I wonder what that thing is going to do when we go under the Katy Under Pass"? Shirley said, " I don't know". And about that time the thing began to glow much brighter and began moving North toward the Kansas border, then for about ten seconds, it gained faster and faster speed until it just vanished into the beautiful star filled Christmas sky. We looked at each other and sighed, a real sigh of relief. We have never seen another of these things since.

Sometime after this experience, I believe it was in the late spring, our twins were only about two years of age when David Lee, being a curious little fellow; stuck his hand in the squirrel cage fan of our evaporation cooler. I was sure that he had lost his hand or at the very least his fingers, but he was lucky that his little hand was so small, that the blades of the fan only spun against the back of his whole hand, forcing it along with his arm down into the cage. Even luckier for David, we pulled the unit's wall plug from the wall in time to keep him from trying to extract his hand and loosing his arm. This accident did result in our taking him to the Doctor's office to get his arm and hand treated for a large scrape of his skin. I mention this, because although, David, never cried over this, it was as though his twin brother, Dennis Lynn could feel David's pain, he began crying from the time Dave's arm entered the fan and cried for sometime when we brought David home from the Doctor!

Dad and I, were both paid by the insurance company each week based on the commissions we had earned the previous Quarter year. So, we made a pack to set a monetary goal for each of us depending on what we felt was both needed and practical. We usually worked two or three days each week, met our goal and enjoyed going to games, fishing, or just being with our families the rest of the week. We dragged his big old boat all over Sand Creek.

Anyone who knows anything about sales will understand what transpired next . Somehow the assistant managers of the insurance company found out how we were operating and greedy devils that they were; decided to increase their percentage of our commissions by making us spend more time in the field. When we refused to do so, they came up with another way to get more production out of us. I should have seen their ploy for what it was, but my ego got the best of me and when they complemented me for the great job I was doing as top salesman in their District by sending Dad and me with our wives to New Orleans for a three day, expenses free, company clinic, I was ripe for their picking. That was when the district manager called me and told me I should move to Bartlesville where the really big money was, and take a promotion to Metropolitan Insurance Consultant. In effect what was really going on was they were busting up Dad and my bird nest and taking away my collection salary. The latter, they would give to the new guy who moved into my Pawhuska position. This also made Dad's job much harder, as I wasn't around to help when problems arose and the new guy didn't give a hang about the fact Pop had given twenty-two years of service to Metropolitan. This move did not happen until late may of 1961 and we had many great times before it came about; one of these great times being the trip to New Orleans with Mom, Dad, Shirley and me. We drove Dad's car with him and me sharing the driving time. Once while it was my turn to drive, during my stop at a red light, I was concentrating to hear their conversation and sat through the next green light. As the light glowed yellow then turned back to red Dad, referring to me said to Mom, "Guess he just doesn't like green." He was subtle and kind but always able to get his point across, especially with his family. We had a fine time in New Orleans; we visited most of the tourist attractions such as Bourbon Street, and watched the ships on the Mississippi River. We also listened to Pete Fountain's music at his nightclub and Al Hirt and his band at his place on the same street. The highlight of the trip was supposed to be the formal dinner, hosted by Metropolitan Life at the Roosevelt Hotel our last night of the convention. It turned out to be a real hoot. Dad's former boss and long time acquaintance, had recently divorced his wife of many years and had remarried a much younger, haughty, woman whose obnoxious, high and mighty attitude obviously made everyone in our dinner party very uncomfortable. Our Company manager for the Tulsa Northland District was to host the Tulsa tables of which there were to be two.

Mr. Welsh's table adjoined ours, as he was presently the manager of the South Tulsa office and had been the host at the convention the previous year. So, all the employees of the Tulsa area were to meet in the Hotel lobby at precisely six o'clock and enter the dinning area and sit together. Everyone was on time except the bosses. They made a grand entrée at six-fifteen with the young wife noisily leading her embarrassed husband into the middle of our group, stating she had to have a bit more time than others to get dressed and flaunting what was obviously a very expensive new gown for all to admire. After Madames' making quite a scene and being generally overbearing, our manager and everyone's host, Lonny Welks, suggested we go in for dinner. When all the party was seated, the wait staff began taking orders for drinks. Naturally since it was a company dinner with the managers' breathing down our necks, the agents and their wives were carefully ordering only soft drinks, Typically, when the waiter asked the new young wife for her order, she noisily replied she would like a martini with two olives, making sure everyone at the table heard her order. For the next thirty minutes the lady monopolized the conversation at our table like a queen holding court and by the time the waiters came to take the orders for the evenings entrée, most people had began to ignore her or at the very least to listen with only one ear. Now, failing to be the center of attention was not one of this ladies best attributes, she was just not to be ignored and as the waiter wiggled between the narrow seating, his tray piled high with food held over his head, and slipping quietly behind the queen's chair she announced, she needed to powder her nose and without looking up suddenly scooted backwards in her chair and tried to stand –up. She hit the waiters tray with her shoulder and it tipped toward her husband's position, the waiter tried to catch it and it came back toward his wife and her expensive gown, the whole table gasped, as the orders of four people sloshed onto the stately ladies back and into her lap as she had fallen back into her chair after bumping the tray. I must say it was all I could do to keep from laughing, even though I was immediately concerned about her well-being. A look of complete and utter disbelief came over her face and cussing like a sailor she stood up and scolded the waiter for his lack of respect and carelessness. She then haughtily stormed out of the dinning room to change out of her fancy attire. As she left, Mom and Dad exchanged a knowing glance. I really wanted to clap but decided it might cost me my job. So, I thought better about it and said to Shirley, so those around could hear, "What a shame!" When the four of us returned to Pawhuska from our enjoyable New Orleans trek, Dad and I were filled with new ideas on how to help more folks receive the benefits of life insurance and we were revitalized in our approach to the business. So, we set our weekly goals about one third higher than in the weeks before the trip. A person would think our new approach would have impressed our superiors. Unfortunately, they merely used this as a sign we could have been working more diligently all along and subtly they began working on me to move to Bartlesville.

Every time I had any contact with one of them they would complement me on my sales, always ending their conversation with how much more I could earn if I was in a wealthier area. They never alluded to the fact I was in my hometown where my family was highly respected and that it was one of the wealthiest small towns in America. Our family continued to enjoy being together in Pawhuska with my brothers coming by every chance they got to count the number of pancakes their nephews, my sons, would eat for breakfast. Making bets on this was a favorite pastime. The managers finally convinced stupid me to leave this utopian situation and move to Bartlesville, with the understanding I would immediately receive a promotion to Metropolitan Life Insurance Consultant, and within six months another promotion to assistant manager. What they did not tell me was the present manager was leaving within six months for a new district and the new one that was to take his place would know none of these promises and would not be bound by them if he did.

Shirley's Dad, Hollis built trailers that looked like they came from a Detroit factory and was always generous each time his daughter and her children were forced to move due to his bumbling son-in-law's rambling. So once again he pulled a flatbed from Pryor to Pawhuska, worked all day moving us and would not take a penny for all his trouble. He did this in the heat of late June, as I had to be in the main office of Metropolitan Life in New York City on the first of July for retraining.

Shirley, the three kids, and I drove to the Tulsa airport on the forth of July, about six days after moving our family to Bartlesville, as I needed to catch a plane to New York City. I wanted the children to see the plane leave the ground, so I ask Shirley to park the car and accompany the kids and me into the terminal. Shirley was reluctant to do so, as it was an extremely hot day and the twins had no water, milk or other provisions and all three were quite young. We parked the car at the airport lot and after a bit of pleading from me, Shirley being the loving wife and knowing we will be apart for over a week capitulated. We got out of the car, locked it and I stuck the only set of car keys in my pocket. We went into the terminal, got my ticketing completed and all sat down in the waiting room with my departure gate number. We watched a number of planes arrive and depart before my plane loaded. Finally my departure number was called and we said our goodbyes, I sure hated to leave my little family even for only a short time, but it was necessary if I was to take on the new job. I got to my seat, buckled in, and the plane took off.

For some reason my leg was hurting near my right pants pocket, I put my hand into my pocket and to my surprise the pain became severe when I discovered it was caused by the car keys which I had failed to leave with the family. Shirley later explained that she was frantic when she realized her true predicament. It was a major holiday, the heat was unbearable, the kids had no food or water, and she was fifty-five miles from home with no car, and she knew no one in this area. All these things she blurted out to me when I called her the next day. Boy, was she put out with me and rightly so; what a dunce I had been. She had finally been able to reach a locksmith in Tulsa, who was boating on the lake, and he took mercy on her because of the children and came into town to fix the key problem.

Our move to Bartlesville was not a total washout, due to the fact we were only eight miles from my Berryhill Grandparents. Although we did not get to visit them as often as I would have preferred, we did get over there once in a while and since they were both getting quite old, any time I could spend with them was treasured by all involved. Also, thanks to Dad's and Mom's helping us save on our rent in Pawhuska, we were able to buy our first house. It was located in southwest Bartlesville, about one mile east and three blocks south of the old lead and zinc smelter, had three large bedrooms plus a garage, and was in a very nice middle class neighborhood. Best of all, the children all along our street played both in the street and in each other's yards. So, our kids had lots of friends to enjoy on a daily basis.

In September of our first year in Bartlesville my brother, Philip, was returning to Phillips University in Enid for his second year of studies. Dad and Mom's car was on the blink so; Shirley and I loaded our kids in our Rambler Station Wagon and took him to school. Bartlesville to Pawhuska was only a short thirty minutes trip, but Pawhuska to Enid was three long hours of bad roads. We left Bartlesville early, about seven thirty am and picked Philip up about eight. Driving pretty fast, which at that time was fifty to sixty miles an hour, we arrived in Enid at about one pm. Feeling quite safe in the Rambler, that was only about a year old, I had been really pushing the speed limits. As we drove up to the first stop sign in Enid, I applied the brakes and we came to a slow stop. I heard a thud under our right front tire. My heart sank, as I thought the tire had gone flat. Only if we had been so lucky! I got out to see what was wrong with the tire and discovered that the whole wheel had broken off the car. If this had happened only seconds earlier our car would have badly wrecked. This disaster happened within sight of Philip's dorm, So, he got out and left, walking the rest of the way. I called a wrecker and took the family to lunch, while a shade tree mechanic who we had never met, but was very considerate, welded the wheel back on the vehicle. We then returned home, driving much slower than before the incident, I learned later from several garages that this particular problem was a regular occurrence associated with this model of car.

Later in this same month, we joined a small First Christian Church located in East Bartlesville and I became its first choir director. Our life was really going well, as I had left Pawhuska assured of my next thirteen weeks income at over two hundred thirty dollars per week, and with my manager's guarantee that I would only have to work on commissions for six months. That meant if I really hustled, I could probably sustain my income over the second quarter then my new promotion would kick in. Sounds great! Well, at the end of the first quarter my income fell to one hundred seventy dollars per week, the end of the second quarter it fell again to one hundred thirty dollars, Shirley took apart one of my uncle Albert's old coats, cleaned, then pressed the beautiful tweed, and made coats for our twins, as we could not afford to purchase winter attire for anyone and by spring 1963 Shirley was getting dog bones from the local meat market to make soup for our evening meals. As I mentioned earlier in this chapter the managers of my district changed and the new guy was not going to honor the first manager's commitments to me. I was stuck and although I worked very diligently from the first day I arrived in Bartlesville, the Redwine name meant little to anyone here. Especially, it meant even less to the biggest employer in town, Phillips Petroleum. The reader can see the handwriting on the wall. So, I will digress from the obvious financial oblivion for a few lines to write of happier moments during these trying times. Claude Staton, my uncle by marriage to my mother's younger sister Alene, was and is a very special fellow. During our time in Bartlesville, he and Aunt Polly, that was what the family called Alene resided in Caney, Kansas, which is located only about twenty-five miles north of Bartlesville on US-75 highway. Claude and I fished often together, one time seining fish for the state game and fish department from the area immediately below the dam of Hula Reservoir. The fish were used to stock surrounding farm ponds. While performing this barefooted task, we stepped on many small fish and learned a very painful lesson. The fins of these fish plus the muddy contaminated water of the river can lead to serious infections, which can take away ones ability to walk and therefore work for a number of days.

We also fished a small farm pond that Claude referred to as the Mud Hole that was our favorite bass reserve. It was alive with bass and a real joy to fish although, it was only about one half acre around. Many times we caught ten or more nice bass while fishing this small pond. Aunt Polly is another story entirely. She loved to dress up my oldest daughter Carla Rene and enter her in every sort of competition, especially homecoming or May-Day Parades and although, she often requested to keep Carla for the week-end, we seldom allowed this practice after Carla recited to us the foods Aunt Polly had fed Carla one week-end. This menu consisted entirely of a large bowl of peanuts, bananas, and mayonnaise mixed together, with all the soft drinks Carla wanted to wash the mess down. In spite of this, we all loved and enjoyed both of them. To further explain what a great guy Claude was; we didn't visit with him for ten years after we moved from Bartlesville, due to his divorce from our aunt, but somehow he managed to keep up with where we were and the warm, January 1969 day, we moved from Fort Gibson back to our home in Muskogee, he surprised us by showing up at our house in Fort Gibson at eight o'clock in the morning, worked all day like a Trojan moving our heavy furniture, and left quietly without even letting us buy his supper. To this day I still do not know how he found out we were moving or where we lived. About ten years after this move Claude, lost his foot due to an infection he acquired as a result of going barefoot and stepping on a sharp object, this loss would have been disastrous for most other men but at ninety years of age, he learned to walk again with the aid of a crutch and then acquired a prosthesis and now regularly attends senior dances. When he is not on the floor cutting a jig, he entertains the crowd and plays his guitar or piano, Claude and Polly were divorced and lived apart for the next forty years but due to their loving daughter Claudia, they now reside in the same rest home in Caney, however not in the same wing of the house!

# We finish the Music Degree

The winter of 1962-1963 was our lowest ebb while living in Bartlesville. No matter how hard I worked I just could not seem to make any headway financially, my sales were really at rock bottom and my salary for the next quarter was going to be about thirty dollars a week. So, after knocking doors in the snow one cold December day, I went home and sat down with Shirley to map out a new strategy. We talked about how our finances were low and that prospects for their recovery did not appear to be forth coming. She asked what I thought would be a good solution and I told her I would like to return to Oklahoma State and finish my music degree. To my surprise, she agreed. Then continued to explain she had figured a way to accomplish this feat if her Dad and Mom were willing to let her and the kids stay upstairs in their home for a short while until we could move everyone to Stillwater. We decided to rent our home to recover enough money to make the mortgage payments. We would sell our Rambler and purchase a much cheaper car, move our furniture and hold a garage sale of our belongings that we needed to discard. We would keep and move most kitchen supplies and equipment. Then I would rent a house with my brothers in Stillwater, Shirley and the children would move to Pryor to live with Shirley's parents and I would enroll in school. All this must be accomplished by the fifteenth of January, (Remember it is cold mid December.) I would need to attend the second semester, which would officially begin in about three weeks in order to get the required classes I needed to complete my degree and receive my teaching certificate by the second semester of the 1963-1964 school year. I called my brothers to ask if they would agree to live together with me, as Shirley and I had agreed this would be necessary for my returning to school. They both said, " lets roll." Jim was already attending O. S. U. and Philip wanted to transfer from Phillips University to begin a new course of study. After getting their approval, we began to work quickly on this new project. Everything seemed to fall into place, as we worked really hard each day to get the pieces fitted to this puzzle. Shirley's Dad found her a great job as head secretary at the National Carbide Company Plant in Pryor. We rented our home to some nice folks and moved the kids and Shirley to Pryor. I convinced Metropolitan to give me a transfer to Stillwater and without their knowing, simultaneously got a job with the Southwestern Insurance Company in Stillwater so, I could write for both companies and give my customers the best deal from either company. In addition, I called my old friend Bill Varnum, who was now the band director at Stillwater Junior High, and asked him to start up our old dance band, so as to make a few extra bucks. He was delighted to be back in the business and we set out immediately to rebuild the old band, using the original book with some updated material and the best musicians on the campus. My brothers and I moved our belongings into a rented house on North Duck Street, immediately across the street from Bennett Hall dormitory and I enrolled along with them in second semester classes.

In spite of all our problems in Bartlesville, things were looking up and I do believe if we had been more successful there our lives would not have been as full, because if we could have stayed there, we would never have accomplished all the myriad of other things we have done.

The spring semester went very well for us and although shirley liked her new job, she had her hands full working and being a full time mother to our three kids. We did not get to see each other very often, as it was a very long drive from Pryor to Stillwater and a real challenge for her to load all the kids and make the trip in our 1940 Buick. We had purchased this car from one of the agents in my office after selling our Rambler to get out of the mortgage on it. Corralling three young kids on such a long trip while driving, took a lot of patience. Our kids still get a laugh out of telling how they learned to duck Shirley's flailing right arm as they played havoc in the back seat of that old car.

The summer classes went well, but Brother Jim decided to pledge the Sigma Nu fraternity, so he moved into the fraternity house for a short time, the Sigma Nus' were widely known on campus, as the most social of social groups and this eventually led to Jim's dropping out of school and his driving to California with a friend, who was also disenchanted with school. Phil and I really missed him, as we had been enjoying the time together. Jim spent some time with our cousin, Claudia Staton Gambino, while he was in California and they have been closer as cousins because of it. He joined the U. S. Air Force shortly after his summer trip and the Air Force stationed him in foreign language school at The University of Indiana at Bloomington

After a short time, he entered pre-law classes there and eventually received his law degree from that school. I have always been very proud of my brother Jim as he is one fine person, but I felt we lost him to Indiana due to his education there, and for that I am sorry, because I miss him greatly. Shirley and the kids moved in with Philip and me at the end of the summer session. Our oldest daughter Carla was entering first grade that fall and we wanted her to feel secure in

her surroundings before she enrolled. Shirley went to work in the city offices of Stillwater, but the work was really hard, with long hours and very little pay, (fifty cents as hour) and a very overbearing female boss.

One day, about two weeks after we enrolled Carla in Will Rogers Grade school for her first taste of formal education,

*Carla, David and mother Shirley at OSU 1963*

Shirley was enjoying her lunch hour at the small café on O. S. U. 's campus and our good friend of many years, Glen Phibbs, saw her there. Glen told her that he had just over heard a conversation in the employment office, and that if she would act on it immediately, he felt she could get a very good job. While he was in line at the employment counter, someone had called for a bookkeeper and tax person to keep records for the construction company that had the contracts for the new buildings being constructed on the campus. He said," If you go quickly, you can probably beat the person being sent from the University employment office to the construction site and you will get the job". Shirley dropped her lunch and almost ran the two city blocks to the site. When she got there, the boss, Mr. Bill Cowan, was inside the office trailer and he asked, "Are you the new bookkeeper"? Shirley replied,"I am." and he growled, " I thought they were sending a man, that could read blue-prints". Shirley then told him she could read them, as her father had taught her some years ago. He stepped back and invited her in, showing her the desk piled high with paper work. He then went out to the job site and left her by herself. Oddly, the person requested from the employment office never showed up to fill the job. Great guns, we eat again!

This job was really a lot of work, but Shirley was in on the very first few days of the new construction, so she was able to gradually add more and more small duties to her total responsibilities. In addition to keeping the hourly payroll for the two new construction sites, reading the blueprints soon became very important because the man who was costing the project on a daily basis **quit!** Mr. Cowen asked Shirley if she could do the costing, and she told him she could, so she took on that major position also. Due to her many duties, the pay was very good and Mr. Cowan held Shirley in very high regard, as he had never had anyone who could perform these many tasks with such efficiency. What he did not know was Shirley was bringing a great deal of her work home to complete late at night after she had cooked dinner, cleaned the house, bathed the kids, and handled our financial responsibilities. When I finished my studies, and received my degree, we left Stillwater for a new teaching job in Broken Bow, Oklahoma. Mr. Cowen tried to get Shirley to stay with him, as he told her he had hired three women to replace her. These three women only worked two days before quitting, because they said, No one could do all that work.

About the end of September, Philip and a classmate of his, Carl Tuck, came to the house one day and I overheard Phil say, " I'm, going to call her"! I looked inquisitively at Tuck and he explained

Phil had discovered another Redwine at O. S. U. and had decided to call and find out if it was a relative. It turned out that some two years later after many dates, that both she and Phil would transfer to another university to complete his undergrad studies and Sarah Redwine, the lady Phil called that day, would become Mrs. Philip Redwine. Even more odd was the fact that after that initial call, which ended in Phil asking Sarah for a coke date, the coke date became a major part of Carl Tuck's life. It seems Carl had been dating a lovely girl from Tulsa, named Sharon, and they decided to get married the same evening of Phil and Sarah's first date, so when Phil went to pick up Sarah his first words to her were," Do you have a hat and gloves"? Sarah said, "Yes". Phil, then told her, "Put them on we are going to a wedding". I know Sharon's folks never believed this, but the wedding was just that (spur of the moment). Sharon asked Carl to marry her about three pm on their wedding day and before four pm. Carl had made arrangements with the preacher to perform the seven pm service at the First Christian Church, one block from our house. Sharon called her shocked parents in Tulsa to ask them to attend, I went to a local Bakery, where I had seen a wedding cake that day, walked in and the lady behind the counter said," Have you come for the cake "? I never hesitated and said, "Yes". I paid her and we had one fine wedding reception at the North Duck residence. Champaign, wedding cake, mints and nuts, no wonder her parents did not believe us when we told them we had not known in advance of this day that their kids were getting so serious. I have often wondered what happened in that Bakery, when the people who ordered that wedding cake came for it.

Shortly after the wedding Philip pledged the Alpha Tau Omega Fraternity and moved into the fraternity house. I am sure his moving out of our small house where he was sharing a bedroom with his four year old twin nephews had nothing to do with his new residence.

Carla, Dennis, and David had some really trying days while we were completing that fall semester, they had baby sitters who mistreated them by locking them outside in the hot sun without anything to drink, and one particular woman threatened Carla with not picking her up at school, if she was not waiting for the woman when the sitter arrived. This so unnerved Carla that she was failing to do her class work in the afternoon. Fortunately, Carla's teacher questioned her as to why she was in such a hurry to leave class and discovered the root of the situation. In the case of the twins, Shirley happened to leave work a bit early one day and saw for herself that they were being locked out of their sitter's house while the sitter was giving her own child ice cream. We diligently and quickly found another sitter, but none of our kids were very happy with her and the boys cried almost everyday because they hated going there.

This situation led the boys to pack their pajamas, old favorite sweatshirts, and extra shoes (they were wearing their favorite cowboy boots) in a sack and run off one day. This escapade transpired one Saturday in November and unfolded thusly; about three pm on this sunny but blustery fall day, a car pulled up in front of our house where I was just arriving from my performance at a home football game. Traffic was really ferocious on Duck, as the stadium was within one block of the house and Duck was a major thoroughfare. I noticed the twins getting out of that car and was quite surprised, as I thought they were in the house. I recognized the driver as one of Phil's fraternity brothers, but I did not know his name, He said," You missing some boys "? And my heart jumped, as he told me, he had spotted both my twin boys who were four years old, out on the extremely busy North Highway # 177, trying to catch a ride to their grandparents who resided in Pryor. He had picked them up and brought them home. I was so thankful God had returned them unharmed I did not even scold them. I just hugged them and took them inside to their mother, who did not know they had slipped away. We immediately questioned them as to where they were headed and why. They began to cry and tell us they were unhappy here and were going to their grandparents. This affair changed our minds from staying for another year to get my masters, to getting the hell out of Stillwater as soon as we could finish my undergrad degree.

Christmas of that year found us doing very well financially, as I was performing two or three nights a week with my dance band, selling a bit of life insurance and Shirley had the bookkeeping job with Cowen Construction. In addition to these incomes I booked a couple of college shows, for which I was paid to write the musical arrangements and provide the musicians to accompany the entertainers. I stayed fairly busy with the twenty-four credit hours I carried that semester. A large number of hours even for me, as I never carried less than eighteen any semester I attended O. S. U. With my performing in the West Side Story Orchestra, the university marching band, and my own band, I had little time left for study but I still pulled a 3.8 grade average that last semester. This made up for those really bad first two semesters of my freshmen year, and helped get me admitted into graduate school some ten years later at Kansas University.

# The Move to Broken Bow

In early January of 1964, Mr. Hiram Henry, the marching band professor at the university and a person to whom I shall always owe a great debt, as he has been a true friend and mentor from the early days of my freshmen year at O. S. U., visited with me and told me of two or three band director/ teaching positions that he had information about that would possibly be available at the end of the month. Mr. Henry suggested I contact the superintendents at these high schools to inquire as to the possibilities of my going to work in their schools as a band director. I called all the schools and the first superintendent to return my call was Mr. Rector Johnson of Broken Bow, Oklahoma. I immediately made an appointment for a face-to-face interview with Mr. Johnson for the coming Saturday at one pm.

I thought Broken Bow was over by Tulsa, I had no idea it was a seven hours drive from Stillwater, in far southeastern Oklahoma. Shirley and I visited about the interview and decided to go that very day and trade in our old car for a newer model, as we did not think it wise to try to drive any distance from Stillwater in the old Buick, especially taking the whole family including Shirley's mother, Ester, who was staying the week with us. The local Ford dealer in Stillwater was advertising a special on some former police patrol cars they had purchased from the state. So, knowing no better, we took a look at them. Then not knowing what to look for in such a vehicle, we bought one. The dealer had repainted our car in red with white trim and it looked really hot, with a four- barrel carburetor and white sidewall tires, we thought we had really made a good deal, as we were given a very good trade amount for our old Buick. What we did not know about our new purchase was that this baby would really fly down the road, but in so doing sucked up gas like crazy.

On our trip to Broken Bow which began at seven am on Saturday, we had to stop four times for gas and about twelve noon found us half way between Antlers and Broken Bow when the large water hose broke on the radiator and the car overheated. I jumped out, rapped the hose with some duct tape, which we had left in the car after we used some of it to repair a carpet in the trunk, then took a pop bottle and refilled the radiator with water from a nearby ditch. We drove more slowly from this point, thinking we would not put as much pressure on the broken hose, but the water was still leaking from the broken area and about twenty miles west of Broken Bow, the car overheated again. Fortunately, there was an old shack on the south side of the highway with signs out front, that denoted this shack was some type of store. I headed to this store on foot, to make a phone call to Mr. Johnson and let him know I could not possibly be on time for our appointment and I certainly was not prepared for what was inside that building. I was later told we had happened onto the store known in these parts as Gangrene Annie's. As I entered the dimly lighted door, which had no screen and was standing wide open, I could see two grubby old men in patchy overalls seated behind a nasty raw wood table with two large live chickens parading on it. The chickens were stepping in their own waste, which obviously had been on the table for some time. As I stepped inside the door, I could now see that this so called store had a dirt floor, and a large rawboned woman of nearly three hundred pounds in a very dirty ragged dress was taking up space just to the right of me. This was squalor that I had heard of, but had never believed existed.

Needing to make my phone contact with Mr. Johnson, I quickly explained, my car was broken down and I needed to use their phone. I asked if they had a phone and all three pointed over to my right in front of the woman, who, when she opened her mouth to speak, revealed many missing and ugly yellow broken teeth. At this time I thought of only two things, the phone and getting back to my car. So, I asked again and the woman said, "We have a phone over in that corner, as she pointed to a pay phone booth on my right. You are welcome to it, if you can make it work, they put it in last week and we have never figured out yet how to use it. I walked over to the phone booth, read the directions and with the aid of a nice new quarter, called Mr. Johnson. He was a bit put out that I was late for our appointment, but told me if I could make it to his office by two-thirty pm, he would still see me. I thanked my lovely and badly needed hosts for the use of their phone and ran back to the car, where I again repaired the hose with duct tape and refilled the radiator, this time filling it to the brim. Then I got in and drove the last twenty miles to my interview as Shirley and her mother told me that while I was inside Annie's store, they had witnessed an in- creditable event. A woman had come by their parked car leading a deer, by it's leash of a rope around it's neck and with a small bell tied to the leash.

When we arrived at the office of Superintendent Johnson, before I went in, I handed the car keys to Shirley, as we had already discussed she would try to see a bit of the town, get the hose fixed, and most importantly get the family a cold drink, as it had been a long trip and everyone was a bit frazzled. When I knocked on his office door, Mr. Johnson surprised me with his greeting. He did not come outside his office or invite me in but requested I wait a few minutes in the outer office while he finished his interview with another applicant. It had not occurred he was interviewing anyone else. Boy, was I naive. However, he must have been with this young man for quite a while before I arrived, as he only had me cool my heels for about ten minutes, then after introducing the young fellow to me, he asked him to go see the town, while we talked, then come back in about two hours and we would all go to dinner.

After Mr. Johnson got passed the first few minutes of our interview, in which he was obviously upset because I was late, he settled into being very cordial and we got along really well. He took me to see the facilities available, they were quite stark, the band room was a small dark area heated with two rattling old steam radiators and there was only one four-drawer metal file that comprised the total music library. I was surprised by the fact that his school, had such a fine reputation, and was so poor in financial resources. He obviously knew something I had not learned, and I could learn a great deal from this real southern gentleman and educator. I was most impressed with the fact he did not show me the football field or any other of his athletic facilities and not once did he mention the fact that his football team and track team had won the state of Oklahoma championships last season. He bragged continuously about the Rhodes and Fulbright scholars that had graduated recently from his high school, and made it clear he wanted a music teacher that would teach fine literature to the students in a manner that the town and he expected would result in their band competing at a very high level at the state and national contests.

The interview lasted about two hours and I asked him many questions about the town and where I could find a place for my family that would be comfortable but not to expensive, as I would want to rent housing. He explained that a band director, Eldon White, who had taught there sometime previously, still owned a house which he was sure would be available, and we settled on salary at five thousand two hundred dollars per year, then he told me not to act as though I had the job, because he wanted to have dinner with the other fellow, then tell him privately that I was his choice for the position.

About four-thirty pm as we were locking the door on the band room the other fellow came back, we three headed to the superintendent's office but never got there, because Shirley and my family were parked just outside of the office and Mr. Johnson stopped to meet them.

After introducing the family to him, he asked us to have dinner with him and his wife. We were thankful to have the invitation to dinner for many reasons; one being it was a great chance to visit further with Mr. Johnson, who had lived in this area for many years, another was he could assure Shirley, that we could find lodging quickly and most importantly we did not have any idea where to find a good place to eat. He suggested we dine at the old Charles Wesley hotel dinning room and explained, that today was the last time we would have the opportunity to eat in this very fine dinning room and take advantage of its long and storied history, as the owners were closing it after this evening's business. They were going to tear it down and rebuild, using newer brick and rustic red cedar materials and also they were changing the method of service from the present family style, which provided the patrons with large bowls of each food served, which the customer would serve themselves and pass the bowl to the guests seated along side at the same table, as one would do in the privacy of one's home as opposed to the procedure used in most current restaurants of ordering through a waitress or waiter.

We really enjoyed the meal of large platters of fried chicken, accompanied to the table by mixing bowls of buttered corn, cold slaw, mashed potatoes, a boat of wonderful gravy, baskets of fluffy angel biscuits, (always a house specialty) and all washed down with the best iced tea I had ever tasted; although, I am sure Mr. And Mrs. Johnson were more nostalgic about the loss of this fine old institution than we, never the less, we felt some anguish at the change. I must admit the owners replaced the old building with a very beautiful and long lasting new hotel and restaurant, just a few yards south of the old location and we ate there many times over the next thirty years. With few exceptions at all those meals, we found the food and service to be very good.

After dinner Mr. Johnson took the other applicant aside and told him of the decision to hire me, then came out on the porch of the old building to tell us he had done so and also bid us adieu, telling me, he would see me on the last Monday of the month for my first day of teaching.

We loaded into the gas- guzzler of a Ford and headed back to Stillwater, all the while filling each other in on what the day's experiences to each of us had been. Shirley and Ester had some great stories about what they had seen in the little community. They both told of seeing a pickup truck parked on main street with a six foot black bear scrolled on its back, lifelessly in the pickup bed, still bleeding from the gun shot wound that had dispatched the huge animal. Shirley reached under the front seat of the car and pulled up a copy of the town's weekly newspaper, The Broken Bow News, dated today, and pointed to a picture of a mountain lion that had been killed on Main Street last week. Ester gasped, and though she was not the dotting mother in law type, quietly stated," I am not sure this is the town for you". Ester whispered this, as Shirley was continuing to explain that all the down town store fronts had corrugated tin awnings held up by rough cedar posts that still had the shoulders of their limbs where the limbs had been sawed from the trunk. Then both ladies in unison recited seeing two wild deer on the north end of main-street while they were driving around the town.

Today's trip had certainly been an eye opener for the whole family, although Shirley and her mother had their doubts about living in so remote an area, the kids were really excited to get to see such a place and even more excited to have the chance to live there. They also were happy to be moving anywhere that took them out of Stillwater.

By the time we could see the lights of Stillwater, on our return trip, we had fairly well decided to move to Broken Bow. So, it was nice not to be forced to call Mr. Johnson and tell him I had changed my mind about taking the position and I was pretty sure this job was the right move for all of us. I had a very good feeling about this opportunity to have a very fine music program, as all the pieces of this puzzle appeared to be present and I was to be proved correct many times during the next three and one half years. I have always thought that there are five essential ingredients that must be present to have an outstanding musical organization. These are capable administrators that truly want the program, mix- in talented students who are ambitious and hard working, add interested understanding parents, then next a capable, kind, but demanding instructor with a wealth of experience and lastly, but not necessarily in this order, good facilities, equipment and fine instruments. Also I believe if any three of these items are present in the same situation with capable students, the results will be very respectable.

# The Early Broken Bow Years

We moved to Broken Bow the day I completed my fall semester at O. S. U. and I met my first classes the next day, accompanied by Mr. Johnson, who was a very hands on administrator. He spoke to every class introducing me to the students in a very professional manner. Mr. Forest Carter, a kind but very straight gentleman, was the high school principal to whom I was to directly report. Mr. Carter had three lovely daughters in the band program. One would have thought, that Mr. Carter would have been the person to introduce me, but at Broken Bow Mr. Johnson commanded such respect from his staff, the parents and students, that when he was within sight or hearing distance the air was stiff with silence from those folks who were in attendance, as they waited patiently for him to speak. It was plain to me, he considered this first day a very important one and he was leaving nothing to chance.

The high school band had been rehearsing The Finale to D'vorshak's New World Symphony in preparation to present it and two other pieces, The first and third movements of Gustov Holst's First Suite for Military Band and His Honor March by Leonard Fillmore at their district contest, which was fast upon them, as the date for the contest was only six weeks from today. I was familiar with all these pieces having either performed each or conducted each at some point in my career and not wanting to strain our relationship anymore than was necessary, I decided then and there to take advantage of the rehearsal hours the band had invested at this point in these fine musical works. When Mr. Johnson finished his kind words, I thanked him and got immediately to work rehearsing the finale, during which

I could tell from listening, that although it was going to be possible for the band to score highly on it, we had a mountain of work ahead of us preparing this major symphonic piece for serious competition.

We met our first rehearsal on Monday as I reiterated earlier. By Thursday we had scheduled a full section rehearsal of one hour or more for every section and the band was really buying into my style and working ambitiously to perform in a winning manner, we appeared to have a really good rapport and I could envision a possible superior rating at the up coming performance.

However, Thursday evening about six o'clock I got a phone call from my Mother. Mom said, "Please come home to Pawhuska at once if I wished to see my father one more time before he died,as he had been diagnosed with terminal cancer that day and had been told he only would live less than six weeks at the most". Unfortunately, he died within three weeks, but I did get to visit one last time with him and he did get to tell all my children good- by. After I hung up the phone from Mom's, call, I called Mr. Carter and told him that I would need Friday off to see Dad and he cancelled my Friday's rehearsals.

We loaded the family in the bright red and white ex-patrol Ford and headed to Pawhuska, a trip that at that time, due to the terrible roads, and the states policy of open range, (live stock did not have to be fenced and if a car hit one the car's owner was liable for payment to the stock's owner.) took nine hours driving time. It did not matter which highways we took.

We arrived in Pawhuska at about seven am and went to the old home place on fourteenth and Ruble, but no one was there as they were still at the hospital. So, we got the kids some breakfast and then all went to visit Pop and Mom in his hospital room at eighteenth and lynn ave. The old two story brick hospital located at this address has since been torn down and the new hospital which served my mother well some years later, was built about a half mile away on fifteenth, four blocks east of the high school.

When we arrived at the hospital, the nurses would not let the kids go into Dad's room, as they said," he was in need of complete quiet". Shirley and I honored their demands and left the children in the car, as it was a fairly nice day for this time of the year. Then we walked to his room where we found him sitting up in bed feeling in much pain, as his cancer had moved into his throat and though the nurses attended him well with his often requested antacids, he was getting no relief from the burning in his throat. When he realized we were there, he managed a smile and nodded his acknowledgment of our presence and as I had watched him do so many times before, reached up to his left ear with his left hand an gave the ear a kind of curling motion. Dad would always do this ear thing when he was happy or when giving some idea a great deal of thought. There were hugs all around and he asked to see the kids, so I went to the nurses and convinced them it mattered little to his well being physically and it mattered greatly to his mental health, to see everyone he wished, as he obviously was not to survive much longer.

From that time until his death three weeks later, the nurses encouraged everyone who came by, to visit with Pop, as he was a very popular guy in that little town. He told Mom later, and she told me at his funeral, how much he appreciated getting to see so many of his friends one last time before his death. I had experienced the deaths of my Grandfather Berryhill, and my Uncle Albert to whom I felt very close so, I thought I could handle the death of my father pretty well, but I will tell you now it's not the same. Every death is a terrible and tragic loss when you love someone like I loved my Father and Mother.

We stayed as long as we could that weekend, but on late Sunday we had to return to Broken Bow, as I had to put in an appearance at the school. Dad, was really cool about the fact we were leaving, we hugged and he told me quietly and sadly these two things, he said, "I don't want to die, but at least I have never had to watch as one of my children died" Then he said," "I hate it that we will not see each other again". I tried to allay his fears of this and said," I'll be back in a week or two". He was far more astute than I and unfortunately correct, as these were his last words to me.

Cancer research was in it's infancy in 1964 and typical of Dad's generous nature, when his doctors explained his medical condition as hopelessly terminal and asked him to submit to che-mo therapy, which was presently a witch doctor type of treatment, very painful, and highly experimental; he immediately told them that if it might help the future of their research and help other patients with the same condition, they should proceed at full throttle, as it was apparent due to his deadline with Michel, the angel, they would have little time to assess their results. The treatments were much more painful than the disease and I watched in horror as the doctors administered a one foot long, two inch round syringe, including it's six inch needle, that was large enough to doctor horses and filled with foul looking liquid into his arm. I've often thought these painful poisons and the treatments hastened my father's death.

Although, I drove like a mad man, the day I got the final call from Mom, who told me, that he would soon be gone; the distance was just too great to cover in the time I had to drive it. I have never forgiven myself for not going back the following weekend and for missing the opportunity to once again say farewell, while placing that silly job in front of what was the most important man in my life. The six weeks that the physicians predicted for Dad to live turned out to be only three, as he passed away on the twenty third of February 1964. Mother, told the family, that he spent his last evening watching the first American performance of the Beetles, televised on the Ed Sullivan Show. He watched the performance from his bed in his bedroom and expired the following morning, as he wished in his own room at home. Dad's full name was Adolphus Carroll Redwine, his mother was Agness Watts Wilson Redwine, and his father was Adolphus Cash Redwine. Dad was born in the old Oklahoma town of Walls, on November ninth, 1905. Walls, was located fairly close to the present towns of Red Oak and Wilburton, Oklahoma. There is a town in present Oklahoma called Walls, but it is not in the same location as the Walls of my father's birth. There is no way for me to adequately explain what a fine man my father was, but there are a few stories I remember that might give the reader some ideas of his kind demeanor, and thoughtful attitude toward others.

My mother had three brothers, I have mentioned somewhat earlier in this family account. Two of these men William, now deceased himself, and Lyle, at present in quite ill health, made the following observations about Dad and passed these verbally on to me shortly after his death.

William, (Bill), told me, that although I never saw this side of my father, as he had mellowed greatly by the time I knew him, that when Dad was young and before he married my mother, my father was a fearsome fellow, and was known around Dewey, Oklahoma as a man one did not cross. He was known to enter the local bars on any given weekend and announce to all inside, " Alright you bastards who wants to be first "! Then he would proceed to empty the place, sometimes fighting two or three at a time.

Uncle Lyle, known to the family as "Buck," recalls and paints an entirely different picture of Dad, Uncle Buck told me more than once, "Your father was the kindest gentleman I ever knew"!

I remember my father loved to play dominoes at Skeet Blanc's domino and pool hall that was located on the west side of Kihikah Avenue just north of the Triangle Building in Pawhuska, he was really good at it also, he played for two dollars a game per person, plus a dollar per hicky.

This pool hall was the hang out for yours truly too and many a quarter of Dad's dominoe winnings was spent by his eldest son at Skeet's snooker tables. Ole Skeet had a gorgeous blond haired daughter, who was four years younger than me, and I wanted to date her but Skeet made it clear his daughter was not dating any of the local riff raft, especially those that hung out in his place. I finally got enough courage to ask her out the second semester of my senior year, and she asked me why it had taken me so long to getting around to requesting a date with her, I lied and said," I really did not know". I could not tell her I was afraid of her father.

Along with his two Brother in law's assessments of Dad, I have a couple of additional stories, one in which I actually participated as a youngster, and one he told me about himself, both occur in the same overall story.

One cold day in the spring of 1949, when I was about twelve years old a Hobo came to our home requesting food, this was fairly unusual by 1949,even though we lived within two blocks of the Katy railroad, as the depression, due to the war economy had waned. After Dad had taken the dirty ragged fellow a plate of food and while he was eating it on our back stoop, I made a foolish remark about him. Snidely I said," I can not understand why anyone would bend so low as to beg for food". Dad looked really sad and told me, "Son, thank God you have never been hungry"! Then he continued to explain, that could have been himself out on the stairs of our back porch, for only a few years earlier, he could not find work and he had been forced to ride the rails as a hobo, surviving on the generosity of others.

He then told me of just how poor and destitute he had been during the depression of 1928, and through nearly the next five years. During this time he was living with and supporting his mother in a small shotgun house with one bedroom in south Dewey.

So, the story unfolded thusly, Dad's mother had ordered some groceries from the local grocer and when the delivery boy brought the items requested, the boy set them on the kitchen table, but told Dad who was in the kitchen cleaning a rabbit he had recently chased from under their home and killed, that the local grocer would not let him leave the delivery unless the Redwines paid something on their outstanding grocery bill. Dad told the young fellow to go see his mother in the front room as his mother paid the bills. Then while the delivery boy was negotiating with my grandmother, Dad, carefully took the string loose from the sack of salt inside the box of groceries, stole a handful of salt and even more carefully sewed the sack back to cover his theft. After the delivery boy left, taking the whole order back to the store, minus the handful of salt, Dad and his mother lived on that rabbit for three days until he got a small job in the neighborhood and earned a few cents working on a local house. Then a few days later he was hired back at the local cement plant.

The death of a loved one so close to you is never a good thing, but sometimes good things occur because of the tragedy and that is what happened to our family at the time of Dad's passing. My youngest brother who had not been home or seen by any of us for over eighteen months was furloughed from the Air Force for ten days in order for him to attend the funeral. Jims coming home, even for that short visit, was a blessing to all of us and especially to our Mother who was devastated by grief at this tragic time.

Shirley, the three children, and I returned to Broken Bow the next day after the funeral and I threw myself into my job, spending every waking hour at the band room. I held full band rehearsals daily from seven am to eight thirty and again Monday through Thursday from one pm to two twenty pm. This last scheduling that excluded Fridays, but was one hour and twenty minutes in duration, was our regularly scheduled school band period. Then I held section rehearsals from three forty-five to six pm each day. These sectionals allowed me to hear,

*Left to right; Carla Rene Redwine age 8 daughter of Shirley Janez Redwine mother of both Carla and twin boys David Lee Redwine and Dennis Lynn Redwine age 6 and standing at far right, Shirley's husband and kid's father Carroll E. Redwine, picture taken at Beaver's Bend State Park, January of 1965*

help, and correct the errors of every student for forty-five minutes at least once each week, and to Build stamina in the performers. After six pm and weekends, we spent a lot of time with the family getting acquainted with this beautifully wild and scenic area.

My fine sons, of which I am duly proud, caught many perch big enough to eat from the drainage ditch in front of our urban home immediately after some of the large rains that regularly fell in this area. They also were very able entrepreneurs, at the age of six, they went throughout the neighborhood inviting the area children to pay one dollar each to attend a proposed birthday party for themselves, as they picked blackberries from the fields near our home and carried them to the local households, where they sold the berries for enough cash in addition to the party contributions to purchase their first bicycle.

The twins received a very big plastic gun for their birthday, they named it big bertha and they were quite proud of big bertha toting it throughout their quests of the neighborhood. The neighborhood bully was two years older than Carla, and lived across the alley from us. This young fellow became a bully due to his age difference and physical stature in relation to the twins and Carla, he delighted in tearing up any toys our kids might leave laying around. So at the first opportunity he gave Big Bertha a good bashing and when the boys found their gun mutilated they came to me crying about the bigger boy and his meanness. I knew that if I did talk to the young man's parents, he would just make my kids lives more filled with problems. So, I told Carla, Dennis, and David that although individually they were no match for a bigger person, together they would be a formidable force and that they must do whatever was necessary to teach this guy a permanent lesson, or his attitude would continue to haunt them throughout their years in Broken Bow. The next day the bully's mother called Shirley to complain that he was afraid to go outside his yard, as Carla, Dennis and David working together, had jumped him with a baseball bat and chased him home, where he had come into the house crying. Shirley told the boy's mother, she was sorry our kids were misbehaving, I apologized to the father and privately, we both congratulated our kids on a job well done! The fellow never bullied them again.

About this time, Carla, decided she was a bad luck charm to those close to her and her mental state was really affected by it. Within the next three weeks she had some very traumatic events for a child of her age. She experienced the death of her dancing instructor, her piano teacher got her leg crushed in an accident at a picnic in the park,

*Carla Rene, David lee, and DennisLynn, 1965*

which Carla witnessed and her grade school teacher was diagnosed with cancer. Shirley spent a great deal of time convincing Carla, that these events had nothing to do with her.

John Axton, the father of Hoyt Axton, both now deceased, was the football coach at Broken Bow High School during these great years I taught the School Bands. We were very good friends and John spent many Monday mornings in his office explaining his up coming Friday nights game stategy to me after I finished Marching Band reheresal and before I left the stadium. Due to this friendship, Johns wife May Axton who wrote *Heartbreak Hotel* for Elvis Presley Came to the Bandroom one day with a very entertaining proposal, She said she was going to Nashville to meet a young man called Elvis Presley and he was going to need a band to do his shows and would I like to play in that band and help her record her new song *Heartbreak Hotel,* I told her I had three kids and a wife, had just moved to Broken Bow and had too many financial responsibilities to leave my teaching job. She ask me two or three more times over the next week to go with her to Nashville ,but I was afraid to leave the security I felt in my present position and so I made what was a very unusal decision for me and choose not to go.

Shirley and I had very little time to rest, as my job, her community activities, and the childrens needs for our care and guidance during their activities required many busy hours. So, it was a rare day indeed when we were fortunate enough to sleep in. On one of these rare days, Shirley woke up late and we were still sleepy eyed, laying in our warm bed, when I realized, we had been awakened by the kids, who were playing in the front room with the television blaring. Suddenly I heard a KER-plunk, and I told a very sleepy Shirley," The twins just shot the T. V. with their B-Bee gun"! Shirley replied," They would not do that"! I wiggled from under the warm covers, and wobbled to a sitting position on our warm bed, slipped into my pants, that I had gingerly thrown in the floor the previous night, gave Shirley a knowing glance that said" oh yes they would", and headed to the living room. The whole house had suddenly become as quiet as a tomb. I could feel the rarified air of tension, as I arrived in the front room to see two very frighten little boys huddled under the rocking chair, with their trusty weapon still aimed at the exact middle of the now very black and silent television screen, which presently

The Chandlers

*L to R Dr. Harold Chandler, daughter Cheryl, wife Jo, daughter Kathy, and son Paul*

displayed a lovely little B-Bee hole in the face of it's glass tube. I figured they were scared enough by the results of their morning rain of terror, so I just went over to them and said," well fellows that will be the end of your watching T. V. for one year "! And that was how our family learned to do many more fun things together. Shirley reminds me often, that our years in Broken Bow were some of our most productive and enjoyable of any years we have been together.

We had many great friends who were of like family background and values and since we were in our late twenties and early thirties life was a continuous party. The friends we had were politically savvy, very astute verbally, intelligent, kind and considerate. They also were very much aware of their obligations to the community and we spent many hours on Junior Chamber of Commerce projects, making Broken Bow, during those shining years, one of the most outstanding places to live in Oklahoma. Although, I will more than likely fail to list some of our fine friends, I feel I must mention for old times sake, some of those closest and most dear.

There were the wonderfully talented Chandler Twins: Rex, the generous, handsome, sometimes totally off the wall, but always thoughtful druggist, who in many ways has been a friend our whole family and his could always depend on. His twin brother Paul who had a wonderful family and devoted his life to helping others as one of the areas few physicians, but the one doctor I would trust with my and my family's lives before any other. Pauls wife Patricia, who is and was a warm, kind, gentle, lady in both actions and attitude. Dr. Harold (Hal) Chandler, (deceased), a brilliant Fulbright scholar who was the most fun-loving dare-devil of us all, and delighted in testing everyone 's patients, and their physical metal and Hals beautiful and gifted wife Jo, Shirleys confidant, who we all loved dearly and who organized us into a cohesive and effective group no matter what the occasion. Donna and Fred Brewer, hard working and gentle friends, whose daughter Tammy replaced Carla as the Broken Bow Band mascot two years after we moved from this great little community. Two other fine folks who we really adored as friends and whom we seldom see, but will never forget were the indefatigueable Charlie Reed and his forever inventive wife, Volga who like the rest of our friends had a house full of talented and gifted children, one of which, Glynnis, their oldest daughter, was my pleasure to teach flute in her fifth grade year, and who performed admirablely, as the bands mascot the year we moved to Muskogee.

A terrible tragedy befell the Reed family a few years later when one of their beautiful girls, I can not say which at this time, although I believe it was Dawn, their youngest was killed in a horrendous traffic accident that occurred on highway 70 during her return to college in Durant.

The local banker is always an important person to everyone and we had a good one who, helped himself admirable as he helped all of us in our financial dealings, he was into every kind of business one could imagine, He rented porta -potties, had a major western wear operation and through the bank, financed most of the building and charities in the town. His name was Melvin Cavendar and his main claim to fame was that he was the nephew of the Cavendar, who developed the recipe for Cavendar's Steak Seasonings, a delicious blend of herbs and spices, which if one has not tried on their steak, is a mis-steak! Melvin's pretty wife was named Dianne and she was a real pleasure with which to associate.

I took David fishing at Lukfata creek on the Sharrock farm just north of Broken Bow one spring afternoon as Dennis was too sick with a cold to go with us. The creek was alive with fish and we had many hours of pleasure catching them, as they were great table fare. We had fished a certain hole about three times, floating through it on our inner tubes and casting toward the banks, when a big ole Cottonmouth Water Moccasin, that had been lying hidden on a log near the bank we were casting towards, decided to open his huge mouth, bare his fangs, and hiss at us. We took the hint and got out of that creek very quickly.

At this time in the history of McCurtain County, Oklahoma, the pine trees which were the economic life of the county were so big that three of them cut into thirty foot logs filled the bed of an eighteen wheeled truck. Since the loggers began clear-cutting practices in the 1970's and The Weyerhaeuser Corporation has been manipulating the U. S. National Forestry Service and The National Park Service, as well as the State of Oklahoma Legislature, the conservation practices of the old Dierk's Company Forester's has been cast off in favor of clear cutting the area's timber. This clear cutting practice has lead to total pollution of the areas once clear streams, which presently are no more than muddy ditches, many of which dry up in the heat of summer, a decline in the average annual rainfall and devastated forests, that when harvested take thirty or more of present days brittle, spindly pine logs to fill the same1960 size truck beds. (And this Company has the audacity to call itself; the tree growing company.) If the reader would like to see what an area looks like after an atom bomb has been exploded over it, just go to this county and take a look at a clear cut, and although you will not have to experience the radiation, the feeling of sickness in the pit of your stomach at the sight of the area, will be comparable, especially if you saw the beauty of the area before the action of clear-cutting.

Making music was the main reason I was in Broken Bow, and about the middle of my second week on the job, I was teaching one of my younger classes when around ten am a large panel van parked in front of the band room and the guy who got out of it came inside, seated himself quietly, and waited for me to finish my class.

At the conclusion of my class I released the students and the man stood up. He was tall, nearly six foot two inches in height, slight of build almost a beanpole, with a wry grin that hailed to you from a pointed chin, and kind eyes that smiled incessantly out of a very thin face. The stranger announced himself, " Howdy, I am Jim Gaylor with the Mckay Music Company in Paris Texas". And that is how I became acquainted with absolutely the finest instrument repairman and hardest working music salesman, not to mention loyal friend, I ever had.

Mr. Gaylor, asked if I had anyone calling on me from the other stores in the area and I told him, he was the first to contact me and if he would promise to take good care of my account and do a good job of caring for the bands instruments, he would be the sole person with which, I would trade. True to his word, he was in my band room every week fixing horns, he traveled to every contest with us and worked all day while there, keeping my performing students at the top of their game and he did this faithfully for the next three and one half years. I attribute much of my continued musical success while in Broken Bow to Jim's loyalty and ability.

During the three and one half years I taught at Broken Bow, the very talented band students there, won almost every award possible, including a sixth place finish in the nation- wide Disneyland Marching and Playing Contest. This contest was very selective, and only accepted two school bands from each state for competition. Also during my tenure there, over five students from our school made the Oklahoma All State band and orchestra, and we averaged over forty students per year who auditioned and were accepted into the South Eastern All District Bands. The final year I taught at Broken Bow Schools, our students captured all the first chairs, and our clarinet section sat first through twelfth chairs; skipped one that was credited to Durant high school and our last chair clarinet player sat fourteenth in a sixteen chair All District section. These four school years, this band never scored lower than an excellent rating at the State of Oklahoma contests and received superior ratings at two of the four State contests in which they competed, while scoring superior ratings at every years district competition.

Jeanie Bunch, later to become Mrs. Jeanie Bunch Johnson, wife of Bruce Johnson, one of my deer camping buddies was the concertmaster and solo chair clarinetist for three of these four years.

I always considered Jeanie, who was a three year Oklahoma All State performer, performing in the solo chair her senior year, to be the finest instrumentalist I have taught and I have taught many truly great student artists. Although, due to her marriage, Jeanie did not continue to perform at the professional level, she was certainly capable of doing so. Almost twenty years later, I had the privilege of teaching Jeanie's two older daughters, the oldest named Natalie, was also a very gifted clarinetist, and like their mother, both Julie, who studied flute and Natalie were a joy to teach.

The Students who studied with me at Broken Bow these three and one half years were a very special group of people and it is difficult for me to resist naming each of them, but for the sake of time and space I must. Summers are tough for teachers, everyone thinks teachers have it made in the summer, as you do not have to work. This concept is not only faulty from an obligation point of view, as there is generally many school related functions the teacher must address, such as advanced classes, student camps, and equipment repair, which not only take a lot of time and are an added financial burden, but most folks fail to realize a teacher's income is generally quite a bit less at this time of year and almost all teachers must take a second job of some menial tasks which provide a relative type of remuneration in order to survive the summer months. This is especially true if the teacher in question has a family to support.

Each summer found me scrambling to provide this income and meet these obligations, the first summer I got a job with the Dierks Company killing brush, which resulted in my body being covered in flea and tick bites, plus some poison Ivy scars. The second summer I fared far better, as although, I went to work immediately after school closed for the summer at Dierks, I was able to quit this brush poisoning job after about two weeks and take a job as a pick and shovel laborer helping to build the concrete spillway on the new dam at what would eventually become Broken Bow Reservoir, one of the south-wests most scenic lakes.

Actually, although I no longer had to fight the bugs and smell of the poison, the work was ten times harder and the day I applied for the job, although the foreman hired me due to my being a teacher in town, he quietly made a bet with his secretary, who was a personal friend of my wife, that I would not last two weeks on this job as the heat of summer and the strenuous task would force me to quit. Fortunately for the secretary I was the only person to last all summer, and she made fifty dollars because of it. Two weeks before school started, I collected my final check from the foreman, a man who had very carefully protected me all summer from being forced to join the local union and pay a portion of my hard earned two dollars and a quarter per hour wages to it. When he handed me my final check, he told me that I was the best worker he had ever had and I could work anywhere in the world Brown and Root Construction Company had a contract, he would personally see to it.

The next day Shirley and I loaded our little family in the car and headed to Indiana to visit my youngest brother, whom I had not seen since Dad's funeral over a year previously.

While at Jim's, Shirley helped Jim write his final paper for his final class as he was working full time at R. C. A. Corporation making T. V. 's.

When we returned to Broken Bow, Shirley decided she needed a job. She applied at a number of places, but in this good ole boy town we did not know that was not how a person obtained employment. After receiving a few rejections, she noticed, in the local paper, an announcement that the city clerks job was coming open in the next election. She also noticed that the day she was reading the announcement was the final day one could register to run for this position. This should have told her something about the local politics, but being young and naïve in this area she thought all political offices were open to all area citizens. Boy, was she to get her eyes opened and both of us would very soon hear new marching orders from very powerful folks such as Mr. Johnson, and all his enemies in the community who wanted to use Shirley to embarrass him. Within an hour after Shirley filed for the Clerks job, I was called to Mr. Johnson's office and told in no uncertain terms to get her to withdraw from the race, as the woman the local machine wanted in that position, was over seventy years old, widowed from a very popular former councilman and had been in this job for over ten years. She also had been assured she would have it as long as she wanted to fill the position.

These strong- arm tactics by my employer, were like raising a red flag in front of a raging bull and I went home where, I told Shirley," Win or loose I did not want her to withdraw," and she did not. Early the next day, I was called to Mr. Johnson's office, where he told me if my wife wanted a job, why had I not told him;so, he could get her one? For the second time I saw red and told him, " I thought Mc Curtain County was still part of America, and everyone had a right to run for office"! To which he replied," They do, but if your wife continues to run we are going to beat her butt"! The fierce manner in which he said these words and his selection of vocabulary stunned me and I just excused myself and left, before I ruined what I thought had been a pretty good employer –employee relationship.

Shirley meanwhile, was receiving donations and hearing all kinds of scuttlebutt about the politics of the county from people she had never met. It was unbelievable how many people suddenly were interested in and willing to finance her campaign. She had women, she did not know who wanted to help her make signs, hand out cards, and make phone calls on her behalf. Everything in, on and around our home, overnight, became Red, White and Blue. Fortunately, she had more help than she knew what to do with, so I could kind of lay low and not get the powers that be any madder than they were at me.

The day of the election, the town was really buzzin. Shirley provided cars to the polls, met her helpers, who were in their blazing colored vests at the Charles Wesley Coffee Shop, where she had free coffee for all persons to whom she could visit, wore her now widely recognized red, white and blue vest, and generally stirred the political pot. I was really proud of her efforts and even with the local machine working 100 % against her she dam near won; losing by 24 votes out of 1600 cast. That meant that if 13 voters had voted differently, she would have won. Pretty fine effort for a first timer, and the following week she was offered a good job as secretary/bookkeeper at the U. S. National Forestry Office. I have thought for many years that the Forestry job was purely a political plumb that was offered as a consolation prize due to the closeness of that Clerks race. No matter why she got it, the income surely made a difference in our family finances. This increase in our income now allowed us to look for a house to purchase, as we had been renting for over the last five years and building no equity. We drove around the county looking for land to build on, or a home place with some land around it.

One evening about five pm we found just what we were looking for. The house was on forty acres at the corner of U. S. 259 and a good county road. This property was located about two miles north of town and was considered prime land. And although, we were dubious about the present owners willingness to sell, we drove to the house and knocked on his door. A kind old gentleman came to the door and after our mutual greetings, we told him we would like to purchase his property, to our delight, he told us he had been thinking of selling and set a price of fifteen thousand dollars, as his asking price. Shirley and I considered this a steal, and told him we would go right to the bank and get the money.

It was at this time we made a fatal error, as we told our banker,( not Melvin), but who was supposedly a friend, (I had been giving his two kids free music lessons for over two years), where the property was located. The banker said, it was late, four thirty and he would need to have until the next day to make the loan, as he would need to visit with the bank's loan committee, before any further paper work could be completed. This explanation sounded plausible, so we went home thinking we had the property. The next day at nine am I went to the bank to see my banker friend and his secretary told me he was unavailable until the next day. This sounded fishy to me, so I went to see the owner of the place I wished to buy. When I drove into his yard he met me and told me he had signed the place over to a nice fellow from the bank in town, as he had offered him fifteen thousand five hundred dollars after I was there last night.

I was fortunate to have many good and loyal friends while living in this beautiful area and I would be remiss if I left out the most notable of them. J. T. Williams lived only two doors to the east of our house. He was my fishing buddy and we spent many a Saturday wadding the cold, clear, fish filled creeks of the county and enjoying the scenic, and majestic pine tree covered mountains where the pine trees were so tall, that darkness fell on these mountain roads about four thirty the year around and while one could hear the whistle of the wind high above, the abundant rains fell straight down. I mentioned where J. T. 's home was located and this is pertinent for a number of reasons, none more important than the fact it was in walking distance of my mischievous four year old twins, who were constantly scouting the entire neighborhood.

My boys brazening walked by J. T. 's bird dog pen every day, admiring the eight or nine beautiful Pointers, as the dogs raised their voices in a horrendous chorus of howls acknowledging the twins presence. After a few times of experiencing this loud den, the twins decided that the penned up dogs were very unhappy, and to J. T. 's dismay, as it took every man in the neighborhood most of an afternoon to retrieve the dogs; the twins gave the expensive hunting dogs a very happy day of wistful freedom.

Although, I did not get to attend his funeral, due to the fact I was on tour with the Haskell American Indian Junior College Band performing concerts in Philadelphia Mississippi. I will remember always, this wonderful friend, who died very young at the age of forty-six. He was a fine hunter and marksman, who complemented my cooking skills. He killed the deer, that I never ever saw and I made chili out it, a dish that he bragged about often. I remember his warm smile and quite knowledgeable woodsman ship which saved my life more than once.

For example, I was fishing a small stream known for it's many small-mouth bass and as was the custom for J.T. and me, he had gone down stream to fish, while I was to proceed upstream from his old ford pick-up. We drove through and over some mighty rough terrain to get to our favorite holes. I had slowly worked my way across the shallow end of the first hole and back to the deepest portion of it and was trying to fish this area from a high bluff about fifteen feet above the surface of the creek, when I stepped on a loose rock and my feet slipped from beneath me. I fell straight down into the water, as I fell I was not worried as I thought the water was deep and I would just swim out the other side of the hole, what I was not aware, was a huge boulder that lurked less than twelve inches immediately below my tail bone and the waters surface. I fell on this with my full body weight impacting my tailbone on the pointed boulder. The pain was so excruciating, that I immediately went unconscious and began the process of drowning. Unbeknown to me, fortunately J. T. had broken a fly and was headed back to the truck, which was parked just across the creek from where I fell. J. heard the loud splash and the anguish of my final yell of pain and came crashing through the brush, as he ran to the creek from the truck He saw my body surface and slowly sink back into the deep water, and realized I was drowning. So, he wadded out into the creek until he was forced by it's depth to swim, then swam to my limp body and pulled me to shallow water; where he splashed my face with the cold creek water and slapped me until I revived enough to walk to the truck. He had a childs blow-up swim ring in the camper portion of his old pick-up that he placed in the truck seat for me, so I could endure the terribly painful ride home.

I could not walk for two days and forty- five years later still have problems with my backside if I sit wrong on it. Add to this a kick in the lower back by a fourteen year old kid with large hob nailed boots, who was allowed to follow me to closely, while completing my turn on the super slide, during one of the many times I took band kids to Six Flags Theme Park in Dallas, Ft. Worth, and one can know why periodically, I have serious back pain.

Every April the teachers of Oklahoma must renew their contracts if they desire to stay at the same school. This practice leads to salary negotiations, which sometimes result in the firing of the teacher or the teacher leaving his post to take a more lucrative position.

Because of the students' success, I was becoming well known around the State of Oklahoma and each year I would find that a bigger school was soliciting my services. So each year I would go to Mr. Johnson and request more money for both my program and me. In addition, I annually requested that he hire me an assistant, as I now had more students than Noah had animals and not enough hours in the week to adequately teach them. Being a cagey administrator, he knew I loved working with the students and therefore, he would annually upgrade the amount of financial resources he budgeted for the music program, but would give me only a pittance of a salary increase and only grin and say no to the idea of an assistant.

In the spring of 1967 I finally got to the point that between my work, plus conducting the choir at the first Christian church, as in every town we lived, and my fishing, but mostly my band job, I was never home, we were in debt to the local grocer, and our general financial health was at a low ebb.

I made my annual trek into see, Mr. Johnson but this time, due to the fact the superintendent of the Muskogee Oklahoma Schools had offered me a thousand and five hundred dollars above my present salary, to head up their instrumental music program, where I would have three assistants, a full time secretary, and over two hundred sophomore, junior and senior boys in my marching band, add to these items I would only teach four classes each day. One of these classes would be a stage band consisting of very selective and gifted students, and a class of beginning music theory. Then after marching season I would be allowed to audition the marching band to select a symphonic and concert band and live in a much more cosmopolitan area, that had a fine hospital and Shirley was presently pregnant with our fourth child. I was just going through the motions of past negotiations and unless Mr. Johnson had something more to offer than I thought, the coming fall season was going to find the Redwine family in Muskogee. He did not and we moved! I must admit, all that glitters is not gold and that to leave those wonderful students and our many close friends was a very difficult decision, and I never had that wonderful atmosphere of musical excellence again; although, I did approach it closely in Fort Gibson Schools three years later.

The twirlers in the Broken Bow Band were a very special group of girls, they were beautiful, physically talented, and academically

*1966 Broken Bow Band queen coronation David and Dennis were twin crown bearers*

*The band members L. to R are John Bruton, Anita Carter, SandraBunch, Jerry Don Campbell and Pam Wolfe, and a tuba player I cannot remember*

gifted students, who had to audition every year against their peers for their positions

These were the most coveted non-academic positions in the school for female students and after the first year I was in charge of the marching band, I went to the twirling corp. and suggested they select a mascot. The mascot would be selected by twirling auditions, which would include fifth grade female band students, who would be required to perform well on a wind instrument. The high school twirlers would judge these auditions, with me having final approval. The older girls thought the mascot idea was really hot, as they were already taking great pride in teaching the grade school girls as private students, and therefore, the whole community respected the mascots position immediately. The high school twirlers took turns being responsible for the young mascot at football games and parades always treating her with kindness and respect, and the mascots were a big hit with the crowds, as they really performed very well; doing the same routines as the older girls in almost every performance. This was truly a great idea as it boosted my recruiting efforts by a wide margin over previous years. (Every little girl in grade school wanted to wear that mascot uniform and twirl at the front of the high school band), including my extremely talented oldest daughter, Carla Rene, who won the audition to do so in the spring of her fourth grade year. Un- fortunately for Carla, we moved to Muskogee that summer and she had to wait until I got the Fort Gibson Band position a year later, to get to strut her stuff. Our move to Muskogee was neither all good nor all bad.

We now had saved enough cash for the down payment on a home and with the help of a G. I. Loan that was moved quickly through federal offices with the aid of Ed Edmondson and my very politically astute Mother, who phoned him personally; we bought a home. Also we had the help of a local realtor, who allowed me to reside in her private residence for the next three weeks, while the present owners of our new residence, settled a dispute over why they should sell or not sell to us; we purchased a fine new story and a half, seven room, home, that also had a fully enclosed, attached double garage. This home was just what our family needed; it was on a full acre, with a ten-acre horse lot, which we immediately put to good use, as we soon were given three horses by Hollis Smith, Shirley's Dad. Dennis and David enjoyed it, because it allowed them to mow lawns in the neighborhood and earn their own cash, and Carla, had her own room. For the first time, since we had moved from Bartlesville, Carla could say she was not living in a rental property. We had sold the Bartlesville house during our second year in Broken Bow, due to the fact it was too difficult to care for it and live so far away. Shirley loved our new home, as it was only five city blocks from the best hospital in eastern Oklahoma and she was going to give birth to our fourth child with in the next four months, also she had her horses for the first time since our wedding.

Shirley had sold her long time pal Shorty, a barrel racing champion horse, she had trained from the time the horse was a colt, won many races on him, and sold her winning horse just before we got married, as she knew she would not have a place to keep him at our home in Maryland. I liked it because it was in a great location, I could afford it, and it made everyone else happy. This home had a lot of lawn to mow, but I now had over two hundred boys who wanted to do me favors. So, the lawn was no problem at all, as my first chair trumpet player and first chair trombone player, Tommy Stout and Charlie, whose last name I just can not remember respectfully, were weekly lawn boys.

Just shortly after the author went to work on this new teaching position he received a peculiar phone call on his school office phone one morning after band reheresal. The male voice on the other end of the phone line said his name was Merle Haggard and he was speaking from his home just south of Muskogee, and did I know of him? I told him I had not heard of him, but then asked what I might do for him? Mr. Haggard said,"I am going to release a record of a very good country song in about three weeks and would you like to put the Muskogee fight song on the other side of the disk?" I was not into country music at that time, as in my infinite wisdom; I considered it to be an inferior art form. This was a position I would shortly learn was quite foolish and one also I certainly no longer hold and not wanting to insult Mr. Haggard, I told him I was sorry ,but I did not want to make any more records of the Muskogee High Band at this time, as I already had about one thousand copies of one I could not sell. Merle pleaded with me to reconsider. He said, If this is what I think its going to be you will never have to sell anything again to raise money for the band program. I continued to be stubborn and told him thanks , but no thanks. About three weeks later he released *Okie From Muskogee* without my help. Meryl was correct, had I taken him up on this deal our school financial woes would have been solved

*Tonya Michelle Redwine at age six months*

*Shirley Janez Smith Redwine "Mother" and Tonya M. Redwine*

*Clarice Iva Cooper Redwine paternal Grandmother and Tonya M. Redwine*

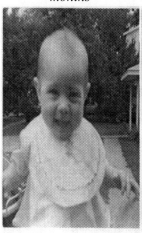  

# Okie to Muskogee

Ester Van Berg, Smith, Miller, Shirley's Mother, was a kind caring person and she was visiting at our home the first week of November, 1967 when in the very early hours, of the fourth day of November, we took Shirley to the Muskogee Hospital, where she would soon give birth to our lovely youngest daughter. After we registered Shirley and got her settled in a room, I went to the high school to teach my morning classes and about ten o'clock am the phone rang in my office and when I answered it Ester said," We have a new baby girl, can you come to the hospital"? I told Ester, "Wait for me, I will be right there"! When I got to the hospital, Ester met me in the lobby at the front door and said, " The nurses said, we can see the baby now".

*Carla Rene Redwine* **wins 1967**
*mascot tryouts*

*Carroll E. Redwine, Father and
Tonya Michelle Redwine Daughter
taken in May, 1967 in Norman,
Oklahoma at Philip W. Redwine's
Law school graduation*

251

*Left to right; David Lee Redwine, his sister Carla Rene' Redwine, pushing baby sister Tonya Michele Redwine, in stroller, and Dennis Lynn Redwine, standing far right. Picture taken Easter 1968 in Muskogee*

So, we both headed toward the maternity ward and the holding room for newborns. The nurse came into the newborn's room just as we arrived and held up Tonya Michele Redwine, who was resting on a piece of brown paper, still bloody from her birth into our world. I understand physicians agree that newborns can not focus their eyes, but Tonya's eyes were open and she appeared to look directly at Ester and me, while with her left hand she reached up to the top of her left ear and pulled on it just as my father used to do. Ester remarked, "That is A.C. Redwine personified", and that was my exact thought. Was an old soul making a new entrance to our world?

Tonya, the only left- handed person in our family at the time of her birth, was always her own person and still is, if you do not want to hear the full truth about any situation do not ask Tonya, but no one loves her family and my Grand babies more and better than our sweet Tonya.

Although there is a ten- year difference in their ages; Carla, and Tonya are loving sisters, as Carla for some years, took care of Tonya while Shirley was unavailable, due to work or other responsibilities. Unfortunately, the sister relationship was damaged some fifteen years later, by Carla's crass, cruel, and totally immoral husband, who threw away his family to run off with his Sister in Law,who was the mother of my first and tremendously gifted Grandson, David Aaron Redwine. Aaron was born to the union of David Lee Redwine and Jeanna Maxwell in Seminole, Oklahoma April tenth 1980. Unethical and immoral, these two ex's get the prize for making every effort to carefully manipulate their sposes against their families and one tried to poison Carla's mind against Tonya , by telling Carla, such things as, that her sister was a spoiled brat and other untruths, for over ten years, while they were married. This subtle manipulation by Carla's husband had it's desired effect for some years and only in recent years have my girls somewhat rediscovered the relationship they once enjoyed. Truthfully, the only good thing that matrimonial relationship accomplished, as I see it, was the birth of my wonderful grandson, Chase Tyler, who was born to this union , August eighteenth, 1989. I don't expect all concerned to see these folks in the same light as I, but (I calls em, as I sees em 'BAD'!) I can tell you for a fact, that Carla's husband did not sit down and eat even one meal with Shirley and me in his home, during the entire time he and Carla were married. Carla often invited us to dinner and prepared many a fine meal for us, but he always found some reason not to come to the table and would even go out for dinner elsewhere, leaving the house, as his young son, wife, and in-laws were sitting down to the meal. (Real cool guy, Huh)?

Shirley, in order to protect her job with a local loan company, that was very unsympathetic to young mothers, went back to work only one week after the birth of Tonya, this was a very difficult thing for Shirley to do, both physically and mentally, as she worried about Tonya's care by her babysitter and she was still recovering from the childbirth, but she felt she had to keep her job, as the job market in this area was presently very lean.

The superintendent of Muskogee Schools who had hired me, failed to inform me, that he was going to retire when school started that year and in my humble opinion his replacement, was without a doubt, the worst administrator of any school, that I have been associated. He started the year off by insulting his staff in a giant all school meeting, that lasted all day, but at which he only brow beat the staff for thirty minutes and went back to his office. Morale at that high school was terrible and the year went down hill from that meeting. I buried myself in my teaching of the students, who tried diligently to make our year a good one and although, we received a superior rating for their efforts at their first district contest in some years, an excellent rating at their first ever attempt at a district marching contest and an excellent rating at the first state contest in which they had participated,they also performed five admirable performances of the Broadway musical, **Oklahoma** with an all school cast, full orchestra, and wonderful choreography. However, the over-all instrumental music program in the school fell short of its outstanding capabilities, due to in my opinion; many blunders by the administrative staff.

A staff that within one month of the start of the fall term had totally lost the confidence of the faculty and duty staff. Although the students and parents were trying hard to have a winning band, the seemingly oblivious administrators, including my high school principal, music supervisor, and superintendent of music for the

Muskogee schools were disregarding, the lack of coordination in the instrumental music program in their school and turned a deaf ear to anyone, including me, who brought it to their attention. I was so distraught over this terrible loosie goosie state of ineptness that I vomited every morning before going to the band room.

About this time, Aubrey Potter a fine musician I had known for some years, phoned me. We had attended the same high school. Aubrey was presently employed at the largest music store in Kansas City and somehow became aware that the Muskogee band job was not to my liking and flew his light two-seater airplane from his home in Kansas City to Hatbox Field.

Hatbox was a small airport about five blocks from my house and after Aubrey taxied in, we had dinner and he asked me to interview for one of the large high school jobs in Kansas City, where he felt he had a great deal of influence due to his relationship with their music department and the superintendent. I agreed, that if he called the superintendent and made me an appointment, I would fly to Kansas City the next morning and visit about the job. Aubrey said, "It is the premier music job in Kansas City", and I fully trusted his judgment on this subject. So, about seven thirty am the next day, we boarded his plane and took off for Kansas City.

I was enjoying the lift off when Aubrey turned to me and said, " I am going to climb to ten thousand feet, there is a three thousand foot tower around here somewhere and I can not see it due to the haze". I guess he read my mind, as I looked a bit scared and he continued," If we have trouble, you will be just as dead at three thousand feet, as you would at ten. I enjoyed the day with Aubrey, but even though the job for which I interviewed was great and they offered it to me, I just did not want to raise my kids in Kansas City. My good friend Aubrey was not very happy, that after the Kansas School offered me the job I did not take it, but he did fly me back to Muskogee and have dinner with us before he flew his return trip.

To try and correct the Muskogee School music situation, I wrote a comprehensive school music program booklet of eighteen hundred pages and took it to the superintendant. Placing it on his desk March first of 1968, in a face-to-face interview. I repeatedly asked if he would read and put it into effect over the next five years, as that is how extensive the program was. He promised to read it and do as much to implement the proposal as he felt the budget could afford, telling me he would need April to read the proposal, as it was lengthy. To make a long story short I went back to his office April third to inquire as to his decision, and he would not see me. So I went back to my office and called him on the phone. When I finally reached him after some shenanigans with his secretary, he admitted he had not read my proposal.

I quickly and politely said good bye to him, jumped in my car and went again to his office, where I asked his secretary to see my personnel file. She smiled unknowingly and went to a file cabinet, where she pulled out a drawer and extracted my singular file, and then she walked over and handed the file to me. I turned around as though to read it in private and sorted through the papers in the file until I found my teaching certificate, which I secretly took from the folder, placing it inside my suit coat pocket. Then, as the secretary had sat back down at her desk and had her head lowered toward the disheveled papers she was sorting, I thanked her and as she looked up, handed her the personnel file minus my teaching certificate.

# On to Ft. Gibson

Then I drove immediately to the superintendent's office of Fort Gibson Schools, went in, met the gentleman, whose name was Leo Donahue and since I knew for a fact, his band teacher was leaving and had announced his future plans to perform on the road with a big name entertainer and also knew for a fact, that Mr. Donahue was in a life and death financial struggle with the Muskogee Schools over the taxes collected from the new O.G.&E. Plant located on the bank of the Arkansas River between the two school districts. I asked Mr. Donahue, "How would you like to have the Muskogee Band director working for your school next year"? He laughed and clapped his hands, then said, " I think that is a great idea" That is how I left Muskogee and became the band director at Fort Gibson, where I again produced a great little band in only three years.

When the Muskogee superintendent found out I had jumped his contract before the April fifteenth release date and had signed with his adversary, Mr. Donahue, he was furious and threatened to have my teaching certificate revoked by the state department of Education. So, I went over to Fort Gibson to tell Mr. Donahue about my dilemma and he told me not to worry about it, as he did not believe even this administrator would stoop that low, but if he did, Mr. Donahue would sign me to a janitorial contract for our agreed salary and we would have the only janitor in Oklahoma who was teaching band. Suddenly I had a new respect for this wily small school administrator. Mr. Donahue knew I had a lovely home in Muskogee located only a few miles from Fort Gibson that would make the trip to his teaching job insignificant. So, when he requested I move to Fort Gibson, I was surprised, until he told me why.

He explained, that he had a problem with a number of his junior high teachers and their principal, who he knew were not doing a very good job and he thought they might quit if he required all his staff to live in his school district, as they had nice homes and even some large farms elsewhere. I thought that was pretty good thinking and agreed to move, as soon as I could find a rental property in his district and rent my home. This I did, immediately after school was out for the summer in Muskogee. The rental property was only a city block from the " Old Texas Road" and directly behind the Fort Gibson band room. It was a terrible place to live, but I did not intend to be in it more that a year, as I figured the other people would probably clear the way for our moving back to Muskogee before spring. Whether they quit or stayed, by then, it would make no difference.

When cold weather arrived the huge fireplace in the front room burned a Rick of wood every four days and the house was still cold, because there was a crack between it and the wall of the house you could put your fist through. The basement under the house was completely full of drainage water from the street in front of the house and there were rats as big as a small cat in the outter walls. Shirley and I looked all over town for a better rental property, as I truly wanted to keep my doors open with the boss, but shortly after Christmas, I went to Mr. Donahue and told him that house was endangering my kids, and since I could find no other housing in his district, I was moving back across the river. He did not seem too upset as his plan to get the junior high folks to move had not been very successful either. So, in January we moved back into our home in Muskogee.

From the first day I took the job in the summer of 1968, I had the confidence of the administrators and town's people of Fort Gibson. They were all helpful and encouraging socially and financially. Mr. Donahue ask me to survey the music department and get back to him, so that we would have the instruments and equipment needed to produce a good band in the fall. I gave him a list of immediate repair, and a second list of long range goals and new instruments I felt we must have to play the type of symphonic music I would be teaching, along with a price-tag of ten thousand dollars for the new percussion equipment that the band desperately needed.

He took one look at it and to my surprise, authorized the whole package immediately. This fellow seriously wanted a good program and was willing to put his money where his mouth was!

Facilities were another real problem, as the present band rehearsal area was an old second world war Quonset hut. It was about sixty feet long, but only about fourteen feet wide, with old fashioned, wooden framed, four foot by four foot glass panes, which when the room was filled with students, must be raised, as this was the only system of cooling in the classroom.

*Carla Rene and her 7ᵗʰ grade band class*

Due to the width of the room, which faced the south, it was necessary to file in the students that sat in the eastern portion of the room and after they were in their seats, the rest of the class would come in. I often wondered what we would do in case of fire or other disaster. However, this situation never seemed to bother the very enthusiastic young folks, who never complained about the crowded conditions or the heat.

We had a very good rapport, the band and me and since I could not get to the back of the room without a great deal of difficulty, as a path would have to be cleared through many students and their equipment, discipline was at times a bit of a problem, especially in the trumpet section, as it was directly in front of my conducting podium and at the very back of the room, between me and the long row of open windows. When these trumpet players would get to rowdy I would, after warning them a couple of times, reach behind me, into a large box where I kept chalk-board erasers, grab one and throw it at the most rowdy of the students.

The first time I did it, the response of the class was one of startled disbelief, but it got the desired results and the band quickly settled down and back into serious study. Subsequent episodes generally provoked a great deal of spontaneous laughter, but always a better classroom effort. However, I do not recommend this as standard classroom procedure, as one day, I had no idea Mr. Donahue and the agriculture instructor were both just out side those windows. The boys acted up, I am positive to provoke me into doing the now famous (Redwine toss), which I obliged and the trumpets, did their by now, usual ducking motion, the missile flew through the window and outside. The flying eraser I thew whacked the agriculture teacher whose lovely daughter was my first chair flutist, and who would soon be promoted to my boss, as he would be the high school principal the next school year!

We had lots of fun working, together, learning routines and music for the football games and Carla Rene' finally got to be in the twirling corp., even though she was only in the sixth grade, as she was the only girl in school who had seriously studied twirling, and I had to have someone teach the other twirlers.

Carla's popularity, as a twirler and member of the high school band, came at some cost to her mental state, as her peers in the same grade became jealous of her success. Little girls have a way of ostracizing anyone whom they feel is rising above the norm of their clique and they can be very cruel in the manner they try to isolate the target of their vendetta.

This happened to Carla as about five of the girls in her class, whom she thought to be her good friends, decided she would be the target of their isolation. Naming these little snipes would serve no purpose at this time, so I will deal with them as a group and not individually. After nearly two weeks of tolerating these little girls snide insults and hurtful attitude, a very distraught Carla, went tearfully crying to her understanding mother, hoping to find a socially acceptable solution to this problem. Shirley consoled Carla and after hearing of how miserable Carla felt, gave some thought to her dilemma. Hoping to get some sage advice as to best how to handle this problem, Shirley visited with Carla's sixth grade teacher, who said," I could intervene in this, but it would probably cause Carla even more grief " Shirley, decided that the best way for Carla to handle the situation was for Carla to develop new friends from the other classroom of sixth graders.

Shirley also prayed diligently for a better solution than the one she had advised, her prayers were answered immediately as Carla's new friends in the other room were much more in tune with her friendship and even more-so when Carla's best friend Johnny Lou moved to her dad's farm in Okay, Oklahoma a small farming community close to Fort Gibson, where she enrolled in the same classes as Carla their seventh grade year.

The irony of this situation was that the mother of the leader in the clique, that had been so mean to Carla, called Shirley, less than two weeks after Carla had revealed her story. The mother sobbingly told Shirley," There is a clique of little girls in my daughters sixth grade class, that are making her life miserable and I do not know what to do about it, my daughter said to call you as Carla is one of her best friends". Shirley, listened as the mother of the girl further said, "My girls would never do such a terrible thing to anyone" Shirley, who had never told anyone other than Mr. James, Carla's teacher, about this situation, told the unsuspecting lady, who was also a close friend, the complete sordid story and her solution to the problem.

While Carla was in the sixth grade, the twins were in the fourth grade and their teacher was Novita Walker, the wife of my good friend Jerry Walker, the schools basketball coach and eventual high school principal. Some years later, after I taught here, Mr. Harrison replaced Mr. Donahue, so Jerry took Mr. Harrison's principal position. Novita was a conscientious teacher, but young and somewhat inexperienced. So she was trying hard to do a good job with the students. She had a few problems with Dennis and David, as both were very intelligent and finished their assignments quickly. Shirley, noticed that the boys had a lot of homework and she found it was not only keeping them up late some nights, but it also was keeping our family from doing activities together. Shirley asked the twins why they did not finish their school work in class and they told her Mrs. Walker, would not give it to them until class was over, because they finished it at school if she did. Shirley thought this unusual, so she went to school to visit with Novita about it. When she told Novita the twin's homework story, Novita confirmed it was correct and told Shirley, she was trying to develop good study habits in the children by giving them assignments they would do outside class. Novita convinced the other fourth grade teacher to have the same policy, but her chickens came home to roost two years later, when Novita's son, Jerry Jr. became a fourth grade student in the other teachers classroom, and Novita was complaining to Shirley one evening about all his homework interfering with their families' social life.

Dennis and David had an unusually good relationship even for twins. Some schools will not let twins take classes in the same classroom, as they feel this policy jeopardizes the academic learning of the weaker of the two. This was the policy of the Muskogee schools, where we enrolled the boys in their third grade year. Shirley tried to explain to the school people these guys did not lean on each other and would be very hard to deal with if they were separated, but the grade school principal; and her third grade teachers were adamant that the twins must be taught in separate classes. In less than two weeks after school started, the teachers changed their minds, as they could see the twins were so despondent they were accomplishing nothing in school.

During the third week of school Dennis came home and told us David was not going to class every morning, as the teacher made David stand in the hall. Shirley made another trip to the grade school to see what was wrong and if David should to be disciplined at home to care for the problem. Shirley asked the teacher why David was being punished? The teacher said he was not being punished, he refused to say the Lords Prayer, and so she had him stand in the hallway during the prayer each day, as she thought we did not agree with prayer in school. Shirley asked to have David come into the interview, so she could ask him about this, as we said the Lords Prayer every Sunday and she did not understand why her wayward son, David, refused to say it in class. When confronted, David, calmly told the teacher and his mother, the class did not say the prayer correctly, and that is why he would not repeat it with them. Shirley ask him to explain what the class was doing wrong and he said," the class says, **(forgive us our debts, as we forgive our debtors)** and the correct words are, **(forgive us our trespasses, as we forgive our trespassers).** Shirley explained, it was alright to say it either way, the teacher smiled, as she realized the problem with our family was over, David went to class happy to be once again part of it, and Shirley went back to work with the biggest problem of the week solved.

I did not hear about this problem and its solution for nearly four days, as I was spending every waking hour at the band room ensuring that my students in the Fort Gibson Band studied sufficiently to score a superior rating at both the district and state contests that first year and they did, for which I was proud. They performed tremendous literature at the competitions and never scored lower than excellent at any contest they entered over the next two years.

When we left from there to teach for Kansas University at the Haskell American Indian Junior College in Lawrence, Kansas the summer of 1971, we left many good friends and a band that would be musically solid for some years, as no students in the band were older than sophomores the following year, and the upcoming younger classes were very talented. However they were losing three fine instrumentalist, David who played fine clarinet, Dennis who was equally as good on Trumpet, and Carla who was their first chair flutist. So reader, this is how our next move came about.

# Rock Chalk Jayhawk- Lawrence Kansas- Our Next Home

In the spring of 1971 Jack Romine, who for some years had been the director of the excellent Alice Robertson Junior High school instrumental music program, and my friend, had worked at A. R. the year I taught at Muskogee High School. Jack called me on the phone to request Shirley and I have dinner with him and his wife Wanda Romine at their home in Southeast Muskogee. We drove over to his house and enjoyed a fine meal after which Jack told us Wanda was leaving in a day or two to teach school

*Tonya at her third  year party*

at an American Indian High School in rural Montana.  She was planning to be in Montana until the end of summer when she would join Jack at their new home in Lawrence, Kansas where he would be on the faculty, as head of the Music Department of the New American Indian Junior College, being developed on the historically significant Haskell Indian Boarding School Campus. Jack and Wanda were both very excited about the future prospects of this new institution as their good friend, Bill Burgess a nationally recognized educational administrator was being appointed  to head up the new school by the Bureau of Indian Affairs in Washington D. C. Bill would be hiring the new faculty and develop the curriculum.

What Jack and Wanda proposed was that, if Jack was allowed to have an assistant band director, and he thought this was a distinct possibility, Shirley and I consider moving to Lawrence, as he would like me to take the assistants position. He explained money was going to be very little problem and I could expect to nearly double my present income, if everything on this deal happened as he expected. The reader might think, after my recent Muskogee experience, I would have been a bit more skeptical of pie in the sky operations, and by now realize, the old cliché' that all that glitters is not golden, has the sound of truth in it's ring. But Jack's enthusiasm and the fact Wanda was leaving her two kids and Jack for the next few months and traipsing all the way to Montana made this idea sound plausible. Plus my greed for doubling my income had a great deal to do with my wanting to believe this beautiful golden apple had no worms. Jack did tell me he wasn't positive that his job was secured yet, but Burgess was to call him when it was confirmed and at that time he would know about the assistants position also.

We left the Romine home thinking how nice it would be to double our income and have Jack handling the pressures of the head director, while I would have the opportunity to teach at the college level and complete my Masters Degree at Kansas University, which at that time, was nationally recognized as one of America's most prestige's music schools. However, we really did not think it would happen as the whole deal just sounded to good to be true. So, we put it out of our minds and both Shirley and I were somewhat surprised, when nearly three weeks later, I got a call from Jack and he told me everything had gone through just as he and Bill Burgess had been told it would by their source in D. C. Jack said Wanda was a happy camper, and doing well, (Jack was not aware how well, or just what she was doing in the camper, but he would eventually find out, after a few months in Kansas, when she asked him for a divorce.)!

When he called, Jack told me I would need to make a decision fairly soon, as he only had a few weeks before the college expected to have its full staff available for the summer session and he would need to assign his music faculty to their classroom responsibilities. I ask him about salary and the possibility of the school paying our moving expenses. He said he would have to see Burgess, as all financial agreements would have to come from Bill. I told Shirley that evening about Jack's recent good fortune and we visited extensively about the pros and cons of the move, a move that would mean we would have to sell our lovely home in Muskogee. We finally agreed to find out what the financial arrangements would be, and if they were as lucrative, as Jack had originally told us, we would make the move.

The next two or three days we heard nothing from my old pal Jack, but finally he called to say Burgess had assured him the B. I. A., could pay at least fourteen thousand per year, but could not help with our moving expenses. Since I was making seven thousand eight hundred annually at that time, the salary sounded pretty good, and I was positive Mr. Donahue would not be able to match that amount, even though he had recently won the law suite with the state over the tax monies from the River Bank O. G & E Plant. Besides, I wanted a crack at teaching older students, thinking I might like teaching at the college level permanently. I was reluctant to tell Mr. Donahue of my future plans, as he had been a very enjoyable man to work for and had made every effort to help my family by paying me well, giving Shirley a very good job, and supporting the music program in grand fashion these past three years. It did get a bit easier to resign, when I found out the new school he was building, as a result of his new- found tax wealth, included a band room that was to be located high up over one end of the gymnasium. In this location, the band would need to negotiate a long fight of narrow metal stairs to get to the ground floor with their heavy equipment. The blaring acoustics of the concrete block room, would only include a glass wall between the athletic noises of the basketball court below and the deliberately delicate, balanced, sounds of the music classes. Also the room was to be only twenty feet wide and fifty feet long with no proposed instrument storage. Somehow this sounded just like the mess we had been teaching in at the Quonset hut, but without windows (for the famous eraser toss) to the outside. However, the glass wall **was** exactly in the same position as the famous Quonset windows. The major reason I was so pissed off about this building, was that Mr. Donahue had requested my input about the plans of this building over a year ago and I had gone into great detail, and spent considerable time drawing him a set of plans for an adequate music facility, which he was either ignoring, or did not read. When I finally found that this was his plan for the new school and he did not tell me until the foundations had been poured, I went to him and said my good byes, without much remorse.

The parents of my students were a fine group and when they heard we were moving organized a lovely evening for Shirley and me at Pete's Restaurant in Krebs, Oklahoma. This is one of the finest places to eat in our state; the menu is outstanding, the generous servings of delicious food are impeccably prepared and the service quite adequate and the prices are very fair. We were very impressed, not only with Pete's restaurant, but even more-so with the fact that over thirty men and women were willing to drive over one hundred fifty miles, to honor us on this occasion. Again these folks made it difficult to move to Kansas, but Shirley and I have always governed our decisions thusly, if a door is opened to you, go through it and find out what is on the other side, however, do not force them open. **The Romines had appeared to open this door for us.**

# Rock Chalk Jayhawk

1971 was a many varied year. Each quarter was either very good to us or teased us with wonder. Shirley and I spent the spring working in Fort Gibson and our three older kids attended school there, but we all enjoyed living across the river in our Muskogee home. That is we enjoyed it other than the problems associated with commuting, we only had one vehicle at this time, so Shirley and the children had to either come back and pick me up or hang around with little to do until I finished teaching the band sectionals and the band students free private lessons every day. This latter free work was a real bone of contention between Shirley, who said, "No one taught our kids free anything", and me, who felt it, was necessary to prepare the band for the difficult material I intended to perform. Shirley was absolutely correct about her position, so it was really a problem to ask her to keep the children, especially baby Tonya, in Fort Gibson each day even though the older kids used their time wisely to complete the days extra school assignments and to practice their instruments, for Shirley it was a wasted two or three hours of the only time she had to do her needed chores and housework. Shirley was darn sure not going to miss this portion of our stay at the Fort Gibson job and she made it very clear that if I taught privately in the future, I should expect financial remuneration. Although, I have at times since leaving Fort Gibson, been lax in collecting a fee or keeping records of my hours spent with my private students, I have expected them to fairly compensate me for my time and knowledge. Most have been more than willing to treat me fairly in this regard.

The second quarter of 1971 was a real whirl-wind, we made the decision to move to Lawrence, closed out the school year, which is always a big deal with inventory and such,but even more-so if a teacher is leaving a school, put our home on the market, sold it for a nice profit, and bought a new home on the golf course at the Lawrence Country Club, which we moved into the first of June.

The realtor who sold us the beautiful home with a full basement in Lawrence, financed the house through his own company and guaranteed us, that should we need to move from this house for any reason within a year, he would return us our full down payment. Although we did not know it at the time we purchased this property, this last guarantee would became extremely important, as we decided due to Carla's situation in the local school system, and the local policies of the Lawrence high band director to move to Baldwin Kansas, a school with a better band teacher and a better program, only twenty minutes outside Lawrence. However, we did not make the move to Baldwin until the end of the fall semester and Carla spent a miserable four months in the junior high band program at the Lawrence schools.

The twins appeared to fare a bit better, but they also were not real happy with the instrumental program at their school. They were somewhat compensated for the weaknesses in this program by the fact they got to practice together at home, and they were enjoying a great boy scout troop that was very active. The boys went camping almost every weekend and learned many valuable lessons from these trips.

Tonya was a very active baby and our full basement allowed her to ride her tricycle and play freely with her toys, while we never worried about her safety. This lovely home was spacious and had tile counters in the kitchen, a tiled entry hall, and two fully tiled bathrooms and was fully carpeted on the ground floor.

The reader would surmise our family to be in tall cotton and happy to be in this new town, we were, and we were not! Remember Bill Burgess, the guy that held the purse strings at the Junior College? Well, it turned out that Mr. Burgess did not have total control of the money! Before we moved to Lawrence, I went to Mr. Burgess and told him I would not sell my home or leave Muskogee, until I had a signed contract guaranteeing my position with the school in Lawrence. Bill agreed that was a good idea and within a week called to ask me to come to Lawrence to check out the new school and sign a teaching contract for the coming summer session. This contract would also contain wording that the fall and spring sessions would be included and I would be rehired on an annual contract. I had no problem with this type of deal as I had been operating on these year to year contracts since my first year in Broken Bow and figured this would be no different. If I did a good job, the school would annually reward my work with a new and better agreement.

So, Shirley and the kids stayed to show our home in Muskogee, while Jack Romine, who was to be my immediate superior, and I went to visit Mr. Burgess at his new school. Bill was very gracious and it appeared to me he was in total control of his surroundings, as he took Jack and me to lunch at his historically significant, beautiful, and stately home located on the campus of Haskell American Indian Junior College, formerly Haskell Indian Boarding School.

After meeting Bills family, a small lunch, and a quick tour in Jack's car of the major sites on the campus, we returned to Bills office to discuss the financial arrangements and hopefully sign an agreement for my teaching services at Haskell. We talked at length about teaching philosophies and about what we all hoped to accomplish at this level with the students of Haskell, whom we knew would have totally different social and economic backgrounds from anyone present. Bill and Jack were real fancy bull-shitters and I should have picked up on it and got to hell out of this mess right then and there, but every time I thought of running away from these guys, they would mention the dollar signs, my greed would raise its ugly head and I would settle back to be showered with more hogwash.

We finally got around to putting my name on the dotted line, and aside from the fact, that Bill assured me he would have a job in his office for Shirley, and that I was going to receive fourteen thousand dollars per year and that I would not get a check for at least thirty days, as the government never pays in advance for services rendered, I can not remember one darn thing about the rest of that contract, except that it was at least three pages in length, and Bill did not sign it, at least not in my presence.

I later learned he was not in total control of his position as to finances, as a guy named Wally Galuzzi, who had previously been the Superintendent of Haskell Boarding School was still living on campus, doing a political side step with the BI A in Washington, and generally throwing a monkey wrench into the paper-work of this new school Burgess thought he would control. Needless to say, the battle lines had been drawn by the time I was introduced to Wally which took place, two months later. Two months that found Shirley still did not work in Bill's office and I had not been paid.

When the time came, that we were in the same room and Jack was forced to introduce me to Wally, the situation became very awkward, as Jack had to tell me Mr. Galuzzi's position at that time in front of Wally. I quickly could ascertain that Wally was in the driver's seat and making life miserable for Bill. Wally had our funds tied up. What better method to insure your job than to control the money of the institution. When I signed that agreement, I had no way of knowing I would be in the middle of a power struggle between two factions, or that this war was so big its battle lines stretched all the way to our nations capitol.

I later viewed this situation thusly, Burgess and his political faction were relatively new to the Washington scene, they should have given Galuzzi a piece of the action early in their planning. They could have included him in the overall scheme of the institution, this probably would have not made the old dog totally happy, but it would have turned him from a biting adversary to just a sleeping grump. Instead Burgess and his group under estimated the political clout wally's group held and they brazenly steam-rolled him after his many creditable years of service to the B I A. This federal agency is notorious for political glad handing, good old boy tactics and this attitude has prevailed since the thieving, skin flint days of the Indian trading posts. They forced him to use every dirty trick he could muster to retain his position and his Washington crony's to save face.

Personally, I did not give a dam about Wally's and Bill's openly spiteful little blood letting. I cared how it affected the educational institution, they and their colleagues were bouncing the faculty around like it was a tennis ball in a country club tennis match. and considered us pawns on a chess board. We were expendable, especially the non-indigenous Americans. It. Appeared either side never minded, that the instructors were mostly highly successful educators in their own fields, with outstanding backgrounds and all with families to consider, only the political power that came from winning, even if the battle left nothing, but scorched earth was worthy of eithers consideration. As I said, I did not care about any of this, except for how I was affected by it. They left me no choice. Remember, I was to receive my first paycheck at the end of thirty days work, well thirty days drug into six months and I still did not get any money. At the end of two months without pay and no job for Shirley, as Bill had promised, I asked Jack to go with me to Bill's office, as I wanted some information, as to what my future would be at Haskell and when I could expect to get my money. By now I was getting pretty shook up about this whole mess and felt they both knew more than they were willing to tell me about my position. Bill was his usual glad- handing self and sitting behind his big shiny desk all puffed up like a big toad his stuffy appearance and seemingly indifferent attitude toward my dilemma made me angry as hell. Until Jack chastised me, when we were in the band room some time after this meeting, I did not even realize I had insulted the boss by pounding my fist on his desk, this was a fax paux, totally beyond my usual actions, but I was truly frustrated and at a loss for some action that could get me out of this mess.

This meeting did result in Bill finding Shirley a temporary position with the extramural Independent Studies Office at K U, and this lead to me finally getting my money by a loan through this office. During these trying times, I had to straddle the fence between these two factions working daily with both sides within ear-shot of each other. Man, what a challenge that was.

Shirley and my family were doing without a lot of seriously needed items, we did ok for the first month or two, due mostly to the fact we had made a nice profit on our home in Muskogee and I got one more monthly check from Fort Gibson Schools after arriving in Lawrence, but by the end of the third month we did not have enough money to meet our house payment and no cash for any miscellaneous purchases, the realtor was very understanding and loaned us the money to pay our house payments for the next three months. Shirley got a better paying job just about a month before Christmas, as secretary to the County Extension Agent in his Lawrence office, where she met a lady named Gussey flory, who became a good friend and to whom we would all be forever indebted, as Gussey eventually, (about six months later), got Shirley a tremendous job as his second in command with Phil Rankin, Personnel Director for Kansas University.

The same week Shirley went to work as a temporary, I got a job at the largest Texaco Station in Lawrence working as night manager and mechanic, which paid me minimum wage of two dollars and seventy-five cents an hour. And I had to work all day at the college and from six pm until one am at the station.

The kids thought this was great and that we were really doing well, but little did they know, due to the fact we did not have money for food, we ran up a five thousand dollar credit card debt over this six month period, eating two meals a day at the Holiday Inn Restaurant, the only restaurant in town that accepted a Texaco card and the only credit card we had.

Since I taught my last class at the college about three thirty every day, and this was the only time I got to see the kids and Shirley other than when we all were sleeping. And since wieners and buns were all we could afford eating. Until the weather got to cold to do so, when I got home I would load the kids and food and wait for Shirley to come home from her new job, Bill Burgess helped her find at the K U extension office. Then we would all go to the county lake for a picnic and swim, before the family dropped me at my second job.

Bill made this effort on behalf of Shirley's employment, to replace the job, he had promised her at Haskell and that Wally was presently blocking by non- appropriation of the funds.

Eventually, this evening swim became quite a party, as the area children asked our kids if they could tag along, so our kids asked their mother if this would be alright and she told them, it would be ok if each person would bring a contribution of food. That next trip we had so much picnic stuff, we had to limit and assign what the guests would bring to the next trip and Shirley and I really were busy caring for the safety of all these children. We finally had to set restrictions on the number of kids that we took, as there was too many to ride safely in our truck.

I was actually hired for Bill Burgess by the University of Kansas Extra Mural Independent Studies Program and I was on the faculty of Kansas University assigned by K. U. to teach at Haskell American Indian Junior College. **The fact that I was not a BIA employee turned out eventually, to be both a credit and a liability.**

We will address the advantage first. The last few days of November I still had not received any money from this teaching position even though I had developed a total curriculum, taught daily five days each week and helped print a catalog of classes for Haskell. About one pm on a beautiful fall afternoon, Jack asked me to get down some of the new percussion equipment he had stored in the second tier wall cabinets eight feet off the floor at the rear of our rehearsal area. Jack was a fine percussionist, and planned to start a new ensemble with some of these field drums. I got a twenty- foot, very unwieldy ladder from the construction site next door, drudgingly dragged it up the sixteen step narrow, metal steps outside our facility, and after some difficulty managed to get it through the second story outside exit door and into the rear of our rehearsal room, positioning the ladder, so that I could open the cabinet doors without knocking myself off my perch on the ladder and still reach the percussion equipment inside, which I would need to sort through before getting the pieces Jack desired.

Undaunted by the heat in the room and impatient to retrieve the drums, I quickly climbed the unsteady ladder and started to open the heavy wooden cabinet doors. Suddenly, due to my extended arm reaching into the cabinet the long ladder, with me at the top of it, began to topple and I reached out with my right hand to try and grab the closet door. Although the ladder did not fall over, I missed the door and keeping my feet on the teetering rungs, fell against the wall with the right side of my body and my right hand, which was now impaled on a large nail that was protruding outward from inside the cabinets. I realized my predicament immediately and since Jack had left a few moments previously to go outside, I knew I had no help getting down from the top of the ladder, even if I figured a way to pull my hand from the nail without going unconscious from the pain and the sight of my blood, that was surely to spew from the resulting open wound. I told myself to calm down and try to figure out how to get out of this mess without ripping my hand apart, and about that time, I got lucky. Jack came back inside and I called him over to where he could stabilize the ladder and told him about the nail and my hand which he now could see. Then I told him to try and break my fall if I passed out and pulling my hand straight off the nail, grabbed the wrist of the hand with the open wound and placed my thumb tightly on the large blood vessel to form a tourniquet and prevent the loss of as much blood as possible, I managed to climb down from the Cabinets without loosing consciousness and Jack rushed me to the infirmary at K. U.

While I was waiting to see a physician, Jack called Shirley, who had just the past week, thanks to Bill, gone to work in the office of Extra Mural Independent Studies as a temporary for which we were truly grateful. The other assistant in her office overheard her harried conversation, as Jack explained my accident and expressed his condolences and shortly after Jacks phone call while in conversation with this gentleman, Shirley mentioned the fact I was having mental problems, due to the fact I had not been paid for six months. He told Shirley the University offices where she worked (Extra Mural Independent Studies), had a special fund for these situations and he did not know why no one had explained this process to us. She had me call this office that immediately paid me all my back pay and explained to me the Haskell people said they were sorry, but my paper work had been lost on Wally's desk, and they did not know how this had transpired. We had become collateral damage! But in this war, take no prisoners is the rule and no one would take the blame or credit for such.

Other than the facts that we lost a lot of money to interest on our Texaco card, and my resulting terrible mental state, nothing else transpired. Because of this fiasco, which the University office told me should never have happened, as they could have paid me every month and replaced the money with my checks as they came in later. We discovered this was common practice for this University office.

Now that we were getting paid regularly and Shirley had a real good position the next quarter was very calm and the whole family was happier except for Carla, who was still having problems with her band teacher, but it would be spring before we could remedy this situation.

Christmas that year was real bleak and the worst holiday ever. Not because of money, which we now were receiving on a regular basis, but because everyone in our little family had the flu virus on Christmas Eve. We were sick all through the holiday. We had called my sister Jane who was living in Trenton, Missouri early in

*Front porch of Bald-win home Girls-front to back Tonya, Carla, Shirley-C. E..-, Dennis*

December and made arrangements for her and Bruce Bartlett, her husband, to spend Christmas Day and have Christmas Dinner with us. They had never seen our new home and although we had invited them in the fall, it had never been convenient for them to drive down to Lawrence until this holiday. Since they were to arrive on Christmas Day, and we had all been sick for three days previous, we thought we might be well by the time they arrived, However, it became obvious on Christmas Eve that we were not going to be well by the next day. So, Shirley called Jane and told her not to come, as we did not want to inflict she and Bruce with our malady. To make this story shorter, caring Jane showed up anyway and fixed dinner for us all, which we really appreciated and fortunately for them, she and Bruce did not catch our flu bug.

In the spring, Shirley went to work in Phil Rankin's office and our income really shot up. The older kids were getting out of school for the summer, and we decided to move outside of Lawrence, to insure Carla would have a better school situation the following fall. We looked at a number of rural properties but none that could compare favorably with our present home. So, we placed an advertisement in the Lawrence paper asking to purchase a home in the country. The day the add first appeared Mr. Dillon a wealthy and kind old gentleman, called to offer us his wonderful working family farm.

Mr. Dillon owned a large piece of farm land, it totaled three hundred eighty acres, twenty minutes drive south of Lawrence and just south of Baldwin, Kansas on an all weather road. This property also included a fifteen- acre lake and two fine homes with numerous well-built, working cattle pins and two large barns for the storage of hay, grain, and farming equipment. The improved pastures were sewn in brome grass, that was three tall and so thick one could barely walk through it. Only minutes before Mr. Dillon called, we had agreed to consider a proposal to purchase another place. When I told the old fellow we had already made other arrangements, he said," You really ought to take a look at my place before you finalize your purchase, it is quite nice". He was so nice and seemed to be hurt by the fact we were not even considering his property that I told him we would come right then to his farm and take a look. Boy, was I glad I did! The place was everything Mr. Dillon said, and more! After he showed us around all the barns, pens, and both houses, the newest of which he refused to accompany us into, as his recently deceased wife had passed away in it, he told us he would sell any portion or all of the property. I told him, although I was very impressed with his beautiful property, I probably could not afford to purchase any portion of it. His gentle face lighted up with a wry grin, and his large, kind, blue eyes twinkled merrily as he said, "I will make it so you can, those four kids need to live on this place". Then he continued, "How much money do you have that you can put down on a note"? I laughed and countered with," How much would you take for the new house and five acres around it"? He told me, "thirty eight thousand". And then he must have seen my face fall, as I realized no banker would carry a note for that amount with no more down than I had available and he quickly said," I will carry the note, but how much money do you have for a down payment"? I said, " I could come up with two thousand eight hundred out of my present home". He said," lets meet tomorrow and we will deal! I could not believe my ears he was seriously going to practically give us his wonderful place. I smiled and said, "Only if you will give me the right to fish in your lake for the next ninety-nine years"? He smiled, understandingly, and said," Sure!

All the way back to our home we visited about this exciting place and its many wonderful attributes. And the next day Mr. Dillon true to his word in every respect made us the deal of a lifetime. We moved the first week of August 1972 into the beautiful new home Mr. Dillon had built for his lifetime love, which never had the good fortune to get to enjoy it. Our kids were treated like his grand kids and they loved him as we all did, who could not love a man who everyday came to your front door step, asking you to take the rest of his place and let him carry a note that would terminate at his demise no matter how or when it came about. He simply wanted us to enjoy the farm as he had.

What a pleasant place to live, and only a relaxing twenty-five minutes commute to our jobs each day, as our kids truly enjoyed attending school in the very progressive Baldwin schools where Carla, would become a Kansas all state flutist. A quaint small town, developed 1839 along the old Santa Fe Trail, where the one cop in town would give you a ticket for missing the towns only four-way stop sign.

While I taught at Haskell I was very fortunate to teach a fair country trumpet player, Sam Neal, whose dad was a minister at the Indian Baptist church in west Shawnee, Oklahoma and who ironically would attain his music teaching degree and teach for many years as the highly liked assistant and eventually successful head band director at my old job in Fort Gibson, Oklahoma.

I liked the students at Haskell they were somewhat naïve in their approach to education, as they seldom went to class on any days but Wednesdays, and Thursdays as Mondays they were still enjoying the past weekend and Fridays they were preparing for the coming weekend. This meant as a band, we seldom planned anything for weekends as you could hardly ever get them to participate. They did like to perform at the football and basketball games, as they liked to watch their teams and make out of town trips, which were totally paid for by the school. One of these young men who was an Alaskan Eskimo, became a frequent visitor to the band hall and after we got pretty well acquainted, I asked him on a hot and muggy afternoon to go downtown with me and get some ice crème. He told me, "There is no ice crème to be had in Lawrence". I told him about the Baskin- Robbins Store and he replied, "That's not ice crème"! I said, Oh no"? Then he said, "Ice crème is made with wild berries and whale blubber"! So much for that days ice crème trip, we had a coke instead.

We started school with six music students in the summer session of 1971, but by fall jack had recruited nearly thirty more instrumentalist from all corners of the U.S.A. The new choir teacher, Jacob Bohannon, who was a Choctaw Indian from Hugo, Oklahoma, had recruited about twenty-five more for the vocal department. So, my first year music theory classes were pretty full and we had a start, although these students were very weak performers musically, toward some performing ensembles. Sam was the best performer we had, but at that time in his musical development, would not have been able to play the solo parts on the materials I had been expecting my high school kids to play.

Jack was a master at smoke and mirror productions and insisted on teaching by rote or any other method that he thought would produce immediate results, as he knew politics were playing a big part in whether or not we would survive Wally's storm. He planned dances for the students on campus and developed a little rock band built around Sam's singing and trumpet playing. Jack performed at the drop of a hat every where he could gather a crowd, even marching his straggling little group dressed appropriately in colorful Navajo costumes in the KU Homecoming Parade. This was a real savvy ploy and brought him much kudos from Burgess and the boys. So his next brainstorm was to recruit the western U.S. by touring the states of

New Mexico and Arizona performing concerts and shaking hands with the parents of what he hoped would be his future students. This worked so well, both in recruiting and with his political hacks, that the BIA in Washington heard about it and with their blessing; the following year he took us all on tour to Mississippi.

On the tour, we performed in Oklahoma and recruited some really good students, who would be coming to Haskell the following fall and when we got back to Haskell, he sent me to Texas and Oklahoma to recruit for two weeks and I got about twenty really fine kids to obligate their selves as future music students at Haskell. By that time we had over fifty instrumentalists and forty vocal students and it appeared we would have a bright future at the new junior college.

Well, appearances and fact are surely not the same, especially in political swamps like Washington D. C., Haskell, and in the Dakotas. Sometime earlier, I alluded to the fact that I was not a BIA employee and this was an advantage at that time, well now I will tell you of how it eventually contributed to my demise at Haskell. My problems at Haskell began specifically miles away in the Dakotas, where that summer on the Rosebud Reservation, a loose canon in the federal FBI shot and killed a native woman standing in the doorway of her home, while she held her infant child in her arms. This incident was just the ticket the militant movement in the western tribes had been waiting for and the yells of hate and prejudice sounded throughout the United States. Most notably this occured in the BIA and other such indigenous government agencies.

My family is part Creek Indian and we are proud of it, some of us are also Cherokee, However, we do not flaunt these wonderful background traits in the face of those who would resent or admire them, as we are Americans and United States citizens first and foremost. So, when the political winds of prejudice began blowing, as back- wash from the killings on the Rosebud and Haskell fired **a large number of teachers, because they were of non- Indian blood,** I told no one and have never told anyone at Haskell I was American Indian. If I could not teach there, because the administrators considered my work with their students to be outstanding, I did not want to remain on their music faculty solely due to my blood- line or skin color.

Jack knew of my Indian heritage and advised me to report it, but I just could not be a party to such petty shenanigans and told him so. Unfortunately, I never did get to work with all those new students I recruited and never knew if they even went to Haskell, as I went out immediately and unsuccessfully to seek local high school employment.

During the entire time I taught at Haskell, I attended master of music therapy and music education classes at the Kansas University music school. I applied and was accepted into the graduate school of music during the fall of 1971, and persevered through some very trying ordeals and an arduous and demanding graduate committee over the next eighteen months, receiving the only Master of Music Education Degree granted that term and the last such degree to be granted from the Kansas University School of Music. A Copy of my Masters Thesis resides in the K U University library, the Library of Congress, and at the KU Music Library. I could not have completed my Masters research or the thesis, without my committee chair, the wonderfully dedicated Dr.Radocy's brilliant expertise,or the generous help of Shirley, who typed many, many nights all night and then went to work at her job during the day, painfully suffering the entire time with severe rheumatoid arthritis in her knees and legs. All these things happened while her wonderfully generous and thoughtful Mother, Esther, cooked for all of us, cleaned and bathed Tonya and delivered the older kids to their school obligations. I received my graduate hood of pink and black in may of 1973, and lost my job at Haskell the same month, what a roller coaster ride!

# Oh Lord, We are Going to be Texans

Checking Kansas High Schools I found that although at Haskell the name Redwine meant white man, to Kansans it meant red man and therefore, had some predjudice about it. I changed course and reverted to calling my old buddy Jim Gaylor, whom I knew would be aware of any music jobs open in his area.

Jim was as usual very knowledgeable and quite willing to help me find employment in his part of northeast Texas. He listed about five schools that were looking for head- band directors and supervisors of music. I took a week off at the college and went to Paris, Texas to get Jims aid in obtaining some interviews, as the semester was winding down and the Indian students, who mostly attended classes as they choose, had pretty well quit coming to class. They also had figured out the firing of the major portion of the faculty, meant they would not have these teachers to deal with in the future. Within three days, I was hired as the supervisor of music and head- band director at Clarksville, Texas. The salary was not what I had been accustomed to at Haskell, but for a small 2-A school system in this part of Texas it was very commensurate with other area secondary institutions.

While in Clarksville I looked at a few homes and purchased one. It was a stately sixty year old two story mansion with original turn of the twentieth century fixtures sitting on a beautiful city block of land that was encircled on the north by producing palm granite trees, the fruit of which was stolen by the local kids before we could harvest them and shaded by thirteen huge sixty to seventy year old pecan trees, a lovely garden spot, and a producing fruit orchard.

When I returned to Baldwin, I sold our lovely farm home to an attorney in Kansas City, to whom; Mr. Dillon had agreed to sell the entire farm. That was a sad day! All I told Shirley and the family about Clarksville was," I bought a house I think you will like it". I had a few more days to teach at Haskell before my contract ran out and the day after I finished there, I got out of bed at seven am and announced to the family," Get in the car we are going to see the Colorado Rocky Mountains"! Shirley said, "We can't do that, we don't have enough cash to make such a trip"! I replied, " I will go to the bank in Baldwin and cash a check". She said, "We have never been in that bank, I do not believe they will cash a check for you". We got in the little yellow Opal station wagon, our new car at the time, drove to the only bank in Baldwin, and when Shirley and I walked inside the teller said, "Good morning Mr. And Mrs. Redwine", as though she had been expecting us and had known us forever! After cashing a check, we returned to the house, grabbed our tooth -brushes, and other toilet supplies and only one change of light summer clothing for each of us in the family, as I told everyone we would purchase what we needed as we needed it and we did not want to be bothered in the crowded car with luggage.

Tonya insisted on taking her large summer hat and teddy bear, which presently accompanied her everywhere. She was quite a sight, as her caring older sister Carla, helped her into the luggage area behind the back seat and handed five year old Tonya the bag of toys and activities Shirley had thoughtfully purchased to keep the child busy on the coming trip. This purchase was the first thing we did after cashing the check in town. Shirley shopped for these items, while I got the car serviced for our journey, our family's first and only real vacation. I figured, and rightly so, that we would not be this close to the mountains again for sometime, as our next move was going to take us far south of our present location, to the Red River Valley.

We were a happy group of tourists, driving and singing our way across the high plains country of western Kansas and into the foothills of the Colorado Rockies. We went first to the Colorado Springs area, stopping at every tourist Mecca available. Taking Kodak pictures of such treasures as Santa's Workshop, The Garden of the Gods, newly created, "old ghost towns", and Pikes Peak, where the ground squirrels were so tame they carefully took food from the kid's hands. Our next big stop was in Denver, where we had a fine dinner at a Steak

*Tonya Michelle Redwine*
*– Tourist 1972*

and Ale restaurant and stayed at the Holiday Inn so the kids could unwind in the swimming pool. Then we headed south and back into Kansas, to see Laura Engel's Wilder and Mary Engel's original Little House on the prairie. Tonya and Carla were very impressed, as they watched this TV show nearly every night while sitting cross legged on the den floor where Carla brushed Tonya's long blond locks. Dennis and David were not as impressed and hardly got out of the car at this attraction. We waved goodbye to the Rockies as they slowly disappeared in the mirror and returned to Baldwin by way of Oklahoma where we picked up Esther, on the first of July.

We arrived home on the same day and finished packing the trucks and trailers with our furniture and other possessions, called the realtor in Clarksville, who had sold me our house there to alert him we were moving down and on the fourth of July, the hottest day of that year 1973, with gasoline prices sky-rocketing and oil companies making huge profits, as they lied to the public about the quantities of gas available, we moved to stifling, muggy, unbelievably humid, Northeast Texas

We had quite a caravan, I was leading and drove the large U-Haul van. Carla, who was sixteen, very inexperienced and only within the last year licensed for driving, was accompanied by her grandmother, Esther Mae, and Tonya, who shuffled alternately between Carla and Shirley, but spent most of her time with Carla and her Granny Esther, followed closely in the fully loaded yellow Opal. Shirley followed Carla in our red and white old Chevy pick-up, that was wildly loaded and piled high with bicycles, lawn mowers, charcoal grills, water hoses and miscellaneous junk, we just could not do without. Dennis was riding shotgun with Shirley and Dave was doing the same for me. We were a page right out of T Vs. Beverly Hillbillies. I had forgotten to give anyone else in our parade, directions to Clarksville. However, the other drivers were doing ok on the open highway until we got to the large city of Tulsa. The four lanes of I-44 that had been no problem for us earlier, was filled with severe traffic congestion and the eighteen-wheelers were in every lane. Shirley lost sight of Carla and me, as Carla was forced off the main highway onto an access ramp by one of the big trucks, in all probability the truck driver never saw the smaller Opal. When Shirley saw Carla being forced off the main highway, she knew she had better follow her, as Carla would really be lost in these unfamiliar streets of Tulsa. I never saw either Carla or Shirley leave I-44. So, by the time I got to the highway US-75 junction and I looked in my rear view mirror for them, I was surprised to find we were no longer together. David watched for them in our mirrors, as I continued slowly down US-75 for nearly fifteen miles. I knew if I went back to hunt for the other two vehicles, we would most likely pass each other at some point and making direct contact with either vehicle was highly unlikely due to the heavy flow of traffic and the wide islands between the lanes of this federal interstate. It was a real dilemma and I quickly decided our only hope of ever getting back together was for David and me to pull over and wait for them to find us. Although, by now I was getting very anxious as to what had happened to them and really doubted they would take the correct highway when they arrived at US-75. This scenario was possible only if something more serious had not occurred. My considered choices of actions, appeared to be limited, to turning around and trying to locate them, or sitting tight and waiting for them, or someone to come along and tell me a message I really did not want to hear. I decided to remain stationary and hope for the best. It was a good decision, as about three and a half hours later both vehicles drove up, everyone inside them justly angrier than hell, that I had failed to give them instructions about our route and no cash to even get a drink on this extremely hot day, but all were quite relieved as was I, to be once again on the correct road and together.

To this day, I still do not know how they figured out to take the correct highway to find me, as they did not have a map and had never taken this route. After they each gave me an ear full, we finished our trip and spent the night in a small motel in Clarksville, as it was too late to unload at our home that evening. There are times, I still get to hear about how scared they all were and anxious they all were, that they might not find David and me, but I somewhat redeemed my status, as negligent father, thoughtless husband, and dumb son-in law the next day, when they all were pleasantly surprised by the house's warm southern charm, as they helped me move into our roomy Clarksville home.

Our family had moved so many times that we could tear down, pack, and move everything we owned, which was a massive amount of stuff, in one day. Then carry the marked and highly organized cartons or furniture inside the next location unpack, set up, and straighten every room, as though it had always been in this location.. So when anyone offered to help us, we accepted their generous offer with a jaundiced eye, and usually made a graceful attempt to thank them for the offer, but we explained, due to our plans they must follow our lead as to placing items in the new house.

The day we moved into the Clarksville residence Monte Boyd, a real klutz according to the local school administrators that wanted me to fire him and who, was to be my assistant band director and general pain in the butt, although I was not aware of this at the time, came by to offer his assistance. He was a big help and as we finished placing our last few items in their special areas, we told Monte thanks for his aid. Mr. Boyd whose small round face was flushed from his recent heavy lifting of a couch, looked up, grinned amicably, and said, " I wanted to get you settled, so you and I can begin to work with this years marching band.". I thought, oh no, this guys too gung ho for me and I told Monte, "Do not worry about that, you will get all the band crap you can handle in a week or two, after I recover from this move and get my house and yard in order." He left shortly after that and I did not expect to see him for a few days, but just like a bad penny, the next day about nine am Mr. Boyd returned to help us with the yard.

I had told Dennis and David to clean up the dead limbs that the wind had blown out of the sixty to seventy foot tall pecan trees in our back yard. We were going to mow the grass under these trees and I did not want to hit them with the lawn mower, which could ruin the blades of the machine. I heard Monte talking to the twins as they worked on their limb project and noticed he had a bow saw in his hand, but being busy inside setting up our kitchen, I did not pay attention to see what he was up to. David came to the back screen door, through which he could see me working in the kitchen, pulled it open far enough to poke his head in and said, "Dad Mr. Boyd is --- ----------". About that instant I heard a loud crash, and a yell of utter anguish. So, I rushed to the door to see if Dennis was hurt. I could see Dennis standing over a big limb and he appeared to be fine, but he was looking at a large limb and someone obviously in pain on the ground. That is when David finished his sentence with, "That's what I was going to tell you, Mr. Boyd was sitting on that big limb sawing it off at the tree, and would not pay any attention to us when we tried to tell him, he was going to come down with it". Come down indeed! Straddling that sucker all the way to the ground from fourteen feet above. Monte could not walk for nearly two days and then he did so very gingerly.

Nearly every day for the next two years we were treated to some idiotic action or verbiage from this amiable knuckle head. He created problems for me I never dreamed could exist, I have never seen anyone who would work so hard at producing useless and unwanted results. Mr. Boyd was to eventually be convicted of murdering his young wife and is currently serving a life sentence in the Oklahoma State prison The irony of this situation was Monte graduated with a four- point grade average from the University of Texas at Austin. That does not say a great deal for U T, (duz **it**)?

The third week in July I could put off going to the band room no longer, as the school was paying me to hold classes and prepare the marching band for football season, which in Texas each fall, is like preparing for the second coming of Christ. Public notice had been printed in the local newspaper alerting the instrumental students to their rehearsal obligations, so all I had to do was show up and keep Monte from making a fool of himself in front of the band and their parents. This I did, by keeping him busy passing out the music I intended to rehearse for our first fall performance, but in spite of my efforts, he managed to insult most of the students, or to make them uncomfortable by referring to the band's failings of the past. Positive thinking was not in his make up, or at least it was wellhidden.

Carla, presently in her junior year was an excellent twirler. She auditioned for and was accepted by the present corps into the twirling line. This was a really obvious effort by the band, especially the twirlers to show both Carla and me they were willing to go the extra mile to have a fine band and work with us. The twins were freshmen this year and since the first chair players of both the clarinet and the trumpet sections were performing this fall as twirlers, their sections welcomed them with open arms. Tonya was starting school for the first time and really looking forward to it. Tonya loved her kindergarten teacher and really had a fine first year of school. The following year however, was a different story. No one in our family was ready for what

*<<Tonya Michelle Redwine, with long braids standing next to her first grade teacher in lower right*

happened, when Tonya enrolled and was the only white child placed in the first grade room of an all black class taught by a black teacher. According to the principal the black lady was one of his best teachers, since he needed to integrate that class he knew we, being new faculty from Kansas, would not mind if Tonya was the sole white student in the class.

Shirley and I would not have known about this situation, but in November of that year, Tonya invited the children of her class to our home for her birthday party and no one came. The whole family was feeling bad that little Tonya's party had gone so badly and her sadness was quite apparent as she cried herself to sleep that night. I happened to visit with Tonya's school principal, a few days later and told him about what had transpired at the birthday party. Then I asked him, why he thought the kids had snubbed her?

The principal informed me that Tonya's classmates were either black, or very poor and most likely their parents thought these children would be uncomfortable in our home. So, the parents did not bring the children to the party. The principal further explained, this was the first year of integration in the Clarksville schools, nearly twenty years after the 1954 Brown vs Board of Ed.U. S. Supreme court decision.

We continued to comply with the schools ridiculess policy and did so for a few weeks until Tonya came home complaining that all the other kids in her class were getting special treatment. Six year old, Tonya could not understand why the other kids had a special ticket at lunch and therefore ate free and she had to pay for her lunch, as the teacher would not give her a ticket. She was most concerned, that her teacher sat and ate lunch with them and helped them read a story, but did not help Tonya, who had to read by herself. I went to visit Tonya's teacher, explained what Tonya's concerns were and the teacher told me Tonya was very intelligent and did not need her help reading. Worse, the teacher ignored the part about the lunch ticket. The whole episode went right over the teacher's head, she did not have a clue as to Tonya's real problem of not understanding social inequality.

That was the last straw; I went to the superintendent and told him if he wanted me to continue as his band teacher, he had better move my kid out of that class and pronto. Lunch was not a problem for Tonya the rest of the school year, as very soon after this class room move, she discovered she loved the ease of preparation and taste of Spigettios, or vegetable soup, so she fixed her own lunch each day, so she could take what she wanted to the lunch room.

Halloween 1973 was a hoot; we decorated our big old house with weird lighting, cobwebs, jack-o-lanterns, which we carved, and shocks of real corn. Shirley dressed up like a witch, stood eerily in the living room her whole body sheaved in a pale veil of green light, her long bony fingers motioning to come inside, as Carla slowly opened the big front door, David controlled the scary sounds and music on the phonograph, and Dennis menaced every guest in his very convincing werewolf costume the whole scene was a page right out of a monster movie, and generally scared the hell out of the trick or treaters, some of which, ran away so fast I never caught them to reward them their treats.

We really had a great time in the Clarksville home, Granny Esther stayed most of the summer and early fall with us, camping out in the beautiful east room that we designated as Granny's sun porch, as it was enclosed on three sides by gloriously big clear windows which allowed the morning sun to wake anyone sleeping in it, starting their day with a bright and cheerful wake-up call. When Granny Esther left us to go home to her husband, Red Miller, in Skiatook north of Tulsa, the room lost a lot of its beauty, and seemed lonesome for a companion.

As a result, when Buddy Bartlett, my oldest nephew called to ask us if he could stay with us while attending junior college in Paris, Texas, which was only twenty-five miles west of Clarksville, we welcomed him as a new family member to the sun porch, as it also had its own private outside entrance. Unfortunately Bud and Junior college were not on the same page and by late spring of 1974 he got a job with

*Carroll"Bud"Bartlett*

the Clarksville Pallet Company and moved from the sun porch to a little house about five blocks down the street. That was a sad time for the sun room, our family and Buddy, he seemed so unhappy, and nothing anyone could do seemed to be able to change his situation, eventually nearly six months later, after trying to find a better job and finding none available, Bud moved to Springfield, Missouri where during the next few years, we made a number of trips to visit him and found him happier each time we went. Buddy was killed in a tragic car crash in 1984 just as he appeared to be really enjoying his life. His death is mentioned earlier in this very incomplete family history.

About this time Bret English a well built, very energetic, fifteen year old with beautiful blue eyes and long, but well groomed blond locks, who played alto sax in the high school band, was close friends with David, and presently lived a few blocks from us with his maternal Grandmother, who was known to all local children, as Granny Bates, candidly asked me, "can I live with you"? We had recently helped Buddy move to his house, so we had the extra room and Bret appeared to be a good kid who wanted and needed two parents. So, that night I visited with Shirley and we both agreed, that if Bret would truly become a part of the family and agree to abide by the rules we had for the rest of our children, we would accept him into our family and he could move into the sun room. Just as my dad had expected all my siblings and mother to attend church every Sunday, I expected the same thing from my family and when I visited with Bret about his responsibilities should he become part of our family, this was made clear to him.

He moved in on the next day after our understanding, which was Saturday and when I awoke the following day, Sunday morning, I was pleasantly surprised to look out the back door and see Bret finishing his generous gift to the family. He had gotten up at sun up and put a fresh coat of bright green paint on the hen house. I yelled to tell him breakfast was ready and he yelled back, "I know, its time for church"! Obviously he desperately wanted to live with us, and was going to fit in very well. We got along well, Bret always held up his end of the agreement and when as a high school senior he decided to move to Lake Highlands, Texas the following summer, so he could graduate from a more prestige's high school; it made us all very sad.

However when we finally began to teach at Seminole Junior College in the summer of 1975 Bret moved with us and lived in our home while he attended S. J. C for the next two years, attaining his associate of arts degree in the spring of 1976. Bret prefers to call himself Nicholas after his natural father who past away some years ago, but he will always be Bretly to me and although we travel separate and somewhat diverse roads at this time I will treasure the many wonderful memories we had together. I must mention Brets little family, as they would find it not only odd, but also hurtful of me not to do so. Bret and his first wife, Sandra, had a lovely daughter, which he raised by himself, but while the baby was still in diapers to our surprise, Sandra moved to North Carolina and abandoned both he and Stephanie, their only child.

Some years later when Stephanie was about five or six years old Bret met and married a beautiful blond divorcée named Alice who was raising two gorgeous young daughters from a previous marriage. Alice's daughters names were Laura and Andrea. Laura was about eight years of age and Andrea was about three when their mother and Bret married. Bret and Alice later had two children together, a boy, Nicholas, aptly named, as he is the image of his father, and just as much his own person and Emily, a beautiful, but somewhat intolerant daughter, whose intolerance is most likely the result of her family's heartbreaking split-up. She and her brother who for the first few years of their lives had been surrounded by a large loving and caring family, have recently suffered through their parents bitter and at times caustic custody statements about one another in divorce court. These two presently live with their mother some miles from their father, who only sees them under supervised visits twice a month and he is forced to travel many miles to do so. The older girls are attending colleges many states apart, but make a special effort to visit one another and do get to see each other occasionally.

Both Christmases we lived in Clarksville were very enjoyable. During the first one which we celebrated in December 1973, the big oil companies throughout our nation purposely withheld production and distribution of fuel oil and gasoline to force their prices to spiral out of control. Additionally they released a flood of lies and propaganda, that were designed to convince the general consuming public, that shortages of these fuels were the reason for the price increases and small quantities at the local outlets. I had well informed friends in the oil business, that frankly told me this nationwide hoax by the oil companies was a huge conspiracy to drive up prices and pile up unbelievable profits. So, when our whole nation was told not to use lighting on our homes to celebrate Christmas that year, as the nation needed to conserve the fuel, it made me furious. These giants of the financial world were so devious, that their financial practices shut down trucking from one side of the nation to the other, and there were little or no goods in our stores to purchase. I remember going to the grocer in Clarksville, and seeing only a few packages of hamburger in the meat counter and nearly empty shelving where normally stocks of can goods were four deep on the shelves. and where there was no bread at all, as the bakeries could not get gasoline to deliver their products to the local stores.

My personal protest was to not only put up the family's normal lighted decorations, but to buy up all the available strings of such lights, and add them to our already gaudy sight. Our house was the only one for blocks around that was lighted, but we certainly made up for all those homes that meekly followed the overwhelming propaganda of the big money. It reminded one of the classic Chevy Chase movies National Lampoon's " <u>A Christmas Vacation</u> ". In addition, we scouted around and found enough gas to drive seventy-five miles to the mountains in Oklahoma both years and cut our Christmas tree from the wild timber, then as one final protest, we covered it from floor to its crowning angel with twinkle lights. This over decorating became a tradition with our kids and for years after this, when they came home to celebrate the birth of Christ with us, they expected to see the house lighted up like a giant Christmas tree.

I started directing the choir at the First Christian Church in Clarksville a few weeks after our 1973 Christmas. This necessitated choir members, and I knew where to get at least five of them. Shirley sang alto, Carla sang soprano, David and Dennis sang tenor, Bret and I sang bass, and that is how I got my boys to learn to sing, as they were not presently enamored with anything vocal. We recruited three more women, two sopranos and another alto, and two of their husbands to sing with David and Dennis and Wham—O, instant church choir!

In January of 1974, Shirley went to work for the Clarksville Furniture Company, a new manufacturer in town, whose Company had relocated here from North Carolina. Her first few months in their new building were interesting as the company was just developing their offices and Shirley's office consisted of a large wooden packing crate, turned on its side and a floor lamp both of which were placed in a back balcony high overlooking the bustling manufacturing floor below. Surprisingly, D. Wayne Barker her manager and boss and Shirley were in total control of the Clarksville operation and they had a very good rapport, both with the workers and each other. For some months this job was great and Shirley was very happy doing it, until a mentally challenged, power crazed, young woman who was extremely envious of Shirley's position, asked to be transferred to the Clarksville office from the factory in North Carolina.

This woman was nutty as a fruitcake and daily made Shirley's life miserable. She pulled all kinds of dirty tricks and eventually got Barker fired, so Shirley decided the income from this job was not worth the daily misery she was enduring, as this manipulating and conniving woman had the ear of the factory's owner in North Carolina, so Shirley went to work for less money, but better conditions at the local Farm Bureau Insurance Office as a secretary for Morris T. Cooper, a real country gentleman, for whom she truly enjoyed working.

The Red River Valley has enjoyed a long and colorful history, as the old Texas road from Ft Smith, Arkansas to Houston, Texas and the Gulf of Mexico passes directly through it and was used as the alley behind our home in Clarksville. This road, developed in the 1820's and 1830's was the major route used to settle the Indian lands of Oklahoma and the republic of Texas by the white settlers and early explorers such as Daniel Boone, David Crockett, Stephen F. Austin and Sam Houston, among many other notables. The fact that I walked that old Texas road everyday, just as these greats did, where so much of this nations history and great men and women trod, eventually bringing our present nation together took place, only dawned on me today while writing this page.

What a legacy those folks left us, and what a price they paid to do so! Although this area has a relatively long history of settlement by white and black people it is still a very rural area and many large native mammals still call the banks of the Red River and surrounding marshes, tributaries, and forests home.

One of these, a panther of considerable size and cunning decided to pay us a visit in Clarksville around the first of May 1974. It terrorized the town for some sixty to seventy days before a local farmer finally shot it. My first experience with this beautiful, but deadly cat was a real hair-raiser.

On a beautiful spring evening, after just finishing my proud carpenter work on our new rabbit hutches that I over built as usual, I used two by fours nailed to four by four posts set in concrete and nailed to our hen house. Then I floored the hutches with half inch wielded wire, trimmed again with two by fours. I headed to the back door of our house to enter and have supper, but stopped to listen as the dogs on the south side of Clarksville had suddenly set up an awful howl, which I could tell was slowly advancing northerly up the creek that runs completely through the town. It was obvious that what ever they were tracking on the creek was coming straight toward our location on the old Texas trail. I was hungry and supper was ready, so I decided to go on in the house, but I noticed as I stepped over him, our dog was cowering deep under the back steps and when I called him, he whined and would not come out. The dog had evidently sniffed something in the wind, which I could not detect.

What ever the dogs south of us were getting as scent they sure were not catching up to, or were not making the effort to catch, as you could hear by the sound of their barks the chase was proceeding closer and closer to our house and had been going on for over thirty minutes. Just after dark we all turned in for the night and had turned out all the house lights when we heard the darndest loud den coming from the hen house and newly built rabbit hutches which contained nine young rabbits we had placed in them. It sounded like something was tearing the hutches away from the hen house, or at the very least trying to.

Bret and the twins got out of bed at the same time I did and we rushed outside just in time to see a huge panther sitting on top of the eight-foot high hen house and the frightened chickens and rabbits scurrying hap-hazardly around their pen and cages. I told the boys to get back inside the back door, but to keep an eye on the big cat, while I went to get my hunting rifle. By the time I got my gun, loaded it and returned, the boys had watched the panther jump down and slink off across the street north of our house into the neighbor's yard that also contained now crazed chickens that were raising a hell of a ruckus. The night was pretty dark by now and I was just as scared of being attacked by the animal as the chickens were, as I could not be sure it was not waiting for me across the street so I had the boys, who now had a big flashlight, to shine it over toward the neighbors' chicken pen. However the cat was not in plain sight and the chickens were settling down, so we figured the cat had moved on, as it had seen us and would not want to have a confrontation with humans. We had a big old fashioned light on the hen house so we turned it on figuring to keep the cat away, then we all went back inside and returned to our beds.

About three hours later Carla, whose upstairs bedroom was a perfect vantage point from which to view the hen house, came running into our bedroom across the hall saying loudly, "Daddy it's back, the panther is out there, I saw it in the light and it is trying to eat the little rabbits". I grabbed my loaded rifle, which I had left close by the door in my room and ran downstairs to the back door, but the cat had already had its supper and the wielded wire on the cages was torn and ripped where the panther had made entry into the rabbit hutches. I hoped to get at least one shot at the devil, but he must have heard me coming, as he had disappeared when I opened the back door to shoot.

The next day I told the principal and superintendent about our night's wild experience, but I could tell they thought I was lying and making up this story. It was hard to believe that such a thing could happen in the middle of town, with so many people around. So that was the last time I told anyone downtown about the big cat, but for the next thirty days, until an area farmer finally killed it, our whole household took turns watching for the cat to come back, which it did four or five times, but we never got a shot at it, the panther was just to smart for us and although it ate the feet off all our little rabbits, by getting below their cages and we had to butcher them. It never tore the cages off the hen house.

Dennis and David had two bicycles apiece and Carla and Tonya each had one, but as sometimes happens they all were in poor working condition with either flats or some small needed repairs. They came to me requesting I find a bike repair shop to fix all the children's bicycles. When I agreed to get these bikes fixed, I did not know there was no repair shop in this area. When I discovered that this was the case, I told the twins they would have to fix their own bikes, which they immediately set out to accomplish. They tore apart one of the oldest bikes and using the parts from it and by ordering new parts from the manufacturer they soon had bikes for the kids in our family running in good shape. When the kids in town saw our twins riding their bikes and found out that they had repaired them, they asked the boys to repair their bikes. Within two weeks our yard was full of bikes, it seemed every kid in town wanted to get their bikes repaired and Dennis and David had a thriving new business, which they aptly named <u>D & D Bike Shop,</u> and hung a big painted sign from a large overhanging limb in the grafted pecan tree at the front of our driveway.

For the next six years the twins kept the bike shop in operation, moving it in 1975, lock, stock and frame to Seminole, Oklahoma where it helped them earn money to finish their college associates degree.

The spring of 1974 was also the spring that Tonya and her mother decided to clean Tonya's closet in her bedroom. Tonya was known to take all kinds of sweets to her room. Since she was the youngest child in the family and a lot of the time played by herself due to the large difference in our kid's ages, she would play in her room and snacks were a large part of the games she played. When she had any of these snacks left over, she just tossed them into the bottom of her closet and seldom cleaned the closet thoroughly, as she was only six and really did not understand the importance of cleanliness. Shirley was helping Tonya clean her room and happened to see the mess in her closet. So, she insisted above Tonya's protest, that together they would give the closet a through cleaning. When they opened the closet door and began to move the debris mice came out of the closet in every direction and Tonya jumped up on her bed yelling and screaming so loud the whole family heard her and came running. The rest of the morning was spent turning over toys, finding mice and batting them with tennis racquets. When we finally got the place cleaned and mice tallied there were more than sixteen dead mice and I am sure we did not get them all. Tonya was finished eating in her room, as Shirley was not having any more mice problems in the upstairs bedrooms.

Carla had a great senior year, she made Texas all state on her flute, got the lead, Eliza Doolittle part in an outstanding high school production of My Fair Lady, was in the twirling corp. and made great grades which allowed her to get a fine scholarship to Southeastern Oklahoma State University.

She also found time to enjoy some fine friends, who have been her friends for many years since, while she received payment for caring for and running the family home, while babysitting part of the summer with Tonya? Carla also got her first taste of the working world, as she blistered her feet, worried about her performance, and tried to please her boss, while working eight hours daily at the School Book Depository for Mr. Schneider, a family friend.

*Carla, Dennis, David, 1975* — *Carla, as Eliza* — *David in center as Doolittle.* — *Carla learning her vowels*

*Left: Dennis and David and Carla doing their nightly homework. Right: Tonya looking on while they do their homework.*

### Boy, I Need to Teach in College Again0.1

David and Dennis also made all region and all state, their sophomore years and all region their freshmen years, and David

performed admirably as Doolittle in My Fair Lady, while Dennis dazzled veryone performing in the orchestra. Carla, Dennis, and David had very active social lives, of which it took a very active father to stay abreast. Sometimes

*My Fair Lady orchestra with Carroll E. Redwine conducting, Dennis L. Redwine is 4th from top left performing first trumpet parts*

having to intervene, much to their chagrin, between them and their altogether too aggressive boy and girl friends.

When Carla graduated, it suddenly occurred to me, my little girl, with whom I had been enjoying life together for the past seventeen years, was about to leave home, and it left an empty spot in my heart that never again would be the same. Only when you experience this trauma can you know its true depth of meaning. I had to move on and I did, but that was one reason I left Clarksville. I had to have a new direction and new experiences to cover this hole in my life. So when my brother Philip called to ask if I would like to again teach at the college level, I jumped at the opportunity to be on the faculty at Seminole Junior College.

Philip was good friends with Jack Mattingly an attorney in Seminole, who was serving on the board of directors for Seminole Junior college, Jack had been Phil's law school classmate at The

University of Oklahoma, some years before and was aware I wanted to return to teaching at the college level. So, when Elmer Tanner, SJC's President who had recently contracted to start construction on S J C 's new music building, told the board he was ready to hire a music department chairman to develop a music school for the fall 1974 semester, Jack called Philip and relayed the information, but Jack also told Phil I should move on this quickly if I was interested, as Tanner had someone else in mind for the job.

*Carla Rene Redwine-Clarksville High -1975*

I called Mr. Tanner that day and he was kind enough to ask for my resume' which I immediately updated and put in the mail to him. I called Elmer on the following Monday to see if he had received my résumé and he said, "I got it today can you come up tomorrow for an interview"? Elmer was not one to mince words and moved swiftly on all matters, especially those that affected his personnel, or teaching faculty. I told Mr. Tanner, I could be in his office anytime after eight am and he agreed to see me at ten am Tuesday. I was early to the appointment and Elmer was there, so the secretary ushered me into see him and I could tell he was a bit frustrated about hiring me, and figured it had something to do with Mattingly calling me after Tanner announced to the board he was looking for a music person and had someone in mind for the job. Mr. Tanner gave me a tour of the school, proudly pointed to the large excavation, partially filled with concrete that was located where the music building was to be and laughed as he said, "That is your future office". We returned to his office where he offered me the position, but three thousand dollars below my current salary at Clarksville, as my resume' revealed. Then he bluntly told me, "Take it or leave it, I need to know by tomorrow, as I want to get this person on board and get the curricula set before we print the fall catalog and whom ever I hire will need to recruit a band and choir this summer".

I am sure that his intent was to make the position appear so undesirable that I would skip happily out of his office and scurry back to Texas, but what he did not know, was that I did not want to go back there at any cost and I also knew that he was getting his teachers a three thousand dollar raise, which would go into effect in January of 1975. And I could expect to receive the raise, as I would have been on his faculty for two sessions by that time. I did not feel it would be in my favor to give him an immediate answer, even though I was ready to do so and asked him for a day or two, so that I might visit with my wife about the move. He agreed to give me twenty-four hours! Generous gentleman, was he not? I called him the next afternoon and took the job, which required another trip to SJC the following day to sign the contracts and look around for some rental property in which my family could live, as we had no prospects at all of selling our Clarksville house.

We searched diligently throughout the Seminole area, but the only housing we could find was a small three bedroom brick in Tecumseh, Oklahoma that was a fifteen minute commute to SJC and a bit longer each day to Seminole High School where the twins would be attending their Junior year. Tonya would be attending, at least for the first semester, second grade in Tecumseh. Shirley looked around for a job in Seminole, but could not find anything suitable, so she went to work at the Goodyear tire store in Shawnee, Oklahoma. The next five months nearly caused us to get a divorce, at least that was as close as we ever came to one as our family was going in every direction, but living together, in a five room house with twelve rooms of furniture stacked inside. Bret had a mattress to sleep on we kept under Dennis and David's bed and pulled it out each night after the twins got in bed for Bret. Tonya and Carla shared a small bedroom that was so crowded the wall- paper had no room to hang. With only one bathroom we had to schedule it on paper, so that everyone could get ready each day for the scattering of the family to each of their destinations, and after I told Bret he could not tie up the bathroom for so long, he then insisted on washing his curly locks daily, he did so each and everyday in the kitchen sink, dirty dishes and all.

Sundays still found us all in the choir that I was directing at the First Christian Church in Seminole and that church attendance probably saved our marriage, as in January the church board, who knew we were commuting each day, insisted we move into the vacant church parsonage in Seminole. We now had seven rooms! Bret found an apartment so he could have more privacy and with the den, which we turned into another bedroom, we now had four bedroom areas. We lived in this house for five years until the church board decided to sell it and we bought a fine new home in North Seminole where we lived until 1981, when we moved back to Broken Bow. But, that is a long time and a lot of good stories later, lets get back to fall 1974.

Carla was attending Southeastern Oklahoma State University

and came home only on Thanksgiving and Christmas, as she had to sleep with Tonya when she did. I hated the fact that she was in such a position and tried to send her a check each month of three hundred and fifty dollars so she would have the things she needed. I only visited her three times that year in Durant and although I was unhappy about it, I was not surprised on one of these visits to find her living with Mark Reasoner in a small house off campus, knowing a number of young men his age and how they responded to their responsibilities, I now knew why Carla never had enough money, and was working every spare minute she could find to make enough income to support both of them.

One of the reasons we could not purchase a home in these lean years was the realtor in Clarksville was trying to get that home for a dime on the dollar. He figured and rightly so, that we could not continue to pay rent in Seminole and house payments in Clarksville and if he was patient, we would forfeit and he would get our home in Texas. He was correct and he did, we finally, after over a year of suffering through month after month of scrimping and saving to pay for that house, had to let it go for what we owed on it and the realtor bought it from the bank. We lost over twenty five thousand dollars in that little transaction and learned that for every Mr. Dillon that exists, there are two villains like the Clarksville realtor lurking in the shadows.

In the spring of 1975 The Seminole Lions Club invited me to become a member and I did. It was one of the best things I did while in Seminole, other than being youth director and choir director at The First Christian Church. My father had been an outstanding Lion member in Pawhuska and I know it must have given him many hours of pleasure to be able to return to the people of his community some of the many good deeds others had provided him. Over the next six years from 1975 to 1981 I held every elected office the Seminole club had and proudly, was unexpectedly selected as the outstanding Seminole Lion in 1979, twenty years exactly after dad had received the same honor from his fellow Pawhuska Lion Club Members. A couple of the activities I was able to help with while a lion member was the annual city wide Halloween carnival, which I chaired and organized for two years, from which we helped raise over ten thousand dollars; and an Oklahoma state wide telethon, which I was able to chair for the Oklahoma State Lions Association in conjunction with channel 52 in Oklahoma City, and for which my college band was the studio band. We backed up such soloists as Candice Bergen and others, generating over fifty thousand dollars in contributions. Both functions raised funds for the Dean A. McGee Eye Institute in Oklahoma City, which Oklahoma Lions annually support.

My position as head of the music department at SJC automatically made me a community leader in the allied arts. I was expected to organize and conduct every parade except the high school Homecoming and football pep parades and to organize or at least advise the organizers on every big name entertainment that came to town. So, I started an annual fall recital series that brought in some very exciting performers, many of which I had to billet in my home, as funds were pretty tight.

1975 was a very exciting year for a number of reasons, two of those were, David and Dennis were new in this area and were very advanced performers for their age. When the All District Band auditions were held at Eastern Oklahoma State University, David threw the judges a curve and auditioned on Bb Clarinet, Alto Clarinet, Bass Clarinet, Alto Saxophone, Tenor Saxophone, and Baritone Saxophone. Worse yet he made first chair on all these instruments.

When the auditions were finished, the judges, who had auditioned the contestants from behind a blind, were surprised to find David's name at the head of every one of those sections. They put their heads together and recalled David to have him declare, in which section he would prefer to perform, then they immediately wrote a new contest rule that stated all contestants would in the future be expected to only audition for one position in the All District Band. Dennis made first chair trumpet in the same auditions and both boys auditioned and were accepted into the Oklahoma All State Band, a feat they also accomplished the following year.

David's senior year was nearly ruined by his very capable, but head strong high school band teacher, who demanded he meet regularly after school and perform simple studies with his peers whose Clarinet techniques were very much below David's in order to earn his grades in band. Dave did not see any reason to do this and got a D on his report card for not completing these elementary assignments, this near tragedy occurred the same term he made the All State Band. It took some real maneuvering with the school counselor to get that straightened out, but they graduated at the top of their class from Seminole High School. In addition to performing with their school band, they performed regularly with my college band.

By the fall of 1978 the SJC music department was really cooking, we had a very capable faculty that included Denny Wade, who taught low brass and electric bass, Brian Alexander, who taught private guitar and electric bass. Mrs. Ross a full time keyboard instructor, who also taught advanced music theory, Mr. Bell, a twirling instructor and myself who taught Band, Private brass and Woodwinds, Music Theory 1 and 2, and Choir, with the aid of a wonderful accompanist, Mrs. Tense Dees. Our little Band of thirty instrumentalists marched two Marde'Gra Parades, in New Orleans, a Sun Bowl parade in San Antonio, and the 89er Day's Parade in Guthrie, Oklahoma, in addition to playing festivals at Prague every year and many dances on and off campus. We performed a major Broadway musical annually with the band accompanying the College Choir, and marched downtown parades on dates the students were in town. We also performed at least two concerts each semester and at every home basketball game, even one or two baseball games. Seminole currently had really great nationally rated baseball teams.

There were many fine people who performed with me during those seven and a half years I taught at SJC and I do not have room to list them all or mention all their stories, which were considerably interesting, but I feel I must mention some of the persons who definitely had an impact on my later life.

There was Carol Reeves, a beautiful and highly talented young lady who traveled side by side with others and me in my pick up truck two or three nights per week and who could belt out a song that anyone would enjoy. Carol performed with Dennis and David for nearly eighteen months in a highly successful group called the Wine Dots Band, then studied and graduated as a nurse.

Three fellows I could not forget due to our long and friendly association, which began at SJC, were Roger Coble a kind and talented song- writer, presently living in Ruidoso, New Mexico,

318

who played excellent guitar, and performed, as a crowd pleasing, featured vocalist with the Wine Dots for over three years. Roger was responsible for recruiting Joe Haynes into the Wine Dots. Although Joe never attended SJC; he performed with us for over four years. Joe was a fine electric bass and solo Rock guitarist; he presently has a highly successful dental practice in Tulsa, Oklahoma. Bronson Hopper, from Okmulgee, Oklahoma was a very talented young man I recruited to perform on guitar, and we became good friends, he got married while in the group and resides in Okmulgee.

Then there was A. J. Ferron, trumpet player deluxe, extremely close friend and country music singer, with a new Jersey accent, who came in to study with me on trumpet, in the fall of 1977, but told me in no uncertain terms he did not want me messing with his embouchure. After I heard him play I understood why. He had a gorgeous tone, a tooth problem that forced him to play off to the right side of his lip and had learned to compensate well for this problem. I fully agreed with A. J. **Do not create a problem where none exists**. We have been the closest of friends; he even lived a short time in my home. I attended his grand-father's funeral, worried about him when he enlisted and again when was flying all over the world for the US Air Force, attended his Air force Retirement ceremony, eagerly looked on over the years, as he and his lovely wife Elizabeth have raised their three wonderful children, Nicole, Ashley, and little Joey. Best of all, I was privileged to perform night after night after night for nearly twenty years with him standing immediately next to me playing that wonderful trumpet and helping me create a delightful solo or back-up line for the vocals or instrumentals we were performing. What a gift he has, and what a generous, kind, positive attitude. Only someone who has had the extreme privilege to enjoy A. J. 's pleasant personality can know what a friend he can be.

In the fall of 1977 the college board, under the recommendation of Mr. Tanner, granted me tenure; this was a big deal, as only ten instructors out of the nearly sixty who were on the faculty at that time were so honored and meant that other than moral terpretude, which must be proven in a court of law, the institution would have to find a position for me as long as the school was open.

In the spring of 1977, I decided to purchase forty acres of land located in the northeast corner of Seminole County very near the Hughes County border, I spent a great deal of time on this place as it was really secluded and quiet. It was so isolated; it was necessary to build a road to it, before it could be developed. After the road was finished we hired the same heavy equipment operator to build a beautiful three-acre lake in the southeast corner of

*A. J. Ferron and us 1989*

*L to R –A. J. Ferron, trp. C. E. Redwine, sax.*
*Tonya Redwine, -singing-w-Earl Lemons, on bass*
*all performing –with- Red Red Wine band 1989*

the property and then stocked it with two hundred channel catfish, three hundred black bass, and one thousand-hybrid bluegill. In the winter of 1977,

I obtained one thousand fast growing pine trees from the Weyhouser Company and planted them on the area around the lake, but in the fall of the following year, 1978 a prairie fire destroyed most of these trees. I also planted fifty fruit trees of assorted varieties in an area just north of the lake in march of 1978, but one of my brazen neighbors made a midnight requisition of my newly planted orchard and dug every one of them up and hauled them away while I was teaching classes one day in town. I searched the area farms, but never found any trace of them. I did find one of my nicest pine trees newly planted in the front yard of one of my neighbors, but after I pulled my old pick-up nearly to his front door jumped out with my deer rifle, knocked on his front door and as he came out threw a shell into the chamber of my gun, he sheepishly admitted to stealing it and offered to replant it back on my property. I told him to keep the tree, as it would probably die due to the manner in which it had been dug up. However, if I ever saw him on my place again, he would be a dead man and I meant every word I said! To slow this stealing, I drove ten-penny nails through a two by four and buried the board, nails sticking skyward, in a small trench I dug across the only access into the property, my lane. Then, I disguised the tire trap by covering it with loose sand. About three days later, I went back out to my property to discover that someone had ruined three tires on this devise and after changing then, had left them lying by the road. Ah-------Sweet JUSTICE! Or atleast REVENGE!

When I sold this farm in 1981 to use the profits from it to build my restaurant in Broken Bow, the catfish weighed over four pounds each and the few pines that survived were quite tall and pretty.

So, in 1979 all this activity finally caught up with me and one

Sunday morning, as the preacher was giving his long and extended alter call, I rose from my chair to lead the congregation in the final hymn, the next thing I knew there I was lying on my back, on the floor of the sanctuary viewing two paramedics through a misty haze, who were pounding on my chest and yelling to me to wake up. When the physician at the Seminole Hospital visited with me the next day, he told me I was obviously under great stress and if I did not want to have a stroke, or worse die from a heart attack, I had better decide immediately what I was no longer going to be doing. Then he asked me to make a list of the things I was involved in and he would go over it with me that afternoon. When he saw the myriad of things I was doing, he could not believe it, and said, "Most folks would crumble under the weight of any three of the items". At that time I was: running the SJC music department, teaching full time, performing one nighters all over Oklahoma at least two and sometimes three nights per week, building my farm, directing the church choir, directing the church youth programs, coaching Tonya's little league softball team, President of the local Lions Club, landscaping my new home, and working with the chamber of commerce in Seminole to promote the parades they were having. Usually I ended up organizing them and guiding them down the street.

At the same time all this is going on David and Dennis are running their bicycle repair and sales shop located on south main street in downtown Seminole and Shirley was director of the Senior Citizens programs in Seminole and Hughes Counties, she had sixty employees and a million dollar annual budget and was responsible for keeping ten sites scattered throughout these two counties, which she developed from the ground up, in full operation.

*From Left -Carroll Redwine, left back-Dennis Redwine, in red blouse-Tonya Redwine, middle white dress-Gina Maxwell, the Graduate- David L. Redwine, holding baby David Aaron Redwine is Shirley Redwine and standing in front-three years old –Kristie Kay Maxwell*

*Carla Rene Redwine Reasoner, "center and husband Mark Reasoner "left" greeting guests at their1974 wedding reception*

Carla Redwine in 1973 left and right

In order to hire the staff she wanted without political interference from the local incumbent state representative, she solicited a young Okema lawyer, Glen Johnson, to run for the office and got her senior citizens in the two counties tohelp elect him. Eventually Glen was elected Speaker of the Oklahoma House of Representatives and is currently President of Southeastern Oklahoma State University in Durant, Oklahoma

Shirley moved to this directors position in the late summer of 1975 from her six month tenure at the Seminole Chamber of Commerce where she was one of the two secretaries to Bob Jones, one of Seminole's most note worthy Chamber Managers. The other secretary and a good friend of both Shirley and me was Mary Jo Stewart, sister of the great song- writer Woody Guthrie of Okemah, Oklahoma and Southern California.

Mary Jo was a frequent guest speaker in my Music appreciation classes at SJC; she was always well received by the students, as she related stories about her childhood with Woody.

1979 was a very eventful year, as Carla graduated from Southeastern, in the spring with her teaching degree in English and drama. She had her beautiful wedding to Mark in June at the First Christian Church in Seminole and accepted a teaching position at Ardmore High School where she would spend the next twenty years building a fine drama department starting with twelve beginning students in the fall of 79 and building to over six sections and two hundred fifty students in her drama classes by 2005. She did all this without an auditorium on her campus. There is no telling what she would have accomplished if the administrators had provided the financial help and incentive her program obviously deserved.

David met Gina that year and after a short court ship, they began living together. Gina had been previously married to a fellow named Maxwell, a soldier, who had tried unsuccessfully to kill her and her new- born daughter, Kristie Kay, Maxwell. When she escaped, accompanied by Kristie from their army camp home, where the attempt on her life failed, her mentally ill military husband took his own life. My oldest Grandson David Aaron Redwine was born to Gina and David during the next year at the hospital in Shawnee, Oklahoma on April tenth, 1980.

Aaron, a fine looking and very talented young man, lives in Dallas, and at the age of twenty five still supports his mother, who can not seem to get her life on tract no matter what he does for her.

In May of 1980, David Graduated from SJC where he had tested out of many advanced courses while attending high school in Seminole. He completed enough college credit hours for two or three degrees, but graduated with an associate of science in electronics where he spent many hours developing his computer skills. David originally entered SJC as a music major, but due to a very talented instructor whom he grew to admire and respect plus the fact that the world economy was moving in this direction, he and Dennis both changed their course of study.

David had prepared himself well in the electronics field and applied for a position at the Will Rogers international Airport in Oklahoma City, keeping up the computers for the FFA Center and moved his little family first to an apartment on Northwest hi-way in OKC, then to a nice brick home in Northeast Norman, Oklahoma, then on to a brick home just off twelfth street in downtown Moore, Oklahoma, where he and his family resided until their move to Dallas some four years later.

Dennis finished three semesters of classes at SJC and dropped out of school to support himself as he wanted the privacy of his own apartment which he would soon share with his close friend David Neal and Neal's coat eating puppy. He worked for the Bob Davis Appliance store repairing stoves, refrigerators, televisions

*L to R –back row –Shirley Redwine, –holding baby -David Aaron Redwine, graduate- Dennis L. Redwine, Gina Maxwell, "Granny" Esther Miller, and leaning to his right- David L. Redwine, just right of Shirley- Tonya M. Redwine and middle front is- Kristie Kay Maxwell*

and anything electronic. Dennis had been employed for a short timeat the Walls Store in Seminole while he was in high school, so he had a bit of experience and his employers including his mother who employed him at her office at the Seminole Senior Citizens Center hauling hot meals to the elderly found him a hard worker and dependable. Dennis moved to Houston Texas shortly after his graduation to take a position with the Hullet Packard Corporation as a computer tech and was sorely missed by the family. A good item did come of this move, as he met and eventually married Katherine Erenzo while living in Houston, something that might not have occurred had Dennis not gone to work there.

One of the most important things that occurred during these seven and a half years was that we as a family were fortunate to be able to spend a great deal of time with Shirley's Mother, who was also my kind Mother-in- Law. Granny Esther, came jauntily walking into Shirley's Goodyear office one mid-morning, about eight weeks after most of us in the family, thought she would not survive the night in her Collinsville, Oklahoma hospital bed. Granny was transferred to Saint Francis Hospital in Tulsa in a frantic rush to obtain better care than Collinsville had available.

The doctors at Saint Francis, determined she had a serious cancer in her abdomen and decided to treat it with an experimental procedure that required a Radium pill be placed inside her stomach, but they were not aware that the radium would eat up the potassium content in her blood and this nearly killed her, before they realized her need for large doses of potassium.

The last time I saw her in the Collinsville facility, I was convinced she would not live until the following morning, but about eight weeks later she came to stay with us in the Seminole parsonage. Granny soon got her own apartment in Seminole and a bit later moved into Senior Citizens housing in east Seminole. The radium implant gave her a few more years of life, but eventually the scar tissue from it, a very week heart, and a serious bout with diabetes caused her to lose her gangrenous leg and this ultimately led to a terribly tragic loss of will and her final demise. Esther Mae- Van Berg- Smith- Miller was born September 8th, 1917, and passed August 24th, 1982.

To give the reader an idea of how responsible Esther truly was, you should be aware, Esther was not eligible to receive social security benefits of any type and the day of her death, she reminded Shirley to be sure and look in her washing machine, as she had saved a few dollars out of each state check to help with her final expenses. To our surprise, when we gathered the family together to move Esther's belongings out of her apartment, we discovered

*Left-Granny Esther and Shirley dressed for cowboy days at Shirley's Senior Citizen's office and program- Right, Granny Esther at the Seminole Farm. both pictures taken fall 1980*

she had saved two thousand two hundred dollars out of her very meager state income. Shirley was speaking eloquently for the whole family, when Esther, with her final earthly breath, weakly whispered, " Goodbye, I love you", and Shirley sadly, but proudly invoked God's blessing, as she prayed," Dear God we are sending you a beautiful flower for your garden, please accept my sweet mother". We sat quietly for some time, as Granny Esther's nurse kindly told Shirley,"

There would be no need to hurry our departure from Granny's Shawnee, Oklahoma hospital room".

Shirley's loving mother now rests in the northeast end of the

*Left; Tonya M. Redwine rifle twirler pictured in front of her new house in north seminole*

*Right: Esther Mae Smith Miller1981*

*1981Seminole High School Color Guard—Tonya in last row center Piper Mills is Drum Major front and center*

Little Cemetery. This cemetery is located at the Corners of hi-way 9and 9A in. Seminole County OklahomaGranny Esther took care of Tonya often, even after she moved from our home into her own apartment, so it seems fitting to address a few of Tonya's Seminole experiences at this time. Tonya was a very happy grade schooler during these Seminole years and in addition to playing organized softball every spring and summer, she worked hard to win many medals in swimming, as well as in her solo performances on oboe, clarinet, and saxophone. When she took up flag twirling in the eight grade, she did so ferverently and became the best rifle twirler and flag girl in her school for which, we thought the local band teacher, rewarded her, by making her captain of the high School Band's Color Guard. Truthfully, he had no control over these young ladies as the judges he hired to audition and select his squad determined that Tonya should be captain of the color guard and he was hoping Tonya would be able to corral these little primo-donnas. Tonya spent many hours working with the other Guard Members trying to make a cohesive ensemble of them, but to no avail, as they just were to lazy and inept. If her band director had backed her when they rebelled the first time, the group would have eventually come together. Instead he browbeat Tonya in front of the color guard, saying the girls looked bad and it was Tonya's fault, as she was in charge and should have gotten the team to respond, this gave the other girls all the ammunition they needed to blame Tonya for their shortcomings and created an impossible situation, which there was no way in the future for Tonya as a leader to overcome. So, at the Band's Homecoming football game performance, Tonya as captain told the group to wear a particular costume and the girls got together privately and deliberately changed to the opposite color. This action was meant to embarrass Tonya, who they supposed would be the only one in the off color uniform, but Tonya a true leader, smelled a rat, so she had taken both uniforms to the performance, and waited until just before going on the field at half time to change, there-by ruining the little snipes plans to embarrass her. After the half time show Tonya told Herb the whole story and he accused her of making up the story to embarrass the other girls, so Tonya gave him the band hat he had issued her to use during the performance and told him to put it where the sun did not shine! That was the end of Tonya's illustrious band career in Seminole.

# Broken Bow and the fulfilling of a lifelong Dream

The next week Seminole High School had an open date on their football schedule, so on Thursday evening when Shirley got off work I fixed supper and, as we were eating; I suggested Tonya, Shirley, and myself treat ourselves to a week-end in Broken Bow, as Tonya had not really had much of a chance to get away from Seminole for some time. We left Seminole as soon as Tonya got out of school on Friday afternoon and pulled into Broken Bow just in time to catch the kick

*Carla R. Redwine Reasoner @ ages 13, 17, 28, & 39*

off of the Savages home football game. All our old friends were there and we had a great visit during and after the game at the parties held in the gracious and generous homes of these long missed friends. As usual our football team won, but we did notice the band was terrible and nothing like the Savage Bands of past memory. Tonya had a wonderful weekend getting acquainted with and visiting the many fine young folks in the immediate families we visited. On the way home, I asked, Shirley and Tonya what they thought about moving to Broken Bow and starting a fine dinning restaurant, this idea was not to much off our flight path, as we had been looking to open such a restaurant in Seminole, but as yet, had not found a satisfactory location. They both said they were ready to make the move, as they really enjoyed this weekend with the Broken Bow people and would like to live and work there. So, a new business is going to be researched, building planned and built, menu planned and printed, employees hired and trained, Home and farm advertised and sold, new housing acquired, family and belongings moved, jobs and schools, either quit, retired from or transferred to. Its time to change our course, and fly higher and farther than ever before, and the next eight years are going to be spectacular, because we were going to make them so! We spent many hours, days, and weeks researching how to build, operate, and manage a fine dining restaurant. Then thousands of dollars pursuing and purchasing the equipment, antiques, and beautiful amenities for it that we stored on the fully covered and enclosed back patio of our large, comfortable, and efficient rented home located in the Ross acres sub-division of Broken Bow. A. J. Ferron and Tonya'sgood friend Ronald Stiffler of Seminole helped us move our belongings from Seminole to Broken Bow and A. J. continued to live with us for some five months, as we had a large home and he originally planned to manage the restaurant when we got it up and running. But, after about five months he decided to enlist in the Air Force instead, as he wanted to marry Elizabeth and needed more income than we could afford to pay him at that time. A. J. also was getting tired of his high-speed trips almost daily to Shawnee and back to see Elizabeth and especially the problems he was having out running the cops on this route that normally took three hours and he was accomplishing in less than one and a half hours each way in his highly visible black Trans-

Am with red and orange flames painted on the hood and above the front finders. The cop in the little town of Rattan patrolled his towns Main Street beat that included about two miles of Oklahoma State highways three and seven in an old ford pick-up with a red light and siren mounted on top. A. J. told me that the first time he sped through Rattan was about six am and he passed the cop doing one hundred, and ten miles per hour on his way to Shawnee, the cop turned on his red light and spun gravel, as he tried to stop J. 's flight, but A. J. was over the hill west of Rattan before the town cop could even get to the first block off main, later that same day A. J. came through Rattan on his return to Broken Bow and expected to have real trouble with this fellow, so he slowed down to about eighty . As he passed the place where the cop usually sat in his pick-up, A. J.looked over to see the cop leisurely puffing a cigarette and waving goodbye to the black streaking Trans-am. That's what I call picking your battles!

Ferron was not always so lucky, as on one of his many such speedy trips an Oklahoma State trooper got after him and he had to drive all the way to DeQueen, Arkansas and hide out for over a half a day before he could return to our house. Finding a location for our restaurant venture was not easy. It seemed that every-time we found a suitable location it was either not available or leased to someone else. Eventually, we found an old farm house that was located on US 259 north of the city limits and adjacent to the federal forestry offices that was ideal, as it was on the way to Broken Bow lake and Beavers Bend State Park, but the owners were deceased and the property was in probate, so we could not lease it and had to purchase it, which used more of our capital than we truly wanted to use for obtaining a location. We gutted the original structure and used every bit of the materials from the building to restructure our restaurant and club, and if I do say so we created a useful and beautiful facility. Shirley designed the sign drew it on the front wall of the building and painted it. As you can see it was really quite nice. We opened the restaurant and began selling Club memberships in November of 1983, after hiring a staff of seventeen persons that we spent three weeks training in food

preparation, table service, health and food sanitation and customer relations. I designed, built, and painted the sign you see left with our nationally registered **Redwine's Hickory Inn** *cloud trademark.* We had a dry run two nights previous to the opening night to which we invited fifty of the county's most prominent personages, and served them each their choice of a free dinner; off what would soon become our highly popular menu. The evening was filled with fine foods and wonderful entertainment and was a huge success as most of these same guests became paying customers sometimes forced to stand in long lines of forty and fifty persons to enter the restaurant on the following weeks and the second year we were in business, I found that our unusually fine service was drawing large wedding receptions and that we needed to accommodate them. So, I searched the area for a creek bed that had lots of easily accessible flat rocks out of which I could build a twenty- foot by forty- foot patio in the early fall before the fall rains came. I was fortunate to find just such a quarry of beautiful black, pink and some reddish black slate that luckily no one had removed. I took my old Chevy pick-up and working daily from sun-up until about noon each day when I had to

*Chopping up some Ribs, um good!*

*Carroll and Shirley Relaxing and enjoying the beautiful park like setting of the grounds around Redwine's*

prep the restaurant's kitchen. I used a long steel bar to pry them apart and generally uncover them and some two inch oil field tubing to roll them to my truck that I took as close to the dry creek bed, as it's banks would allow, then rolled them carefully up into the pick-up bed. It was quite an operation, but the result was well worth the effort, as I leveled them in sand and brushed them with concrete between their cracks. The whole project took me from September to Christmas to finish. That spring I had Kenneth Mays, one of my former band students and a good friend, build a twenty two- foot by forty- foot three level deck in the yard, not far from the patio which was just out of the kitchen door and waitress friendly. Then I wired the whole yard area with soft colored lighting and the deck with hidden outlets for steam tables and sound systems. It was quite a project and the first night we opened it, in addition to dinner, our guests danced on the

*James D. Redwine and wife Gina enjoying some fine bar-b- q ribs on the fourth of July at Redwines*

deck to the music of David Redwine and the Wine Dot Band. We served over seven hundred paying guests, one hundred fifty inside, the rest outside, where I set up a special outdoor cooking operation, but we had to have almost the whole Redwine family to handle the crowd. Even my lovely mother came to help, so we put her to work as cashier and security person and she caught a woman stealing the table- ware in a large handbag. I was so tired I called a friend to go quail hunting, but he said his dog's feet were sore and we would need to borrow a dog from the farmer on whose land we usually hunted. I told him the only dog that farmer owned was an old bulldog and bulldogs do not hunt birds. ( *by now you should recognize this is a joke.*)

My friend assured me that this dog was really good and he would

*Redwine's fully functioning bar in the shape of a grand piano*

prove it when we got to the farm. I did not believe it, but not wanting to call my friend a liar, I agreed to go out to the farm and let him show me this wonder dog. When we arrived the farmer agreed to loan us the old bulldog and even said he would accompany us while the dog did his thing. He whistled to the lazy old dog that was lying in a hole it had dug in the yard, and the dog lazily got up shook itself and ambled over close to the farmer, stopping to pea on the large tree under which it had been resting, yawned and moved slowly toward the barn gate, which was only yards from the farmhouse. The farmer said, "put a shell in your gun and get ready to shoot when I open this gate." Amazingly we killed six birds, then walked to where the old dog was on point to find he had run all those birds into a gopher hole and was letting them out with his paw, one at a time. How's your leg? The downstairs tables in the bar were highly prized as they allowed for alcoholic drinks to be consumed and no children to be present-The bright light in the top left is a reflection of a table lamp in the mirrors that surrounded the corner table.

The sign on the front of our restaurant was drawn free hand on butcher paper by Shirley and after transferring the stencil to the front of the forty-foot long wall, I helped her paint it, the family did almost

*L= Carla and Tonya with Security Jane Mannequin in center—Jane was placed in window every night to prevent theft R=most folks favorite table for two*

all this type of decorating, and designing of the business including the hanging of the very unusual news-print wall-paper by Tonya and her

*Carroll and his daughters having dinner in the bar at Redwine's*

friend Julie Byrd. I personally designed a wood-burning grill and had a local welder fabricate it out of one-eighth inch metal sheeting. Steaks and Chops seasoned with a secret blend of herbs and spices and cooked on this grill, which used hickory chips and oak charcoal, were especially tasty and could be found in no other restaurant. Old family recipes were used to develop our menu that was rated by an Oklahoma magazine as four- star, and the restaurant was highly recommended. After a surprise visit by the State of Oklahoma Magazine Outdoor Oklahoma, as recognized in it's

*Redwine's Hickory Inn Guests favorite Table for 3*

October issue that year, Redwine's, was the number one restaurant recommended by the Chambers of commerce in both Idabel and Broken Bow. We had Guests who flew into the Broken Bow and Idabel airports from Shreveport Louisiana, Dallas Texas and Spokane, Washington on a regular basis who ate with us. Dennis Redwine spent at least one week of his spring vacation every year for the duration of the business, helping to reconfigure the Restaurant's kitchen and processes and was a major factor in it's continued success. Many times our beautiful daughter- in law and Denny's wife Katherine, our "Kathy", helped also.

Tonya entered her sophomore year of high school at the Broken Bow Schools, and as a Redwine is expected too, she enrolled in the Band program. However about three weeks into the fall semester, I noticed she was not taking her clarinet to class and was leaving it home on her dresser each day. I figured since she was a twirler that maybe she was not participating in the playing portion of rehearsals,

*Broken Bow Bandroom Door 1984*

but due to the fall season was spending her class time working the twirling routines with the other twirlers. I did not think that such use of her class time was appropriate, as she was not developing her ability to perform on the instrument, so I asked her why she was not taking

her horn to class. Tonya told me she had taken the horn to class for the first week of school, but her instructor did not rehearse the band, as he fell asleep each day on the podium and then the students were expected to be quiet while he slept.

KaDee Marie Bramlett

**Bramlett Recent UCO Graduate**

KaDee Marie Bramlett of Sulphur graduated Saturday, December 17, 2005, from the University of Central Oklahoma. KaDee was honored at a reception as one of the five Class Marshals who led the graduates. She represented the College of Arts, Media & Design. Her degree is in music performance. She plays the oboe and is planning to go on to get her Masters Degree. She is the daughter of Laurie Bramlett and granddaughter of Bill and Helen Chitwood.

*One of my success stories, I taught Ka-Dee oboe for 5 years.*

Knowing this was a daily occurrence; Tonya had decided not to bother taking the instrument to class, as she and the other twirlers slipped out side to practice their baton routines when the teacher went to sleep. I could not believe I was getting the full and complete story and was truly surprised to find the administrators knew and were fully aware of this problem. When I went to discuss Tonya's revelations with her high school principal, the principal told me Tonya's band director weighed over three hundred pounds, was very despondent over a recent divorce and had developed Narcolepsy. The administrators did not want to fire him due to these problems and they did not think it would matter to the students, as it was just a band class!

I left the School offices in a very bad mood, but decided to

341

develop a wait and see attitude, as being a former teacher in this system I did not want to be perceived as meddling. I did not have to wait long for serious results.

The fall season in Broken Bow is a wet time of year and about a week after I visited with the principal the rains came down with a vengeance. The band director had a standing order with his band students to be at early morning rehearsals daily at seven thirty am. When I took Tonya to the band hall for her rehearsal, it was pouring rain and all the soaking wet little kids were standing outside the band hall waiting for the director. In order to keep Tonya as dry as possible I waited in our car with her for the teacher to open the building. He did not show up until eight – thirty and then did not have his keys that he had to go back home and find. That was the last straw, I called Paul Chandler my trusted school board member and friend and I told him the whole story. Within two weeks Paul, who was very insistent I return to teaching, had polled the not altogether agreeable, football first, school board, and the lack-a-daisical administrators and I was regretablely back teaching high school band!

Here we go again getting over involved, I would not have done it, but Paul said the board could not find anyone to teach at this late date and I just could not stand by and see Tonya's year in such a musical disaster. Unfortunately I was still running the Redwine's Restaurant and had taken on the major task of rebuilding a band that at the first football game was playing an unrecognizable version of what they said was the national anthem and could not even play their own school fight song. A higher power must have decided to get even with me!

I expected Tonya to work as one third owner in the restaurant and go to school full time, she was only sixteen and in much better health than me, I reasoned. Also she was the only one making any money out of the restaurant. Although I had to sell my farm, cash my life insurance, cash my retirement and IRAs and worked twenty-four hours, seven days a week just as she and Shirley, neither Shirley nor I was getting a salary. At least Tonya was getting tips for her waiting of the tables!

The high school band was really bad and I had to recruit young people back into it that had recently quit, this due to the ineptness of the former director and his uncaring attitude. Norris Harkey, a fine gentleman, and a good musician was the junior high school band teacher, who worked diligently to help Harley Thomas our outstanding drum line teacher and me recruit and prepare their former students, for each performance at the football halftimes. About three weeks after I took over the band in what was fast becoming a good rebuilding year, our first trumpet player, a beautiful and very talented young lady named Jennifer, who was the outstanding leader in the band, lost her life in a tragic car wreck and it devastated the whole school, not to mention our band and its teachers. I had not experienced a death of one of my students in over twenty –five years of teaching, so it was really hard for me also. Working with two very capable women teachers, Mrs. Joy Orr, and the high school choir director, Mrs. Annett Auld, we developed a very entertaining color guard and drill team that took a lot of pressure off the marching band's performance. All in all, the band was really quite inexperienced, but they were working harder than they had been accustomed to for many years, trying to perform well, and we as teachers, were pleased with their efforts that first football season.

The next year we had kids everywhere, over eighty students enrolled in the band program and we were really on our way to having a great year. The football season went so well I decided to reward the students with a trip to **World's of Fun** theme park in Kansas City. This was the biggest mistake I ever made and boy did I misjudge the parents of my present students. We worked hard to prepare for the Kansas City contest, which was held in April. I remember many extra rehearsals that took all our teachers many extra hours to prepare the students and their parts. The day we packed up and left I told the students to remember they were representing their school and town and not to do anything that might embarrass either. They seemed to understand what I was saying, so I did not explain further about the importance of their behavior. I had taken this age students on trips many times and never had any problems with them as to alcohol or drugs, but what I did not know was a lot of these students had parents that kept beer and liquor readily accessible to their kids and they did not check to see if the children were using same. I took an adult chaperone for each eight students on the busses with us, but when we arrived in Kansas City, Mr. Harkey came to me with a discovery that completely caught me off guard. Norris came to my room shortly after we arrived in the motel and said," You and I must go to room number 121, as it is filled with booze". When we got to that room there was booze everywhere. An inventory showed four cases of beer and thirty bottles of rum, gin whiskey and etc. and one eighth grade girl, who was drunker than a skunk, throwing up all over the room. She had been drinking cherry vodka all the way to Kansas City and no adult on the bus had caught her. When we finally got to the bottom of how these kids had acquired all this liquor, we found out one eighth grade boy had taken orders for it from all the junior high kids and purchased about half the amount we confiscated. The rest, which was a considerable amount, came from the homes of a number of the students, some even told us their parents had given it to them, a statement which I found hard to believe, until I visited with their parents, after which I was not so sure they were lying.

This trip that was meant to foster a good rapport and enhance the membership of the band, now had become the bands and my worst nightmare. The coaches who were worried about seeing all those students joining the band and not playing athletics had a field day, quietly dropping words of advice all over town and when we got home although the parents had more to do with their kids actions than I did; they wanted to neither take the blame nor to place it on their little darlings. So they did what all folks do when embarrassed, they took their kids, all thirty- two of them, except for the one who ordered the booze for the others, out of the band the next year. It took me almost two years to recover the bands position in the community and I never did over come the loss of instrumentation or performance ability I would have had if some of these students had matured in my program.

In spite of this fiasco, I was really proud of the fact I was able to return to teaching and retire in1989 from the same school, where twenty-five years previously I had begun my teaching career and due to Mr.Harkey, who took the band and before he retired, made it even better than it was after I retired. Thanks also to Harley Thomas, who sacrificed much to return to the University and complete his music teaching certification, so he could continue both of our efforts to rebuild the Broken Bow band. Harley now leads them as their very able director and they are once again one of the outstanding bands in Oklahoma.

For years Shirley has been an avid reader, reading every type of book she could find on any subject, but especially the classic authors and their best works. She had dropped out of college due to finances at the end of her freshman year at Oklahoma State University, but over the next thirty years had taken many seminars, short courses and single classes that helped her acquire quite a few college credit hours and her love of good literature had been a positive influence in her life; plus it had developed her quest for knowledge.

Although she did not have a degree per se, she was highly self-educated. During our stay in Broken Bow, I visited with her about completing her degree and she agreed it was something she was thinking about, but she thought at her age going back to college after not using her mental faculties in a controlled environment for many years would be very difficult and she thought she would have to take a full load of courses to get back into school. I convinced her to go to the Higher Learning Center and to take just one course. Anything in which she might think she was interested. She went out to the Center in Idabel just to check it out and the counselor there explained she had enough credit hours already completed, according to her overall transcripts, to finish a degree in sociology and psychology in five full semesters of classes. In addition if she wanted to go slower she could take most of these courses at the Higher Learning Center by television from Southeastern Oklahoma State University, but she would eventually need to spend at least one semester on the University campus.

She was dubious at first, but enrolled in a humanities course and to her surprise was able, due to her many years of reading to test out of the course. This bolstered her confidence greatly and she began to get very serious about obtaining her degree, she car-pooled and commuted to Durant for a year then lived on the University Campus for one semester in Durant, Oklahoma. Shirley commuted to Broken Bow most weekends, while living in the college dorm.

She proudly finished all necessary courses for her degree, except for an ( I ) in one advanced course that the instructor was trying to make into two different courses and force the University to change the names of each. So he gave all sixteen students who took the course with Shirley an( I ) and told them they could get it off their transcript, only by taking his next course, which would not be offered until the following spring semester, that shirley was not planning to attend.

The school finally issued Shirley's degree two years later, after the professor agreed to accept her paper on the next course, which she submitted directly to the professor, who subsequently granted her an A in the course. For those two years she was working in Okc. with a temporary degree, and working on the paper for the course she had completed earlier at the higher Learning Center,

Tonya was finishing high School and Graduated from Broken Bow High in the1985 –86 School year. She Graduated in the spring of 1986 and that same fall she entered college at East Central Oklahoma University, where her intentions were to complete a pre-law course and eventually attend law school and become an attorney. She graduated from the Ada, Oklahoma University with a political science degree at the end of the 1990 fall semester, but found that she was not cut out to practice law after serving two years, as a clerk in one of the most prestige law firms in Oklahoma City. She did not want to parallel those female lawyers she watched, go through the daily grind of being a mother, who was never home or end up as a wife, who never saw her husband.

Carla who has since completed her certification for an administrators certificate, received her master's degree at the same graduation ceremony in which, Tonya received her Bachelors degree from East Central State University.

With two thirds of the Restaurant's owners in college I tried to run it for a while by myself, but my heart was not in it and they had too much to do to work in it, so we closed it and used it for a family gathering spot for the next four years until we finally sold it in 1992 due to it's need of care and repairs that we really could not afford, and we were living over four hours driving time from it's location.

# Time to Move on to New Adventures in the Big City

When Shirley graduated she found a position at the Department of Commerce in Oklahoma City and moved to North Okc, where she lived in an apartment and commuted to Broken Bow on weekends. I finally realized she was not coming back and since I had retired and she liked her job so very much, I moved to the apartment in Oklahoma City.

My retirement from the field of public education came at an opportune time, as the reader will no doubt recognize from past paragraphs and was a direct result of my friendship with Mike Vadnais, the Broken Bow High School principal, for whom I had been working as the head band director for the past three years and for whom I had come to highly respect for his sound advise and thoughtful methods of handling difficult situations with our students. About two weeks before the students were to be taking their Christmas break, Mike and I were visiting in his office one cold December morning and he mentioned, " I have been reading the new Oklahoma Teachers Retirement Law and have found it will affect a number of our present faculty". Then he went on to say, " Would you like for me to check and see if you are eligible to retire under this new law"? I told Mike, that as of January first 1989, I would have taught twenty- seven years in the public schools and with my three years military service credited would probably qualify for retirement under the new system. He seemed to agree, but stated, " I will check with the State Department of Education and find out the exact particulars about your situation if you wish"? I requested he do so and let me know as soon as possible.

It did not take Mike long to find out and over a cup of coffee at the Charles Wesley two days later he told me," you are eligible to retire in three weeks, if you wish, but since you cashed your retirement funds out each time you left the State to teach in Kansas and Texas, you owe the fund sixteen thousand dollars, which they will allow you to pay back if you do so this year". He continued, "If you decide to retire, your annual retirement will be over twelve thousand dollars". That was only four thousand dollars less than I was presently taking home after taxes and I would not have to spend any time to receive it. Now the bad news, I was broke dew to the loss I recently took in the Redwine's Restaurant and did not know where I was going to get one hundred dollars, much less **sixteen thousand** dollars.

This was when I found out just how generous and loving my Mother, Sister, and both Brothers are. When I told them I needed the sixteen thousand dollars they collectively signed a note for that amount at my Mothers bank in Pawhuska and entered into an agreement with me that allowed me to apply for my retirement and use the monthly checks I received over the next two years to repay the retirement funds I had taken some years earlier. So that the students in the band were not adversely affected, I held off my retirement until the end of the spring semester in May of 1989. As I relate this information to you it now has been sixteen years and one hundred ninety thousand dollars since the state began delivering those monthly checks. They have allowed me to do many good deeds for my family and friends that without this money would not have been possible.

I mentioned this retirement situation for two reasons, one to explain how close my family remains and also to show why I could not accompany my lovely wife on her original move to accept her new position with the Oklahoma Department of Commerce in Oklahoma City.

Shirley moved into her Rain Dance apartment at 122<sup>nd</sup> and Pennsylvania Ave. in March, as it was necessary for her to begin her new job immediately. Commuting four hours each way each week for three months was really difficult for Shirley, lonely for me as I closed this chapter of our lives slowly, and expensive for us both, as it necessitated we purchase a new vehicle.

Shirley's move to Okie City was fairly sudden due to the fact she was required to be on the job one week after her interview with the Commerce Department. This resulted in her renting an apartment that included a fridge and kitchen stove. She then rented some necessary furniture, i.e. A bed, mattress, kitchen table, four chairs and a couch to use until I could get time to move some of our furniture from Broken Bow when I moved in with her in June of that year. She truly had a pretty nice little abode as the apartment complex harbored mostly single adults (no kids allowed) and included a game room and nice, though small swimming pool.

When I retired and moved from Broken Bow, to the Rain Dance apartment # 121,in June of 1989 we both truly enjoyed the wide range of freedom from daily responsibilities that living in the apartment afforded each of us. It was as though a great rock had been lifted from our shoulders after the past seven and more years of the daily grind in Redwine's. We loved our quality Restaurant as rated by <u>Oklahoma Today Magazine</u> and all it offered our guests, but it's Quality of service and menu truly required a huge undertaking and our undivided attention twenty-four hours daily and seven days weekly. Now we could make our bed, vacuum the two rooms and we were free as a bird to attend the theater, see a baseball game, go shopping, which we did leisurely and often, or any myriad of other pleasures. Even though Shirley was working forty hours per week she

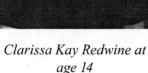

*Clarissa Kay Redwine at age 14*

*<<Each plate served at Redwine's was truly a beautiful work of art. An example of those being served at a summer women's luncheon in 1987 in seen on the left*

had much more free time and was in a happier state of mind, now that she was again in an office where her peers obviously respected her for her multitude of wonderful talents in the business world. She was on the road at least three days a week auditing the federal and state grants to many different communities around our beautiful state, juxtaposed amide her continuous travels to conferences in Florida, Arizona, California, Tennessee, Texas and Washington D. C. among others too numerous to mention. While Shirley enjoyed her position with the Department of Commerce, our son Dennis and daughter in law Kathy were working on a much more important project, one that resulted in the birth of our beautiful granddaughter Clarissa Kay Redwine on may 14th 1990. Just as Shirley and I were so very pleased to have this family addition, I was also very happy for Shirley and her

352

newly acquired office prestige. However, I was only fifty three years old and certainly not ready to sit in a rocker every day watching the world go by, but the age discrimination that I was about to experience for the next few months was truly an un-welcomed surprise. As a highly educated person who had always been a singularly valued employee in every endeavor I had attempted and residing at the very top of my field as a band leader, musician, restaurateur, educator, and entrepreneur, I was expecting the businesses in Oklahoma City to welcome me with open arms and salary negotiation would of course be my most immediate concern. (Boy, was I in for a wake up call)! Money would be my most pressing problem, but not because anyone was negotiating with me over it. Absolutely no one in the City wanted my gray haired services in any capacity. I mailed over one hundred twenty copies of my beautiful resume to prospective employers and never got one return call for any type of job interview. Additionally, I followed up every newspaper job possibility listed in the Daily Oklahoman for the next four months, all my efforts were in vain and my self-esteem was at it's lowest ebb when I called the corporate offices of a Taco- shop to inquire about a news add they had placed for help at any of their three locations City wide and was told by a haughty young woman of some twenty years old she would send me a reply in the mail. When her letter reached me some ten days later, it said there was nothing The Taco Shop did that I was capable of doing! I suppose owning and running every facet of your own restaurant for over seven years does not qualify one for fast food service employment, even making Tacos. Eventually I convinced a small add agency to allow me to make and sell television commercials on commission basis only and finally had to quit this totally financial disaster, when the owners required me to sit and answer their office phones, but would not compensate me to do it.

Shirley was doing quite well in her new position and we decided to move from the Rain-Dance apartments into a nice three bedroom duplex, which was located at the end of the cols- de-sac in the 1900 block of Northwest 42$^{nd}$ just off Penn so that our youngest daughter could live with us, as she had recently graduated from East Central Oklahoma University in Ada and taken a position with Musser and Bunch, the most prestiges law firm in Oklahoma City. This move was one of the best things we did, as living with Tonya was really fun and never a dull moment. Before we moved, we had a really serious problem with the cities drainage system and learned a costly lesson one stormy evening while trying to enjoy a movie. A friend and co-worker told Shirley about a theatre at the corner of NW 63$^{rd}$ and Northwest Expressway that presented first rate movies for the admission price of one dollar, so shortly after being told of this unusual opportunity we decided to check it out. Since all the showings began at 5:45 pm and Shirley worked until five o'clock we barely had time to get across town to the movie before it started so we decided to skip dinner and eat a late sandwich after the movie was finished. The skies appeared fairly ominous, as we parked on the steeply sloping lot of the theater, hurriedly made our way to the theater's ticket booth and jostled through the bustling crowd and into the double glass doors that opened into the large crowded, concession area with it's neon signs flashing, wonderful smells of freshly popped corn and those delicious wieners roasting round and round in their own drippings, an area that must be hungrily negotiated, then stumble down the darkened hallway to find the lighted title above the door of the particular screen entrance and all the while eagerly anticipating the movie we had only paid a buck to see. I can not remember what the movie was about, but I sure remember that about one hour into the showing of it, the theater manager came hastily into what was now a dimly lighted room with the movie still flashing hauntingly and announced to his patrons of which we were two, that due to an on-going storm and the seven inch rain it had produced, the buildings' ceiling had collapsed and as we were watching, water began to cascade down the inside walls like a major waterfall. The movie manager shouted this showing was cancelled and the theater must immediately be evacuated. Shirley and I still were not fully aware of the present danger, but followed the manager's instructions to evacuate the building and when we got outside, we began to understand just how serious the situation had been. The area had experienced a small tornado and a cloud- burst from which the heavy skies had dropped seven inches of water in less than an hour. This was our first urban experience with any storms and their resulting flooding of the cities streets. It seems that Oklahoma City has so much hard top area, that there is no place for and little or no planning for storm drainage, so they just let it wash down the streets and into major creeks. The resulting flooding of all low intersections causes millions of dollars in vehicle damage every year. This being our first time to have this delightful experience, we naively got in our car and left the only safe hill top parking lot in the area, immediately putting our new car and ourselves in extreme danger, as we drove onto the northwest expressway at the bottom of the hill, we were washed into a major creek. As the car began to float, I realized we must get out of it or we would be washed away with it and drown in the ever deepening swirls. With water already up to the dashboard inside our car, we quickly opened both the driver and passenger doors letting the swirling flood gush through. Luckily for us some young men in a pick-up were just behind us and they jumped in the creek and tied a chain onto our car then helped pull the car and us to safety. Our new 1989 Grand- Am was drowned out of course and we had to call an associate of Shirley to pick us up and take us to the apartment. The following day we had a wrecker service tow our now inoperable new car to a shop where it cost us a great deal of money to have the motor taken apart and cleaned, but the car was never the same again, as inside the floor boards and upholstery had been totally soaked.

*The three musketeers of the Red Red Wine Band left to right: A. J. Ferron with his gorgeous trumpet, C. E. Redwine and his tenor Sax, and Tonya M. "Redwine" Clevenger playing lead Alto sax, one of the many instruments on which she performed*

Shortly after this stormy movie episode we moved into the duplex in the 1900 block of NW 42nd and Penn and Tonya moved home from her Ada, Oklahoma residence. This new residence was really convenient for Shirley and Tonya, as it was in the middle of Oklahoma City and only five minutes from either of their employers. It also included a double garage that was unattached to the living quarters that was available for rehearsals of the new band I decided to put together. I had tried everything I knew to find employment and as a last resort had accepted a position with the state of Oklahoma Department of Human Services in the office of child welfare. Naively, I thought if I worked hard enough I might get some of these indigent mothers off welfare and into the work force. It never crossed my mind that the bureaucrats in charge of these offices were promoted on the basis of how many cases they could conjure for their employees, or that my job depended on how many cases were added to the welfare rolls each month. The whole system is set up not to get folks off the dole, but to get more and more of the poor and down-trodden on the list, so that the directors of the program can hire more people and there-in justify and receive larger salaries. This program needs a serious overhaul, the original intent and its stated purpose is commendable, but in its' present form it promotes the breaking up of the family structure, continued generational poverty, and expectation of entitlement rather than escape from desperation and frustration by those it is supposed to be liberating. Additionally it is perpetually and purposely growing larger and larger as it feeds on the very rules and regulations that were once placed to control its growth. A person not closely affiliated with this boondoggle, most likely would not be aware that to receive a monthly check of less than one hundred and sixty dollars, which in itself is totally inadequate, a child must have only one parent in the home and that parent can have no more than three hundred dollars gross monthly income. This regulation results in clients refusing labor or employment, marriages being dissolved, second parents committing fraud, and families being humiliated. I personally witnessed families where the fifth generation was presently participating in welfare and when asked what this child wanted to be when he grew up; he said, "I do not want to be anything,

I receives a check in the mail"! Although I could never prove it, I knew many cases where the fathers were hanging around just enough to inseminate the mother so as to produce another family check, but this same adult felt no responsibility of any type to help rear the resulting off spring. Crime is rampant in these neighborhoods, as no one works, so everyone is free all day and night to do drugs, steal, and plunder the rest of us and although no one admits to it a general feeling of low self- esteem pervades every household and most of these indignant indigents.

Needing to both supplement my income and a diversion from my degrading and depressing welfare job, I decided to revive the old Wine-Dots Band, but when my illustrious ex-son –in- law heard I was going to do so, he informed me I could not use that name, as he now somehow owned it. Never mind that I had started that band and hired him into it nearly fifteen years previously, and he had stolen the band from David Redwine, his brother-in-law and my son, whom I had given ownership of the band when I left it, to start my Restaurant. When Mark Reasoner told me he was using this name and I could not do so it made me furious, but my family was having real problems with this fellow, so I quietly changed the name of my group to Red-Red-Wine and moved on.

With-in a year, this band that was centered around the beautiful vocals of Tonya, the great trumpet of A. J. Ferron, and my leadership became one of the most sot-after dance bands in the City and surrounding State. We did have many problems for the first eighteen months, as we auditioned and performed with over twenty different guitarists, electric bassists, keyboardists, and drummers. Some of these were very capable performers, but they had serious personality problems or were unreliable. This problem became so persistent, that the standing joke between A. J., Tonya, and me was," Who is the bass and guitarist of the month"?

*Tonya singing with Red- Red -Wine*

We eventually found C. J. Wilson and his wife Jane, two wonderfully talented musicians who played guitar and electric bass and three very talented drummers and Carol Morrison a fine keyboard player who performed with us very regularly for the next seven years and this solidified the band. This band performed at nearly every country club, Moose lodge, Eagles lodge and Elks lodge in Oklahoma and took pride in being selected to perform at the Oklahoma Elks State convention for five straight years. This was in addition to performances as far away as Texarkanna, Arkansas and border towns in Kansas with concerts in such theaters as Pawhuska's grand old Constantine.

One of the reasons our family leased the duplex was it had a really private and relaxing back yard that included a very pleasant and secluded patio area. Tonya especially enjoyed sunbathing on this patio and since it did not have a pool, she purchased a small six- foot blow-up baby pool to cool off in as she did her daily sunbath. This led to a very funny event when one evening, she was invited by a young male associate, whom she did not want to accompany, to have dinner and a movie with him. As a dodge, she told him she was going to spend her evening in her pool. The young man immediately asked if he could come to her home and swim with her. Tonya without blinking replied to him," Sure, come on over"! After he followed her to the duplex in his fancy little car, she ushered him into our guest bedroom to change into his swimming trunks and then casually out the kitchen door onto the patio, where she promptly splashed into the kiddy pool and invited him to join her. For some reason we never got to meet this fellow, as he never came back.

Our lease was to be renewed shortly and Tonya, Shirley, and I all wanted to own a home again, so we began searching for property in northwest Oklahoma City that we felt we could afford and enjoy. Shirley found a small vacant 1940's brick not a mile from our present location, but not being really familiar with City realtors and property values she really got stung when she put up a five hundred dollar deposit in escrow to hold it for purchase. The realtor required her to repair the broken walls inside, then would not sell it to her, but would not return her deposit either. The property turned out to be on a restricted government list and she not only lost her escrow but also her one hundred dollars in repair supplies and tools, which some neighborhood kids, stole from the unlocked house.

We finally found a great deal on some property in Bethany, War Acres. The two story buff brick home sat on a large lot in a very good neighborhood, second lot from the corner, located at Barr and NW 42nd. It was in a bit of disrepair, but I felt I could fix it up with a minimum amount of work and expense. The owners, who had sold this house three times previously, agreed to sell us the house with three very important stipulations, 1. We would rent it for three months, if we liked it our rental fees paid to the owner would apply as a down payment toward the total purchase price, which they would finance through a local savings and loan. And 2. They would buy it back at anytime from us for what we paid for it. And 3. They would furnish the house with a new refrigerator, gas range and dishwasher of our choice before we moved in. This deal appeared too good to be true, but turned out to be just as these gracious people said it would. Hallelujah! There are more people like Mr. Dillon in this world!

Within a month after we moved in we agreed to purchase the house, as it was even better than we thought structurally and the location was wonderful. I took a job as choir director at the Memorial Christian Church on 16th and Meridian right away and we became

*Redwine home at 42 & Barr in Oklahoma city*

*Chase at age 4 years*

very active in the community, while I spent the next two years improving our lovely property and enjoying the City while I did it. While we spent the next six years at this address, we were to experience many wonderful events and some quite tragic as well. Four of the most outstanding things we enjoyed were a delightful family Christmas in New York, a wonderful vacation with Tonya and the Varnum Family in Hawaii, Tonya's wedding to our fine son in law Charles (Sam) Clevenger and the birth of our fine grandson,

Chase Tyler Reasoner on August 18th of 1989. Although there were many smaller but delightful occurrences in our lives, such as Ryan Redwine's performances on the baseball diamond, there was also the terrible tragedy of the April 14th 1994 terrorist bombing of Oklahoma City when two hundred eighty three souls were lost on a spring day that dawned beautifully and by two minutes after nine am found even the birds were flittering crazily around in the air outside our house. For many days when I would need to traverse by the downtown area the gloom of sadness that hang over the city was devastating and could actually be felt even by travelers on the interstate highways as they passed through our city.

Returning to more pleasant memories, I would like to elaborate on our family Christmas spent in New York where we met our son Dennis's in-laws Katherine, Erenzo (deceased) and Jim Erenzo who so graciously invited us

*Beth and Beau Clevenger in 2005*

*A family portrait of Dennis Lynn Redwine- his wife Katherine "Erenzo" Redwine and their five-year-old daughter Clarissa Kay Redwine*

to enjoy their home for two days and nights, and where we got to meet a number of their children. Then guided by our very favorite New Yorker, Kathy Erenzo Redwine; we spent two nights and three days in New York City where one of the high lights of the trip was watching the Radio City Music Hall Christmas Show on Christmas Eve and jostling through the bustle of the cavorting crowds, as we window shopped the stores of the Cities' Streets.

Thanks also should be given to Kathy's older brother Ralph who allowed us to sleep in his downtown apartment after the show and to that unknown man who made a pass at Shirley in one of the nightspots we attended while he tried to give her some pot.

*A 2004 family portrait of Tonya M."Redwine," Clevenger, Charles "Sam" Clevenger and their children Elizabeth Jene` and Beau Casson Clevenger*

Additionally, I would like to mention our delightful excursion to Hawaii: planned, guided, shepparded, worried about, and enjoyed by our youngest daughter, Tonya. Tonya made sure we purchased tickets at the very best possible prices and from the most reliable carriers, planned every detail of the trip ensuring that we saw and enjoyed the sights available, meals of the highest quality and spent our relaxed days and nights in total comfort.

She contacted our friends, Bill and Judy Varnum in Hawaii and they were the most gracious hosts anyone could imagine. We stayed ten days in Hawaii, during which time Bill took us to see nearly every possible sight, from the inside of an active seven thousand foot volcano on Hilo to the pineapple plantations of Lanai, to the beautiful Island of Maui and even the secluded black sand beaches of Lanai. Tonya took us to see the whales, as they nearly capsized our small fishing boat on the open ocean and sandwiched in a charter flight hop between the big and small Islands. It was the trip of a lifetime and I shall never forget it. Then after we came home Tonya planned her wedding and we all enjoyed it in Ada on May twenty eighth, 1994. She Sam and their expanded family that consists presently in 2005 of Elizabeth Jene' a daughter age six and Beau Casson a fine

son who is two years old still reside in Ada. When Tonya moved from our home in Oklahoma City she continued to perform with our band for sometime until she became pregnant with Beth and found traveling to be too strenuous and we

*Red Red Wine performing on News Years Eve 1998*

had to hire another lead singer for about a year until she recovered from childbirth. Then she performed with us for about two years and we had to retire the band as it just was not feasible to continue for a number of reasons, one of which I was getting to old and weak to move the equipment and we lived to far apart to rehearse. In the interim, I began booking over sixty acts and developed many fine entertainers in my booking agency known on the web as Great acts. Com. I taught some wonderfully talented people and some of them are still performing today in Nashville, Branson and New York City. To name them all would take more space than I can allow, but some of the most memorable were Zack and Mark Roberts, not blood related, Jennifer Scully, the most talented blues singer I have known, Cassie Stout, Jana Van Landing ham, Tara McKee, and Ashley Wilson four wonderfully talented sopranos and Ross Chitwood who will graduate this coming spring from the Julliard school of Music in New York City. Every one of these people has professional quality voices and if given the opportunity will excel greatly. In December of 1995 we had occasion to witness a robbery and ensuing parking lot murder less that six blocks from our lovely home at the Buy For Less Grocery located at 39th and Mac Arthur

*Tonya dancing with Uncle Bruce at her wedding*

*Ross Chitwood in 2003*

That day we decided to call the folks that had sold us this home and inquire as to their willingness to fulfill their original agreement and buy back the property. They said they would like to see how well we had taken care of the place and if it was in good shape they would certainly purchase it. We set an appointment date for their inspection during the coming January and began searching around the many rural lakes in southeast Oklahoma for a new place to live.

Our buyers were very pleased with how we had improved the property both inside and out and upon their inspection agreed to give us six months to find another home then take possession of this one as they stated back in 1992. We searched diligently for over six months and finally decided to move into a much smaller rural residence that would require a monumental amount of repair and redecorating.

# Sulphur Oklahoma Receives Benefit of Oklahoma City's loss

*Shirley and Carroll visiting the rose gardens in Will Rogers park of Oklahoma City summer 1994*

Although we decided to move from our lovely Oklahoma City home in December 1995, it took us until June of 1996 to prepare and perform the actual event. Each weekend from just after January 1st, 1996 until July of 1996,if I was not performing and some weekends when I was, we would travel to a rural lake area exploring

*David Lee Redwine holding his lovely wife Terry and standing to their left, their daughter, and my granddaughter--- Nicole Johnson 1999*

the possible locations to either build or purchase an existing home. We diligently searched every major south central and south eastern lakeshore and considered most north eastern Oklahoma lakes to a small degree. In each case we determined available area medical facilities, as their availability would have a large part in our final decision.

This was due to our advancing ages and slowly

declining health conditions. After about two months of touring the major lakes of Texoma, Murray, and others and not finding anything even close to what we had in mind for our future home, we stumbled onto our dream without realizing we were there. We were driving north on I- 35, returning home from one of our excursions on a warm early spring Sunday afternoon, when just a few miles north of Ardmore, Shirley, who had been checking our location on the atlas we always carried and marked so

*Family portrait of the Nicholas Brett English family Brett is centered between his Three standing daughters; Andrea, Laura, and Stephanie seated on his left is his son Nicholas, and to his right is his wife Alice and their daughter, Emily this picture was taken in 2000.*

we would know where we had explored, held the atlas up for me to survey, as she pointed to a small lake just East of I- 35 located south and east of our immediate location and off the Oklahoma Highway Number Seven. She stated she would like to check this area as we had not explored this possibility and since it was early afternoon her suggestion seemed quite plausible, so we took the next exit and headed toward the lake of the Arbuckle's, a beautiful area lying quietly on the north side of the Arbuckle Mountains. We explored the West side of the lake, as that was the first area we were to incur and not knowing our way around, got lost often on the many crooks and crannies of the lakes multitude of available entries from the state highways. Somehow each time we got lost and then found our way back to the highway; we past the same dilapidated little cabin just outside and adjoining the Chickasaw National Refuge. We looked at many other properties that had for sale signs posted, but this one kept cropping up each time we tried to find our way back to civilization. There was a smudged phone number listed on the faded for sale sign, and the place had obviously been listed in this manner for some time, as the weeds and brush had taken over the entire landscape around the cabin. After passing the property some three or four times, Shirley asked me to stop, so she could get a closer look at the place and possibly, if so inclined, take down the phone number for future reference. We determined that the listed number must be a Norman, Oklahoma exchange, but I was not very interested, as the place was in terrible condition and I knew who was going to be the person to make any changes in it. Shirley stated it had quite a bit of possibility and I knew that was not a good sign When we finally arrived at our home in Okc. Shirley went in and called the listing right away. **Another bad sign!** The owner, who admitted he had posted the listing some twelve months previously, seemed evasive about setting a sales price, but finally told Shirley he would sell the property for cash only and told her if she wanted to view the inside of the house, the key to the front door was on a ledge over the door, where he left

*Four seasons of our love—C. E. and Shirley*

*These 1983 pictures taken in Broken Bow*

it on a permanent basis (so much for security!) and we would soon know why he did not care to secure the house.

The following weekend we drove back down to the property to check out the inside of the house. What a revelation and what a shock we got when we walked inside. The house was a total disaster area. It contained five small rooms; two of those were being used as bedrooms and were across a small hallway from each other. The hallway also provided access to a very small bathroom and exited into the larger living area, we had made entry into this area by opening the weather beaten, paint peeling front door. The walls were partially covered with the ugliest peeling, violet colored, hap-hazard torn wallpaper I had ever seen. The floors were creaky hardwood, badly scared, untrimmed, and in serious need of a coat of varnish. There were the most god awful looking faded purplish blue drapes hanging crazily from some cheap metal curtain rods over the large inoperable turn- screw windows, and the west wall that adjoined the filthy one car garage with it's broken overhead door, had a three foot by two and a half foot gapping hole directly in the center about five feet above the floor, that at one time possibly held a window unit for the room air conditioning. About six steps to the right of this hole was a door that exited into the garage and the door stood awkwardly open allowing all to view the concrete block that was placed below it for ankle breaking entry to the garage. Oddly, immediately next to this open door on the same wall was a second door that led from what I light-heartedly surmised was the kitchen area into the same filthy area of the garage. Only an unpainted four inch two by four stud separated the two doors that both performed the same function. The whole place wreaked of rat urine seen on the kitchen floors and the 1930's totally rusted out kitchen metal cabinet units, held bushels of rat nests and displayed enough dead roaches to feed all the fish in the Red River. I mentioned the overhead garage door, but forgot to mention it was unhinged on one side and therefore hung lazily and unusable from the side still attached. The garage had a termite damaged wooden door on its northwest corner that opened into a one car sized metal lean too building that had been used for boat storage and it was littered everywhere with old boat anchors, rotting life vests piled high, and broken bottles that looked like someone had used the area for a dump.

I told Shirley this was not the place for us, and she just laughed and said, "It does need a coat of paint or two doesn't it?" I knew she was seriously considering this place and it scared the hell out of me, so I began to call her attention to the many problems and their financial needs. She then said, "That place just needs a good cleaning and some paint and it will make an excellent place to live". Man, what an understatement that was. It took me ten years and forty thousand dollars to get that sucker livable. Truthfully, it would have been cheaper and a hell of a lot easier to burn it down and start over on a new foundation. By now you know my lovely wife loves a challenge and in this property she reveled. It took her four more weeks of haggling with the Norman owner, but she finally wore him down and he sold her the place and for her price, as you would expect. She even convinced the fellow to carry the note on it, getting his guarantee that if she paid it off in a year he would rebate her three thousand dollars.

I had been carefully packing each room of our home everyday since early December. I labeled each box, or container and marked them for the specific room in which they should be moved, but of course I had to leave quite a few items unpacked until the last minute, as we used these on a daily basis. This was especially true as to Shirley's beautiful wardrobe and accessories, because she needed them to dress for her job. I figured our kids were going to help us move, as they had many times previously and I knew they were aware of how important it was to carefully pack, label, and place like items together in the moving van.

I did not plan on Alice or Bret's handling of a large portion of our

*Shirley, standing at the front door and under the new sign I had just built for her newest business venture, "The Gift Basket" located on West Broadway in Sulphur, Oklahoma December, 1996*

belongings on the final day. I forgot that they had never helped us move. Due to this fact and Bret's love to tease attitude, he loaded many unrelated items in unmarked boxes, containers, and baskets along with some of our most expensive furniture in his large but carelessly packed horse trailer. I begged him and David among others, who were loading or packing and sometimes performing both operations to be more careful with our belongings some of which were quite delicate and expensive, but they simply laughed teasingly and continued to cram and toss the items into that darn trailer. When we unloaded the vehicles at our new address, available safe, dry, clean storage areas were at a premium and we lost or destroyed many life long cherished items. We could not even find basic kitchen tools to use in food preparation for months after the move. The whole family was tired and hungry upon arriving at the new residence and unloaded the vehicles as soon as possible, leaving most of our belongings on the patio. I had intended to treat all the family to a good meal in town, but Bret had stopped to purchase some tamales in Davis and since they were all in a hurry to get to their homes after this very long and trying day, everyone ate a quick meal of tamales and crackers, while standing around outside our new home. Then after David, Sam and Bret moved the really big furniture inside for us along with quite a few of the largest containers, a favor which we truly appreciated, as we were very tired by this time, the crew jumped back into the trucks and cars and left Shirley and me to try and store as much of the stuff as possible before it got ruined by the weather. Nearly all the containers we placed in the metal boat- house received some weather damage. This occurred primarily due to the fact we did not know what was in the boxes stored there-in, had we known a great deal of them contained Shirley's expensive suits, sweaters, and accessories we would not have placed these containers in that leaky bar, but inside the dusty, but dry rooms of the main house. We were finding items we thought lost, as many as ten years later. Shirley and I worked diligently for some days moving unopened boxes and cases from the patio into the metal shed, but this shed was quite small and we decided to create a loft in it, thinking that if we placed our belongings higher, they would be better protected and we could utilize the space of the shed move efficiently. This little idea was a real mistake and nearly cost Shirley her life. I had three sheets of half- inch plywood, that I placed above the open rafters of the shed, making what I thought was a very nice loft on which we could place the many boxes, suitcases, and other containers; we were trying to store, while we refurbished the main dwelling.

The process of storing these many bulky and heavy containers was going pretty well and we had worked for two days placing nearly all our remaining belongings in this cheaply acquired attic when the ceiling joists, that were made to hold up only a few pounds broke and the whole attic with all our storage came crashing down. I was standing on the floor at the far end of the building, as I had gone to get one of the few small boxes that had yet to be stored. As I reached down to pick up the box, I heard the slowly creaking sound of breaking timbers. I immediately looked up to see the attic full of heavy goods slowly sliding toward where Shirley was working. Fortunately she fell backward off the ten- foot aluminum ladder and landed awkwardly on a large chest. The ladder caught the sheet of plywood and stopped its decent toward Shirley, but the stuff stored on it began to cascade down around her and although she was hit by some of the stuff, none of it fell heavily on her. She was encased in a great pile of boxes and they captured her legs, to the extent she appeared to be really hurt. I hurriedly started moving the debris away and cleared a path to get Shirley out of her predicament of which I was very concerned, as she appeared to be badly hurt. When I got to her and moved the boxes that had constrained her legs, she gave me a reassuring look and told me that although she had been banged around; she did not think she was badly hurt. I helped her out of the mess and we quit for the day, as the disappointment of our two days work being lost and the chaos of the storage area was just too much mental fatigue for one day.

Our first repairs to the place were made in that storage shed, but shortly thereafter we began to clean and clear the area around the house. I found a fellow with a tractor, bush-hog and eighteen-feet low- boy trailer and he helped us haul off three tremendous loads of old car bodies, busted motors tires and other trash from the property. The loads were stacked so high on his trailer, that when he headed to the landfill with them it looked like a scene from the Beverly

Hillbillies. Then he bush-hogged the entire yard around the house. He could not cut the brush on the rest of the place, as the brush was too big to use his equipment. We did find we had neighbors that adjoined us to the west of our property, something we did not realize until we had made these improvements. After beginning our major clean up of the place we hired an exterminator from Ardmore to fumigate the house for all types of varmints including termites, level the floors and walls, replace the rotting boards on which it was sitting with concrete piers. Replaced the lead water pipes with PVC and connected the bath tub and air conditioning system to the main sewage, as both had been flowing freely under the house. Simultaneously, while I was working on the six, vintage 1940, screw type windows; sometimes needing as much as ten days to clean, chip, and repair, then repaint only one window on our new property and little cabin, Shirley was soliciting and writing community block grants for some of the areas counties and cities. She also had me helping her develop and build a new business called **The Gift Basket** that she was locating in a small shopping center across the street from the Braums store on West Broadway in Sulphur, Oklahoma.

*The Gift Basket was truly a beautiful small store and people from this area came in often just to browse and enjoy the color of the displays. Shirley also had her grant writing office in a room behind this popular shop.*

As I helped her realize her dream and build the display racks, shelving, and cases, I developed a private voice and instrumental lessons studio in a nice large room that adjoined the rear of her shop. Not finding these many difficult tasks enough to keep her off the streets she led a group of concerned business citizens of the Sulphur downtown in the quest for developing a full fledged *Main Street Program* that she would eventually get sanctioned by the State of Oklahoma Department of Commerce, and become it's first full time, compensated, Director.

In my spare time I finished building the electric fence around the western half of our property and considered it time to purchase some goats that I hoped would help us clear the very brushy area I had enclosed. Thinking that the animals would respect the fences charge and it's owner's fence building prowess, I called to answer an add I had noticed in a Sunday issue of the **Daily Oklahoman**, an add for the sale of five pigmy goats. These goats were presently residing on a farm in Choctaw, Oklahoma. The add stated these small animals were docile, easily trained, and quite social in character. They sounded to good to be true,just what the inexperienced goatherd should select for his first taste of raising nice quiet show animals and what a bargain, they would eat their way to a beautiful goat pen. However, someone forgot to inform the goats!

They turned out not docile, but rude, and scared as hell of Shirley and me. They were not a bargain as our local sale barn auctioned some for less than thirty dollars the week before I paid forty dollars a piece for mine and I had to feed them a half gallon of expensive feed, plus a small block of high priced alfalfa hay each day. Worst of all, they were totally untrainable and spent most of their free time standing with their sharp hooves dug deeply in the paint on the hood and cab of my new Dodge truck, as they added insult to injury by bleating noisily from their expensive roost. My neighbors and I had to chase them down, or get them untangled from the brush they wound tightly around if I left them tethered. This was an exasperating almost hourly adventure and required much time and sweat.

This foolishness lasted nearly three weeks, as my electric fence chargers just would not hold these critters. That is until Joey finally brought me the solution, which I will relate after describing how we actually became goat masters. (No one owns a goat! The goat owns the person!) I had an extra long fully carpeted Ford Van, that I had been using for sometime as a band bus, driving it heavily, but carefully loaded over three hundred fifty thousand miles to the performances of Red-Red-Wine. Not owning a cage to haul the goats I was about to purchase, I put plywood on the walls, floor, and ceiling of the van from just behind the driver's seat and right side passenger's seat to the back doors and after making a call to let the farmer in Choctaw know we were on our way to purchase the goats she had advertised and with Shirley riding shotgun, we embarked on the great goat adventure.

All the way to the goat farm I envisioned the magnificent Pigmy goats that I was sure, as owner would make me the envy of our rural, brushy neighborhood.

When we arrived at the Choctaw farm where the goats were stabled, a young stout looking lady about thirty years old met us in the yard and proudly and immediately pointed out five of her most beautifully fully horned animals. Naively I asked, "Do you have some little ones that don't have horns?" These suckers looked pretty ominous to me! Not that I was scared of a goat or anything------The lady shot me an incredulous look of disgust, then quickly grinned as she explained, "All goats, both male and female have horns, and are quite adept at butting their handlers and each other." She continued, "That is their way of socializing, their way of playing." I was quickly to learn the goats use their horns very well, and can whack the stuffins out of a person if one did not pay close attention to them when the animals were close by. This was especially true if the little darlins thought you were not suspecting them to whack you or they had you cornered. The lady finally slipped a cotton rope around a magnificent looking all white male, that was sporting a long white beard, two perfectly formed rams horns, and a surprisingly large bag of male gentilia. As she pulled him toward her he bleated loudly, but she gently began to quiet his fear as she talked softly, "Come Billy." and soothingly to him, "Good Billy." Then assuring the fellow she meant him no harm, she began to stroke his neck and he immediately settled down and leaned against her leg. She then tied him to the fence and got another heavily knotted small rope, that she hid behind her leg and walked slowly toward the other goats, that had been curiously watching her catch Billy.

The farmer again spoke very softly, as she moved slowly through the pen and when she was close enough slipped the hidden rope over the neck of a very friendly young female, she called Fay. When she brought Fay over and tied her to the fence, the lady turned to us and said, "On the phone you said you wanted five" Before she could finish the sentence, I interrupted her saying, "Two will be quite enough, as I can see I have a lot to learn about goats before I try to care for more of them." She was obviously disappointed, that I was only going to purchase two of the goats, but I could see I had my work cut out for me just caring for these two and certainly did not need more at this time. It was getting on in the afternoon and I wanted to release the goats in their pen in the light of day, so we wrote the unhappy lady a check and excused ourselves. Then we helped her load the goats in the van, where after I opened the back doors, she pushed, dragged, shoved, and generally forced both the small, highly agitated goats into my hastily made and crudely appearing plywood cage, quickly, the goat-herd took their ropes off and they promptly went berserk: crazily running and sliding on the plywood, while we slammed the doors and locked them inside my fully carpeted van.

Their first order of the hour was to work hard changing the color of my beautiful blue carpet to a foul smelling and sickenly putrid urine yellow, that was amply laced with small black round marbles. Then they both slid as far toward the drivers seat as the plywood allowed, straining and craning their necks above it to see what was available for them to get into. All this action was accompanied by the loudest, most horrible sounding bas and bleats one could imagine and continued for the next fifteen or twenty minutes, as I tried to find my way out of the Choctaw community and onto the I- 40 interstate that I planned to use on our return to highway 177 in Shawnee and back to the Sulphur area.

Every few minutes one or both of our horny passengers would make a run at and bang the sides or back of the van so hard that it felt like the van might turn over. However about thirty minutes into the trip they settled down and seemed resolved to their fate of becoming rural goats that would have to put up with greenhorn goatherds.

When we arrived at the gate to the goat pen and its electric fence,

I told Shirley not to worry I had fixed it so we could drive the van inside the pen to unload the goats. I got out of the vehicle, opened the gate, then returned to my chauffeur's position inside the van and drove the van inside the goat pen. Now I was going to open the back doors and release the goats into their new home, which I felt confident would be secure and appreciated by our new guests. I failed to put the ropes back around the goats neck, as I felt their was no need to fight that battle, since they would be constrained by the electric fence that I had spent so much time these last few weeks preparing. When I opened those back van doors, **(the fit hit the shan!)**

We then found out just what a great neighbor we had in Debra Campbell. She lived just west of the goat pen and it was her place we had discovered when we cleaned the brush around ours. The two goats nearly trampled me, as they made a mad dash to exit the van and spun me around where I noticed, although it had become dusky dark, a husky, but small figure coming toward the van through the light of the fading western horizon. While this all happened in an instant, I remember thinking, I sure hope those goats do not get out of this pen, as they are unfamiliar with this area and we might never find them if they were to get lost across the federal road, that separated our home place from the federal park or into the brush that surrounded this whole place.

The goats bolted from the van, as I earlier mentioned and headed immediately south where about twenty feet from the van they would encounter the electric fence. I hoped they did not jump over it. Jump it! Heck, they ran right through my wonderful barrier, as if it was not even there. Then the illusive little devils made another mad dash toward crossing the lane that bordered our place on the south.

Suddenly that shadowy figure came out of nowhere and tackled Fay, the small female and holding on for dear life, while being dragged across the painful gravel road, pulled the goat to the ground. That figure that had just saved Fay from certain death at the jaws of the local coyotes, should Fay have escaped, was our illustrious neighbor, Debra.

Debra had seen us pull up to our house from her yard, she had been mowing, and when she realized we were unloading the goats, had come to help. Man, was I glad to see her!

I yelled to her to hang on tight to the female, as I was running to her with a piece of the cotton rope we had used earlier to load the animals. Rope that I had so stupidly failed to tie around them before releasing the goats in their ineffective pen. I helped Debra tie the cord to Fay and as Debra was securing Fay to a nearby tree, I headed south across the lane where I had last seen Billy crashing through the dense brush. I was in luck and could barely make out the two little eyes glowing like green candles some thirty yards into his thick safe haven. I slowly and cautiously battled the briers and brambles, as I circled about twenty yards south of where I had last caught a glimpse of those impish glowing eyes and sure enough, there was Billy, standing very still and watching me sneak up on him. I was sure he would run deeper into the forest if I did not do something quickly to prevent it, so I hurriedly headed farther south, running like a banshee, yelling at the top of my lungs, throwing caution to the wind, while waving my hands wildly (hands that Billy or no one could see in this darkness).

Billy, who was really frightened by now, decided to run back to familiar territory and headed toward the van. While the thorn vines, blackberry brambles, and scrub brush did a number of lovely slashes on any areas I had not clothed and some that I had, I crashed awkwardly through the brush and at full run chased Billy toward the van and his pen. Just as he started to cross the lane south of his pen, nearly in the same place Debra had caught Fay, I got close enough to Billy to fully extend my body in a flying leap, that allowed me to tackle the loudly bleating and violently struggling horny headed creature. Clamped together like a giant trussed beef roast; we rolled and skidded on the gravel of the lane. Skinning nearly every exposed place on either of us. I knew I had to hold on and not let him escape, as there would darn sure not be a second chance to catch this angry and frightened little goat if he got loose in this darkness.

We came to a rolling stop, my many scratches stinging and bleeding, my every muscle aching, and with Billy still struggling and noisily bleating, as though I was cutting his throat, which right now did not seem like such a bad idea. Debra came running over to us with a piece of that rope I had failed to use when it would have prevented

*The white goat is Fay when she was about ten years old and the black goat is Blackie, the animal purchased by Dennis that had been dehorned and neutered before joining our herd. Billy had been sold by this picture taking.*

this problem, and tied it around Billy's neck just behind his magnificent rack of horns. I thumped his rump just for frustrations sake and quickly got out of his way, as he missed in his effort to get even and butt me one last time.

Then as the two goats, who now were securely tied to a couple of trees inside their ineffective fence gradually quieted down, the three of us Debra, Shirley, and myself sat down on the back end of the van and rubbing our many bruises; had a good laugh, quite reminiscent of the great rat chase of many years previous, while we were moving into the house at 805 E. 13th in Pawhuska. The giant difference was of course, unfortunately our wonderful children were now all no longer around to cheerlead us in the chase. How we missed their yells of "Whack Em, Dad"! Or " Poke Em out, Dad"! But we did get the neighborhood together this time! Billy and Fay's escapes and constant entanglement in the brush when tethered, would continue to present quite a problem for about the next six weeks until as I earlier mentioned, Joey showed up with an old used fence charger; he assured me would kill or cure those ongoing escapes.

I had purchased and installed four different models of electric fence chargers and found none to be effective, as Billy especially would delight in politely walking through the fence anytime he took a notion. I hesitated to install Joey's **final solution,** as I did not know what I would do with the bodies of two dead goats should their lives be forfeited before their freedom was curtailed. However, when Billy got out the next day and I had to spend half the hot August morning chasing him through the briers and thorn bushes of the forest; I decided his demise might just be the adequate and fair method of ending my goat problems. So with Joey's help I installed the ultimate fence charger, while the goats remained on a twenty foot tether, which was staked to the ground inside their pen.

When we finished the installation and after we had turned on the electricity to it we left the tether on each goat, as we took both of them loose from their stakes in case the ultimate solution was not so ultimate. **After chasing these critters for these many weeks, we had finally figured out you could leave the ropes around their necks**. Brilliant, Huh? When we released both the goats from the ground stakes, they each immediately figured out they were loose and shot like two cannon balls toward the fence and sweet freedom. Fay managed to escape the fence, though she obviously got the shock of her young life, as she ran and kicked her back end high in the air, twisting her body and bleating wildly, as she headed toward the east woods. We did not worry about her, as we could easily catch the end of her tether anytime we wished. Billy was not so lucky and got his large bag of maleness caught between two of the four electric lines, that had twisted together, as Fay forced her way to freedom, and his right leg was tightly wound into the other two wires.

Poor Billy, I did think he was going to die before I could get the fence turned off. What serious kicking and wailing he did and as he lay stunned still entangled in the wires, I thought for sure we had killed him. As I got him loose he slowly began to breath and tried hard to extricate himself from his predicament, but he was just to banged up to free himself. Finally he shakily stood up and when I gave him a bit of a push, he wobbled toward the inside of his pen. I then caught Fay and released her back inside her pen. Hallelujah! That was the last time we had to chase either goat, as they never would go close to that fence again.

Due to Billy's male prowess and Fay's tolerance of it, we eventually had eleven goats, who thanks to their voracious appetite cleared the brush inside their pen which now looks like a large public park. I must say they both were quite a sight to behold, we watched as Billy, with his magnificent rack and long regal beard would rise to the very tips of his back toes and stretching his body fully as though he was a primate; he would curl back his lips exposing his sharp teeth, that he would use to snatch a cedar branch and pull it to the ground, or as near to the ground as needed, to allow Fay to munch on its tender green leaves. Then after she finished feasting she would take her turn holding the same branch for Billy to gobble. We eventually sold all the goats, but Fay and Blackie. Blackie was a eunuch that my son Dennis purchased some years ago while checking out the local Dog Trade. Blackie was supposed to clear the brush from behind Debra's house, which Denny purchased, but Blackie failed to fulfill his destiny and just stands around eating and bleating. Somewhat poetic I think!

The Dog Trade is a local phenomenon located on the south bank of Rock Creek, East of the state highway 177 Bridge, just North of Sulphur. Area folk gather every Sunday morning around five thirty am to trade every type of item one could imagine. It truly is quite a show and you can buy, sell, or trade, goods, animals, fowl, house- hold items, guns, produce, or anything else one can think of. The Dog Trade occurs weekly the year around, but always closes promptly at eleven thirty am.

Shirley was offered and accepted the director's position with the recently developed Sulphur Main Street Program about a year after we moved to this area, and shortly there-after she moved her *Gift Basket Store* to it's second address at 204 East Main in the historic portion of old east Sulphur.

The *Gift Basket* store offered specialty coffees, teas, and home

*Shirley's fine gift baskets were a hit everywhere, as she shipped them worldwide. Above, C. E. can be seen wrapping one, as Shirley attends the front of the store. Santa, i.e. Charlie Wright a good friend, made frequent appearances at the Gift Basket*

*The Gift Basket had many beautiful and useful items and a fine lunch& catering business*

made gourmet chocolates. It was the gourmet chocolates, that due to their labor intensive production and their popularity with our guests, finally resulted in Shirley selling the store. The store required attention twenty-four hours daily seven days a week. Sounds just like past Redwine businesses does it not? We had a wonderful and very lucrative lunch business, as well as a fine catering clientele. This required a great deal of time to prepare the extraordinarily colorful and delicious foods. We probably would have continued to run the store longer, but two situations occurred that caused us to feel like it was a good time to sell it. First, in the fall before we decided to sell, some folks put in a cookie store next door to us and we lost a great deal of that segment of the business. Then Christmas came and we had a tremendous spurt of income, as we sold nearly all our stock. Rather than restock the store, we decided to take our profits and sell the fixtures, plus the name.

A number of people had inquired as to weather we might be interested in selling our business. During the time we owned the *Gift Basket,* we enjoyed the kindness and consideration of many fine people, who either traded with us regularly, or helped us find unusual items to sell, or recommended the store to their friends. However, we also were the brunt of some vicious and disturbing acts of unethical business practices. Two of these included acts by the clerks of a local grocery and the clerks of the local discount store who came into our store, had lunch as they used their time inside to see what stock we had and either copied our work, or found out where we were getting our stock, then ordered hundreds of the same items, which they promptly displayed and sold in those stores. For the first time, both those stores began selling gift baskets, that looked surprisingly

*Above R: Philip W., James D. &*
*Clarice I. Redwine 07-04-85*

*Left; Bruce Bartlett 07-04-2003*
*relaxing in the grape arbor*

*C. E. Redwine finally hit the green-Peg Redwine, and Janie Bartlett look on from behind and Philip W. waits patiently as usual. Ah, the annual golf tourney! 07-04-2002*

*Faces sunburned, but obviously very happy to be together. 07-04-2005 left to right: front row Bruce Bartlett, Philip W. Redwine, second row: D. Janie Bartlett, C. E. Redwine, Peg Redwine, back row Shirley J. Redwine, and James M. Redwine.*

*James D. Redwine (center) returns triumphantly to us after leading tanks into Basra in first Iraq war. 07-04-1988*

similar to ours, and shortly after we went out of business both stores oddly quit selling them.

The past ten years that we have lived in this area have been very enjoyable as we took care to celebrate Christmas and the fourth of

*Clarice I. Redwine and her granddaughter Tonya M. Redwine Christmas 1967*

*Grandmother Shirley J. Redwine and her first grandson, David Aaron Redwine Christmas 1981*

*Carroll and Shirley in the Gift Basket on Christmas Eve 2000*

*Christmas 1965 taken as our family left Mom's home at 14th and Ruble in Pawhuska L to R: Carroll E. (twin sons) David L. and Dennis L. daughter, Carla R. wife and mother, Shirley J." Smith" Redwine and Shirley's Mom, Esther Mae Van Berg "Smith" Miller the gas eater in background*

July with our families and friends. Some of the pictures showing these great times follow.

These pictures attempt to tell the wonderful relationships of our family and it's striving to continue the legacy of our wonderful mother, who worked daily to keep us together.

*Christmas at Mom's was always a great time: L to R: D.Jane Bartlett, Momma Clarice I. Redwine Tonya M. Redwine, and Carla R. Redwine Reasoner Xmas 1990*

We celebrated many other holidays together, and reveled in everyone, always thrilled to be together.

Shirley and I have spent a great deal of time making what we feel are improvements to this lake cabin and the property around it. We planted over twenty trees the first spring after we moved here. Trees that included pines, that are now thirty feet tall, fruit trees that included three different varieties of apple, two varieties of cherry, pear, plum and peach. All the fruit trees have provided us with ample deserts, jellies and wines except the apple trees, which have not as yet born fruit. The grape arbor was especially fun to build and develop and we have truly enjoyed the great jellies and delicious wines resulting from its very prolific production. We have been able to share these benefits with many family members and a number of friends and have given starts from these two wonderful vines to them also.

Christmas was always a very warm and tender time for all of us and some special moments were shared here. When we first moved to this hillside we noticed there were no birds and very little wild life, we finally decided that this was a result of the lack of water available on this mountain,even though the major lake was only a quarter of a mile from us. We immediately set out to remedy this by building a number of temporary fountains around the cabin; one of these became a major five year project which was just completed in 2005 It is a small creek and is built on the north to south slope of the back yard, it runs the year around and has really brought in many beautiful birds and small wildlife plus even the deer drink from it at times. We have also developed a fine garden that has provided us much produce and many hours of pleasurably hard work

There are many, many more experiences that have taken place in our lives, than I have alluded to in this accounting of these seventy years. Some very wonderful and exhilarating, some very sad and somber, some extremely disappointing, and some that show promise of a tremendous future for our family, and friends, as well as those

*Xmas 1999 picture taken afternoon of New Years Day on porch of lake cabin L to R. Sarah Redwine, Alice English Philip W. Redwine holding his first granddaughter, Haley Redwine, seated next to Haley is Bruce Bartlett, right of Bruce is Haley's mother: Dedra Redwine, then right is Ryan Redwine, D. Jane Bartlett, Chuck- a family friend, and up front right is Carroll E. Redwine, and standing to the far left is Peg Redwine wife of James M. Redwine who is directly behind her and to James's right is Philip jr. Redwine*

*L to R: Brook and Haley Redwine holding their new brother Philip the third, children of Phil Jr. and Dedra Redwine and Grand children of Philip W. and Sarah A. Redwine*

who sadly we find are against us. I have elected to recite only those that I felt have come directly to bear on my life and those that reflect how I have reacted to their perpetuity. It is my fond hope that when my family and friends of that group read this

391

account they will in some small manner see the people, places and experiences, that I have visited about and feel the closeness I felt, as I recounted to the best I could remember an accurate rendition of them. What a tremendous ride this has been, it is my contention I have lived and partaken of the absolute best of times and wonder of all wonders, the bell has not rung its final tone.

*L to R: Tillman Beau and Brysan Redwine Sons of Ryan and Stacy Redwine and grandsons of Sarah A. and Philip W. Redwine December2005*

In addition to working to improve this property, I was given the opportunity to continue my love of music by directing the delightful Sulphur United Church Choir. These people were truly a Christian group and it has for over three years been a high light of our living in this area. The best thing about directing this group was their eagerness to sing good music and do so accurately. Fortunately I was simultaneously offered and accepted the position of music director for the highly successful Ardmore Little Theater production of the musical *Jesus Christ Super Star,* this after enjoying the musical production of *Annie* By the same theater and in which I performed the reed one parts in it's orchestra. In addition for the past six years I managed and with others judged; the *Arbuckle's Wilderness* Band and Choir Contest, getting to enjoy the company of some of the best musicians and gentlemen anyone could know. Two of these fellows Denny Wade and Donny Franks have become my very good friends.

I recently quipped to my brother Philip that I was having problems closing out this book, as his family was growing faster than I could write about it!

I can not recognize everyone who has crossed our path in this lifetime, but I would be really remise if I failed to include A. J. Ferron's children as they have been a big part of our lives, and they

| Joey ferron | Ashley Ferron | Nicole Ferron |

have spent many hours waiting up for their Dad to come home from his evening performing in our bands. Thanks kids for sharing your father's great talent with our fans and us.

Before I close these last few pages I want to tell the reader about

Shirley's and my latest venture into the business world. Nearly two years ago, Shirley and our daughter in law Terry Redwine who is married to our Son David and who moved with him to a home next door to us from their home in Dallas, where Terry had been studying horticulture at a local junior college, decided to put Terry's

Far left gutted metal building being shored up—Right, Nicole and C. E. getting a sheet of paneling ready to install

knowledge of plants and Shirley's knowledge and experience in the gift shop business together and they formed a partnership to develop their ideas into a new business, that would be known, as *The Garden Patch.* Some months and a lot of planning went by and after a great deal of research that resulted in volumes of garden books being devoured, hundreds of gallons of gasoline burned in their quest to view the like stores of others, and many hours of drawings and discussion what, how, and where; they could and would find the wares they would display, They settled on refurbishing an old tire shop that was located on the west entrance to Sulphur on the north side of State Highway 7. This property was in an ideal location as it was easily seen from the very highly traveled road, five city blocks west of the only Wal-Mart store within thirty miles in any direction, and everyone entering or leaving the town of Sulphur was forced to

Far left gutted metal building being shored up—Right, Nicole and C. E. getting a sheet of paneling ready to install

pass it. However, it did have its problems, a few of these included; it had been a tire shop for over forty years. The place was covered in old screws, nails, metal car parts of all descriptions, a dilapidated seventy foot trailer home, that was in such disarray that it could not be moved, but had to be burned to get rid of it, over two hundred old tires piled around in no specific manner, and that no one would haul away, because the local landfill would not accept them, weeds over two feet high in some places and ticks, fleas, rats, mice, aplenty, plus bushels of bird nests containing a fine supply of lice, that had been piling up for the last forty years in every nook and cranny of the old sheds. When I saw it for the first time, I figured Shirley was going to lease it when as usual she said, "**All it needs is a coat of paint**". However, I still had a small measure of hope she would not, as Terry was such a stickler for cleanliness and I knew how Terry hated mice, spiders, and all those others varmints that came with this operation.

I forgot, where Shirley had only one slave to offer in the refurbishing of the property, Terry had two and one half, these included David, Nicole, (Terry's beautiful daughter,) and *the clincher,* Nicole's able boyfriend Manuel Orsornio who would eventually be a

*Manuel and Nicole cleaning and painting the roof*

really integral part of the slave team. In April of 2005 after almost two years of research and planning the women leased the property described and got the owner, our good friend, Charlie Schwake to agree as part of the lease to: 1. get rid of all the old tires. 2. Burn the old trailer and remove it's steel frame and chassis. 3.Plumb the old bathroom and replace the front door. 4. Remove and clean up the spilled five hundred gallon leaking oil tank from the area of the front door. 5. Leave the lumber that was salvageable around the place, so they could have their slaves clean and use it in the repairs of the buildings. 6. Then they got him to agree not to collect any of the rent until these items were addressed, and they felt it was fair to do so, which turned out to be six months later. This sounds like Charlie might have gotten

*David preparing a sheet of paneling to be paced in the vaulted ceiling, a project he mostly did by himself*

*Shirley, Terry, Nicole and Manny put a coat of purple and red paint on anything that didn't move and some that did.*

*Terry, on opening day. The 25th of November 2005. What a happy camper!*

*First shipment of poinsettias to the Garden Patch, on opening day*

*Candy case, waiting for stock on opening weekend.*

*On page 217 Nicole and C. E. are seen installing paneling in the N W corner of the old metal building—left is that same spot on opening day oddly, since our main boss (Shirley) took all the pictures she is not in them, believe me she worked harder than any of us*

the short end of the stick on this deal, but let me assure you, it was the slaves who over the next nine months cleaned, painted, repaired, rebuilt, and above all: paid good money for the materials of this mess who, if anyone, were short-changed. When the girls opened their beautiful new shop the first week in December 2005, Charlie was then the owner of a property that nine months earlier was worth less than seventy-five thousand dollars, now it was at least worth treetimes that figure.

A number of friends and relatives have requested that I include some of the most used and enjoyed family recipes, as when we all visit each other much time and effort is devoted to preparing and eating fine foods  As in most American homes we have many traditional dishes that are prepared and the family expects to be served at certain family functions or holidays.  I will try to list these in a manner that will make them readily accessible should anyone desire to use and enjoy their results.  I am certain most of the older family members have most of these committed to memory, but some of our younger or newer members and friends might find them useful.

# Recipes Listed Alphabetically, as to Food Type

**Breads, Casseroles, Deserts, Dressings,**

**Fishes, Gravies, Meats, Salads, Sauces, Soups, and Stews.**

*Breads:*

### Redwine's hot rolls:

(Must use heavy electric mixer with dough hook to have success with this recipe) 3 cups warn water---110 to 120 degrees, 3 Tbs. Red Star dry yeast, 6 Tbs. Granulated sugar, 6 & ¾ cups flour, 3 tsp salt, 3 eggs, 6 Tbs. Vegetable shortening. Process—In electric mixer bowl-sprinkle yeast in water- stir in sugar, 3 cups of flour, and salt---Beat three to five minutes----add eggs, remaining flour, and shortening, --Beat until thoroughly mixed—take mixer bowl off mixer and cover with clothe-let rise 30 minutes or until batter is double in size—stir down—spoon into prepared muffin pans filling each hole one third to one half full-let rise until double (about 15 minutes) bake in 410 degree preheated oven until brown about 20 to 25 minutes. Yield= approx-36 rolls.

### Hush Puppies:

(These are essential when serving fish!)

1cup corn meal mix, ¼ cup flour, 1 egg, ½ cup finely diced onion, ¼ cup finely diced bell pepper, ½ cup buttermilk, ½ tsp salt---- mix thoroughly all ingredients—drop a few spoonfuls at a time into 350 degree hot oil- watch carefully these are easily burned. Yield = 3 to 4 servings

*Casseroles:*

### Chicken and Dumplins:

Select a very fat chicken, wash and clean thoroughly, cook slowly over medium heat in pot large enough to add at least 8 cups of water.

Add 3 to 4 finely chopped stalks of celery, 1 medium onion finely chopped, 1 tsp poultry seasoning, 1 tsp black pepper, 1 Tbs salt. Cook until chicken is tender (about 1&1/2 hours) remove chicken and bones from pot, let cool and de-bone, cut meat into bite sized pieces, and **give bones to the cats**, place meat back into broth, bring to boil over medium heat while you make dumplings (you can use any commercial canned biscuits, as your dumplings if you are in a hurry, just be sure you cut them in bite sized pieces before you drop them into the boiling broth.) Dumplings----1&1/2 cups flour, 1 egg (beaten), 3 Tbs water, 3 Tbs shortening, ½ t salt---mix and roll out dough, let dry 20 minutes cut in 2inch by 1 inch pieces and drop into the boiling broth. (Optional-cut up small chunks of boiled eggs into dumplings before rolling out). Do not overcook dumplings!!! Yield= 8 to10 servings.

**Holiday stuffing:**

(Dressing to our family):

Two loaves of day old white bread cut into ¾ inch cubes toasted in 410-degree oven until slightly brown. —Place toasted cubes in large mixing bowl –add 6 to 8 small stalks of Celery chopped in ½ inch cubes, 1 large onion finely chopped—3 tsp rubbed sage, 1 tsp black pepper, 2 tsp salt, --3 to 4 cups chicken broth or turkey stock, mix thoroughly and bake in slow oven (350 degrees) until brown on top (about 25-30 minutes) for more southern style replace one loaf of white bread with pan of crumbled cornbread— for moreYankee taste add a can of fresh oysters & leave off the cornbread! Yield= 18 to 20 servings

**Baked Beans:**

1 Gallon can of Campbell's or Van Camps pork and beans (I

prefer Campbell's) –2 cups onions finely chopped, 1 cup green bell pepper finely chopped, 1&1/2 cup light brown sugar, 2/3 cup yellow mustard, 1 medium bottle Heinz catsup, 1 Tbs salt, ½ tsp Black pepper, --Mix all ingredients thoroughly—place in baking pan—put 4 long strips of bacon on top—drizzle additional catsup to color top and bake in 350 degree oven until bacon is browned well. Yield= 20 to 25 yummy servings

### Goulash;

(This was a favorite of the Redwine's when the kids were home) In a very large cast iron skillet brown 1 finely chopped onion and 1 coarsely chopped bell pepper, with 1&1/2 lbs ground beef, add 2 cups of V8 juice and 1 small can chopped tomatoes--- simmer this mixture, (stir this frequently, while you cook a 1 pound bag of macaroni in a separate pan. (GO STIR THE MIXTURE !!) After the macaroni is tender drain & add it to the skillet- mix it thoroughly—let simmer 5 minutes and enjoy the fruits of your labor. We liked this served with lots of bread and butter. Yield=5 to 7 servings depending on hunger of family.

### Macaroni and cheese:

*As preferred by the Redwine grand children*: Buy 2 boxes of Kraft *Mac and cheese* follow directions on boxes!!! Serve often. *Deserts:*

### Grandma Berryhill's Banana Cake:

½ cup margarine, 1 & ½ cup sugar, 2 unbeaten eggs, 4 tsp sour milk or buttermilk, 1 tsp soda, 1cup mashed very ripe bananas, 1 tsp vanilla, and 1 & ½ cup flour. Mix all ingredients—pour into prepared cake baking pan –bake in medium oven (350) degrees until brown and toothpick removes cleanly, Iced or not iced this is a great cake!

### Granny Redwine's Brownies:

Crème ½ cup margarine and 1 cup sugar—Beat 2 eggs til fluffy—stir them into the mixture—mix 3 Tbs cocoa with ½ cup flour add ½ cup finely chopped Black Walnuts or pecans and 1tsp vanilla to mix, then add these two mixes together. Bake in slow oven (350) til tooth- pick inserted is clear when pulled out. Recipe doesn't work well when doubled. *Be sure and bake these in an 8x8x2 inch pan.*

### Momma Shirley's Christmas morning Cinnamon Rolls:

In a large mixing bowl put 3 cups warm water (110-120 degrees), 2/3cup plus 1 tsp sugar, 3

Tbs dry yeast or 3 pkg of cake yeast, 2/3-cup vegetable shortening, 3 eggs 2 tsp salt, and 8 to 9 cups Flour—mix this thoroughly and roll Out on heavily floured counter until dough is about 1/4th to 3/8ths inch thick. --- In clean mixingBowl make a filling of 1 stick-melted butter, 1 cup sugar, and 1 ½ tsp cinnamon. Using a rubber paddle gently and generously cover the rolled out dough with this mixture—Carefully roll the dough into a long roll with the mixture inside and starting at one end cut ½ to ¾ inch pieces across the entire roll. Lay them on their side in a greased and floured cake pan--- bake them at 350 until brown –Cont'd on next page---

Ice them with this icing; ½ cup soft butter, 3 cups powdered sugar, 1 tsp ofVanilla, and 3 Tbs heavy cream. Merry Christmas!! Yield= about 24 rolls (serve with sausage, crisp bacon and ham)

### Hot Fudge Pudding Cake:

In a large mixing bowl mix 1-cup buttermilk baking mix 1-cup sugar 3 Tbs plus 1/3-cup cocoa, ½ cup milk 1 tsp vanilla, 1& 2/3 cup hot water

### No Bake Cookies:

(This was David's and especially Dennis's favorite cookie)

2 cups sugar- ½ cup milk- ¼ cup butter- 4 Tbs cocoa--- bring ingredients to hard boil for 3 minutes--- add ½ cup peanut butter- 3 cups uncooked Quaker oats- 1 tsp vanilla--- mix well—drop onto wax paper to cool. Yield= 24 servings

### Yum Yum Cake:

This sounds difficult, ITS NOT, and it is really worth your efforts!!!

2eggs, 2cups sugar, 2 cups flour, and 2 cups crushed pineapple, 2&½ tsp baking powder. In large mixing bowl beat eggs and sugar till fluffy—stir in pineapple—add flour and baking powder--mix well—put in greased and floured 13 x 9x 2 baking pan— then into pre-heated 350 degree oven for about 25 to 30 minutes. (Use tooth-pick trick) to check cake--- make a topping with 1cup sugar, 1 stick margarine, 1 cup coconut, 1 cup pecans, 1/2tsp vanilla, 1/2tsp lemon juice. Boil sugar, margarine, and milk for 2 minutes remove from heat add coconut, pecans, vanilla, and lemon juice--- Spread carefully on hot cake.

*Dressings:*

### Blue Cheese salad dressing:

1 qt buttermilk, 1 qt Helman's mayonaisse, ¾ lbs blue cheese crumbles, ½ cup chives, 1 Tbs garlic powder, 1 & ½ Tbs lemon juice, 1 & ½ tsp salt, 2 tsp freshly ground black pepper. In large mixing bowl-using wire whip- mix well the buttermilk, chives, garlic, salt, pepper and lemon juice—add the mayonnaise—whip until smooth—gently fold in the blue cheese crumbles—*don't mix hard, it will break up the cheese* Yield = 2quarts that will keep up to 14 days in 35 degree refrigerator.

### French salad dressing:

1 medium bottle Heinz catsup, 1qt Helman's mayonnaise, 1 Tbs onion powder 2 tsp salt 1 tsp black pepper—Mix all ingredients with wire whip until smooth—Yield = about 1 ½ qts. Will keep up 10 to 14 days in 35-degree refrigerator.

### Italian Salad dressing:

1/3 cup Italian seasonings, 2/3 cup lemon juice, 1/3 cup extra virgin Olive oil, 1/3 cup wine vinegar, 1/3 cup water, 2 tsp salt. 1 tsp freshly ground black pepper. Shake well in 1-quart fruit jar. Yield =2 & ¼ cups. Keeps forever!

### Thousand Island Salad Dressing:

1 qt Helman's mayonaisse, 1 cup sweet pickle relish, ½ cup catsup, 1 Tbs onion powder, 3 tsp fresh lemon juice, 1tsp fresh black pepper, 1 tsp salt. Whip all ingredients until smooth. Yield1&1/2 quarts. Will keep up to 10 days in 35degree refrigerator.

*Fishes:*

### Shrimp Cocktail:

To prepare boiled shrimp you must know that shrimp are sold so many pieces to a pound, i.e.: 10-12's meaning there will be 10 to 12 shrimp in the pound you purchase. These are the size I prefer for deep- frying, however for cocktail or (boil and peel), I prefer the 36 – 40 size. I hate those very small shrimp known as popcorn shrimp, as they are so labor intensive, I do like 20-30's for making Scampi, as they have a lot of flavor, and are still not too small. To prepare shrimp for cocktail, --**leave the shells on them until after they are cooked** –Put a pot of water on to boil big enough to hold the wire basket you will fill with the shrimp you are going to drop in the water. Place a package of Zartarand's Seafood boil in the water with 1 tsp cayenne pepper. *Do not break the bag of spices, as you do not want to have the mess all over your shrimp.* **Do not wash the shrimp before you cook them. They will not have any flavor if you do!!** After the spicy water comes to a good boil place your basket of shrimp into it, for no more than 3 to 3&1/2 minutes. Shake the basket gently to get the shrimp to cook more evenly—after you take these out of the water peel and de-vain them, de-veining is the process of making a small cut on the top of the shrimp and pulling out the remaining gut. Leave on the tails, they are customarily served this way. About ½ way up the body make a very small thin cut across the underside of the shrimp, it will help it stay on the cocktail glass rim, fill the bottom of a glass bowl with ice, place your cocktail glass in the ice filled bowl—place a very fluffy piece of green lettuce or other color leafy plant in the glass, letting it hang gracefully out of the cocktail—Add your cocktail sauce to the glass partially covering the leaf and hang your prepared shrimp on the rim of the glass, Place a piece or two of lemon wedge on the lower ice or on the rim with the shrimp, which ever best dresses the serving. **Recipe for Redwine's red sauce is included in the Sauces!**

**Fried Shrimp:**

**Refer to above recipe for purchasing shrimp,** preparing shrimp for frying is totally different from boiling, Select the number of shrimp you feel your guests will consume, generally most servings include 6 to 7-- 20/30counts, but if you are serving 10/12's 3 to 4 will be more than ample per guest. Peel, de-vein, and clean your shrimp then using a sharp knife, butterfly each of them. To butterfly a shrimp hold it in one hand with the back toward your other hand and make a slice down it's back but not all the way through the flesh it will now lay open flatly and then you will place all your butter-flied pieces into a jar of ice water to which you will add the juice of one lemon and it's rinds, Refrigerate these pieces until just before you fry them (no more than 8 hours) Shrimp spoils easily! **Frying procedure:** use three shallow pans, pie pans are good for this work –put buttermilk in one, flour in the next one and cracker meal mixed with Redwines Rolls meal in the third pan, *just cracker meal will work if you have not made rolls*, Take butterfly shrimp from the lemon water and pat fairly dry on a paper towel then holding it by the tail, draw it through the buttermilk, then lay it down in the flour and gently kneed it until it is covered in flour, run it through the buttermilk a second time and then cover it in the cracker meal/bread crumbs.  Your Shrimp is ready to be submerged in the hot oil (350) degrees until cooked to desired color of golden brown.  Serve this with the wonderful Redwine's red sauce for which a recipe is included under sauces on pages 207/208.

**Broiled Lobster tails:**

If tails are frozen you must carefully thaw them in the microwave being careful not to cook them in any manner, as it will make the flesh tougher than a boot, if they are fresh or you now have them thawed, place one upside down on a cutting board and using a very sharp knife make a cut down the middle of <u>the **under side of the shell, only,**</u> (do *not damage the shell, except for this cut, as we are going to use it later)* Cut from the fleshy area to the end of the tail, this will allow you to remove the flesh in one piece from the shell surrounding it, turn the piece of tail you have removed over, so that you can make a slit with your knife the length of what was once the top of the lobster's back, and de-vein the meat,--- place the de-veined and **slightly** butterflied flesh on top of the shell it was once in, with the meat following the original configuration of the tail on a shallow baking pan , pizza pans work well for this—squeeze ½ a lemon over the flesh—pour on 1/3 cup melted butter over it, gently shake paprika over it for color and broil it until it no longer has a **clear** fleshy color, (usually about 5 to 8) minutes. Serve this wonderful offering on a bed of lettuce leaves and along side a baked potato with hot melted garlic butter, or leave out the garlic if you choose.

### Broiled Trout:

Select fresh trout, wash under cold water until very clean inside and out, lay fish on it's back and slice down middle from head to tail making two open halves—place these on pizza pan flesh- up skin down. --- Squeeze a lemon over the flesh—sprinkle ½ tsp seasoned salt, ½ tsp lemon pepper, ¼ tsp paprika over the flesh, broil until flesh is no longer clear and has a flaky white color, usually, not very long. Serve on bed of lettuce, along side baked potato with carrot curls and radish roses, and one scallion for color with side dish of Redwine's tartar sauce. Recipe for tartar sauce can be found in sauces on pages 207/208.

Baked Carp:

**This dish is best served around April first; carp are very elusive and are gluttons in the spring.** Take one finely sanded Red Cedar board; rub it gently with a lemon you have cut in half. (Please use the whole lemon?) Smash 2 large cloves of garlic with the side of a large kitchen knife; rub them firmly into the board (same side as the lemon). —Since Carp are a scale fish, I recommend for best results you skin this fish, you can do this by making a skin deep cut from just at the top of the head circling under the pictorial fin to the bottom of the gills, turn the Carp's head so that it's body lies with it's head toward you and tail is away from you, --now slide the knife inside the slit you made behind the fishes head just under the skin, (don't damage the flesh) and cutting under the skin, loosen the skin from the flesh, by sliding your knife all the way to the Carps tail. Eviscerate the fish, cutting away the entire stomach area, there is not much eatable flesh in this area and there are many small bones. Take a pair of pliers and carefully pull out all remaining fins—lay the fish on it's back and cutting all the way through the fish follow the back bone from it's head to it's tail, Good job! Now you have it cut in half, -- place the two pieces on the prepared Cedar board, Sprinkle it with lemon juice, lemon pepper, Cayenne pepper, and a bit of onion powder (not to much!), mixed with paprika. Put it in a 350degree oven for about 30 minutes. Take it out, _throw away the Carp_ and serve the board, which you must cut with a jig- saw! Sorry about that, I could not miss this opportunity to pull a few legs and if you are this far into the book, you must really be a **good** friend, so I will probably get away with it.

*Gravies:*

### Red Eye Gravy:

Must use a wrought iron skillet to get best results! Cut off enough fresh or cured ham to feed four people, using about 2 Tbs of lard or vegetable shortening, fry it in this skillet until it is browned—remove the meat and keeping as much of the grease and ham juices as possible in the pan, add about 2 Tbs of flour to make a good rue, when rue is fairly thick add 2 cups of hot coffee from your morning coffee pot. —Stir this mixture until it thickens a bit and serve on the side with hot biscuits and the ham you cooked. M_M_mmmmmm, Good!!!

**White-Onion Gravy:**

Using what ever pan drippings available—i.e.; from frying any type meats, add or subtract grease in hot pan making sure you have about 2-3 Tbs left in the pan---add about 2 tablespoons of finely chopped onion to the hot grease & sautee til onions are clear—then add 2 to3 Tbs of flour and make a fairly thick rue. Add about 3 cups of milk to this, -- stirring constantly or your gravy will be lumpy, you can use a wire whip it helps rid your dish of lumps also. Cook over medium heat till gravy takes on desired thickness, usually until it begins to boil. If you get it too thick add a bit of hot water and continue to stir, if it is too thin simmer it until it thickens--- The more you make this dish the more popular you will get with your family and the better you will know how to put it together, and the more rotund we will all get. Serves about 5-6. Suggest serving with biscuits early in the morning, when coffee and sleepy heads are at odds.

**Meats:**

**Bar- B- Q pork ribs or chicken:**

Wash meats thoroughly with cold water, drain on paper towels, pat dry—applying Mc Cormick's Bar- B- Q spice is the only difference here: Rub it on the ribs---Cut the chickens into ½'s or ¼'s drop into brown bag or plastic shopping bag and add ½ cup of the spices--- shake thoroughly until meat is covered. Place in smoker (**not on steak grill**) use pecan or hickory wood fire for best taste. Be patient; good Bar-B –Q takes a long time to process, as fire must be between 275 and 350 degrees for best results. Use a thermometer, check it often, and tend the fire to keep it even, the meat should reach an internal reading of 180 degrees before it can be safely eaten.

**Chicken Supreme:**

(2 pkgs mushrooms, -sliced), 6 chicken breasts -1 large onion finely diced, -2 bell peppers cut into 1&1/2inch pieces, -1/3 cup butter, - 3 Tbs Worcestershire sauce, 3 pieces of chicken and enough water to make 2 cups of stock, -1 tsp garlic powder, -1 tsp celery salt, 1 tsp black pepper, -Sauté' mushrooms and onion in butter with garlic, -- sauté 6' chicken breasts until tender with the mixture--- cook chicken stock, -- thicken stock with a couple spoons of flour mixed into cold water, and then dropped into boiling stock cook until stock is desired thickness.—season with celery-salt, salt, and pepper. Combine thickened stock with mushroom and chicken mixture and add green peppers, cook only until peppers are tender.

**Chile:**

*Choose heat desired ---Mild= 0 cayenne—warm= 1 tsp cayenne—hot= 2 tsp cayenne—very hot= 3to4 tsp cayenne,* In large stew pot place 3 Tbs olive oil, ½ lb beef suet, (ground coarsely), bring to a boil over medium heat. The suet usually turns to oily consistency when boiled, add 2 lbs Chile plate ground beef Chuck or Arm roast, (instead of grinding, you may cube this in ½ inch cubes if you prefer.) **In a separate bowl** --- mix thoroughly ½ cup ground Chile powder, ¼ cup ground cumin, 1/8 cup ground oregano, 2 medium onions finely chopped, 7 to 9 fresh garlic buds very finely chopped, and 1 cup V-8 juice plus the desired amount of cayenne pepper. Add this mixture to the pot----Stir often and thoroughly until pot begins to boil. Turn fire down to simmer---simmer for 1 hour, stirring often to keep meat from sticking. If it appears the meat is sticking, add enough V-8 juice to keep it moist while it simmers. For those folks who prefer them, serve your Chile over a big spoonful of brown beans, rice, Fritos, or even macaroni. Okie Purists eat their Chile with hot pickled peppers and saltines,but grated cheddar cheese and chopped onions are sometimes used as toppings and cornbread is used at times to replace the saltines.

### Meatloaf:

There are many ways to prepare good meatloaf, but this is the taste our family prefers.

1 & ½ lbs lean ground beef, 1 medium yellow onion, 1 medium bell pepper finely chopped, 2 eggs, 2 sleeves saltines, (crushed finely), 1 cup V-8 juice, 1 small can drained diced tomatoes, 4 strips of thick sliced Hickory smoked bacon, 1 small jar Heinz catsup, 1 Tbs salt, 1 tsp black pepper. Combine all the ingredients **except** the catsup V-8 juice draining from the tomatos and the bacon. Add most of the jar of catsup keeping back about 6 tablespoons. ---Mix well---put your mixture in a meatloaf-baking pan if you have one, if not a Pyrex baking dish will work. Lay the bacon on top of the formed meatloaf, and drizzle the remaining catsup& V-8 juice and tomato drainings over it. Bake in a 350 degree oven until internal temperature of the loaf reaches 180 degrees (about 45 minutes) Yield = 8 to10 servings

### Beef or Pork Roast, With Vegetables:

2 lbs Beef chuck "or" arm roast (or) 2 lbs Pork shoulder "or" loin roast, 4 Tbs olive oil, 2 cups flour, 2 Tbs salt, 3 tsp Black Pepper, four large white potatoes (peeled and cut into1&1/2 inch pieces) 5 large carrots (peeled and cut into1&1/4 inch pieces, 3 stalks of celery cleaned and striped, then cut into 1 inch pieces, 2 small onions peeled and quartered, 2 cups of water:

Rub the preferred roast with 1 Tbs salt & 1 tsp black pepper; be sure to cover all sides of the roast. Roll and pat it to coat it with the flour. Set your electric skillet on a large cutting board with newspaper tucked neatly under and **around** the cutting board, to avoid the real mess that this process will make when the food pops out of the pan onto the counter. Place the olive oil in a large 300 degree **electric** (very important) skillet, ---when the oil begins to smoke--- brown the roast on both sides. Place the vegetables evenly around and next to the meat--- carefully pour the water into the skillet avoiding the meat---put the lid on **loosely** and turn the heat down to 250 cook until meat is tender (about 1&1/2 hours) yield =5 to 6 servings.

*Salads:*

**Cold Slaw:**

1 head green cabbage (cored and grated), 1/3 head purple cabbage cored and grated, 3 medium carrots cleaned, scraped, and grated, 1 green bell pepper brushed, cored, and grated. In a separate pan mix together 2/3 cup vinegar, 2/3 cup sugar, 2/3 cup Helman's Mayonnaise, 1 & ½ tsp salt, ½ tsp black pepper, 2 tsp celery seed 1 tsp crushed mustard seed. Whip this mixture until it is smooth and pour over grated vegetables—fold together gently. Serve chilled if posible.

**Potato Salad:**

6 large potatoes, ( baked, cooled, peeled, and cut into ½ inch cubes). Two bundles of green onions (cleaned, chopped into ¼ inch pieces) 3 medium bell peppers one each green, red, and yellow all chopped like the green onions and 5 stalks of cleaned and finely chopped celery. Place all the above in a large mixing bowl and in a separate bowl mix these next ingredients---1/3 cup yellow mustard, ½ cup chopped dill pickle 1 & ½ cup sweet pickle relish, 1&1/2 cup Helman's Mayonnaise ¼ cup sugar 1& ½ Tbs salt, 1 tsp black pepper.

Mix these well and pour into other vegetables then mix them well together. Yield= 15 to 16 servings this will keep under 35 degree refrigeration approximately 10 days Some folks like to add a few chopped, boiled eggs to this, if you do, it will not keep more than 3 to 4 days.

**Chicken or Turkey salad:**

**For a great chicken or Turkey salad use the Potato Salad recipe above (*leaving out the mustard and the potatoes*) and adding two pounds of finely chopped chicken or two pounds of finely chopped Turkey.**

**Sauces and Pickles (and some good tricks):**

**Bar-B-Q Sauce**

1 #10 can of tomato sauce, 1 Tbs liquid smoke, 1 tsp kitchen bouquet, ½ cup Worcestershire sauce, ¼ lb Mc McCormick's Bar-B-Q spices, 1 Tbs salt, ½ Tbs season salt, 1 Tbs cavendar's steak seasoning, 12 oz. Light brown sugar, 1 Tbs garlic powder, 2 Tbs fresh lemon juice.

Mix all the above together in a large 5 qt sauce pan with a wire whip ---stir often to prevent scorching. Slowly bring to boil over **very low** heat – **Stirring often, simmer over low heat for about 30 minutes.** Yield= one Gallon This recipe was developed and served in Redwine's Restaurant

**Steak and chop basting butter: (*and some great cooking tips)*

1 lb cheap margarine, 1 Tbs Garlic powder, 3 Tbs Cavendar's steak seasoning.

Heat margarine until liquid, **absolutely do not heat spices** with the margarine--- mix in spices, and brush generously onto meat, continue to brush the broiling meat with this mixture until it reaches desired firmness, **do not fear the flames they are your friend,** and will make your steak taste even better if you learn how to use them. Test for how well your steak is done, by feeling with your fingers pushing on the meat. **Use no forks! Do not cut meat to check doneness, feel it! The more stable or firm the meat feels the more it is done!** Use a pair of long tongs to work your steaks.

**Restaurant butter:**

1 lb margarine, 1 cup vegetable oil, 1 cup Buttermilk, Blend together and refrigerate.

This recipe is excellent for use with hot rolls and baked potatoes, as the great tasting butter, which is much more economical than regular margarine or real butter, **doesn't tear up your hot rolls**

**Restaurant Sour Cream**: 2 Tbs skim milk, 1 carton (16 oz.) cottage cheese, 1 Tbs lemon juice, and ¼ tsp salt, --blend until creamy- store in refrigeration. Excellent on baked potatoes.

**Red Sauce:**

6 cups Heinz catsup, juice of 1&1/2 lemons, 2 cups sweet pickle relish, 1&1/2 tsp salt, 1 tsp black pepper, 2 Tbs Worcestershire, 1 Tbs kitchen bouquet, 3 Tbs grated fresh horseradish

Mix all ingredients together well using a wire whip. Serve generously with fried "or" boiled shrimp. Yield about 8 cups, keep refrigerated—will keep about 8 days.

*For Cajon style, replace the sweet relish with 4 tsp powdered cayenne pepper and 1TbsTabasco Sauce!*

**Spaghetti Sauce: serves 20 with the added meat**

1 bell pepper, 4 stalks celery, 1 cup yellow onion, (all finely chopped) # 10 can tomato sauce, 1 cup Italian seasoning, 2 Tbs

granulated or fresh finely diced garlic, 1Tbs salt.

Sautee the bell pepper, celery onion and garlic, add rest of ingredients and simmer. Some folks like to add a cup of red wine to the sautéed mixture before putting the other stuff in. For those who like meat in their spaghetti sauce add 1&1/2 pounds of ground beef to your sautéing mixture

Tartar Sauce:

*(Great with fried or broiled fish).* Do not serve with lobster or **carp!**

4 cups Helman's mayonnaise, 1&1/2 cups sweet pickle relish, juice of 1&1/2 lemons, ¾ cup very finely chopped green onions, 1 tsp black pepper 2 tsp salt. Whip together with wire whip keep refrigerated will keep up to 14 days

**Dad's famous Cajon pickles;**

1 gallon Sliced dill chips, 4 lbs sugar, 1 small bottle Tabasco sauce, 3 Jalapeno peppers sliced thinly across the pepper, 3 large onions cut into rings and the rings separated, 1 large carrot cut in thin rounds. Mix all ingredients together in a crock and let them set at cool room temperature for 48 hours, stirring them every 12 hours to get a good mix. Will keep 30 to 60 days in refrigeration 20 to 30 days without. *Never screw a lid on these tightly, and leave for a long period of time, it could lead to botulism!*

**Soups and Stew:**

**Beef Stew:**

! & ½ lbs of Beef arm "or" chuck de-boned and cubed 1 inch cubes, ---2 medium onions, 1 finely chopped and 1 cut into quarters- -3/4 cup chopped green cabbage, - ½ cup chopped green bell pepper, ½ cup finely chopped celery and 1 cup celery stringed and cut into

1 inch pieces. —2 large potatoes peeled and cut into 1 inch pieces, 3 large carrots cut in 1 inch pieces, 2 cups V-8 juice, 2 cups diced tomatoes, 1&1/2 Tbs salt, 2 tsp black pepper.

(Browning mix---1/2 Tbs cumin, ½ tsp black pepper 1 Tbs salt, 2 cups flour.) PUT THIS SEASONING MIX IN A BAG WITH YOUR CUBED STEW MEAT--- SHAKE IT WELL COATING THE CUBES THEN BROWN THEM IN A SKILLET WITH A BIT OF OLIVE OIL—USE A SLOTTED SPOON TO REMOVE THE BROWNED CUBES FROM THE SKILLET AND PLACE THEM ON A PAPER TOWEL TO DRAIN ---WHILE THEY ARE GETTING RID OF THE EXCESS OIL, SAUTEE THE CHOPPED ONION, CABBAGE, DICED CELERY, AND GREEN PEPPER---PUT THE MEAT BACK ON THE HEAT IN A 5 QUART STEW PAN –COVER IT WITH THE SAUTEED MIX—ADD 6 CUPS OF CHICKEN OR BEEF STOCK –BRING TO BOIL OVER MEDIUM HEAT –SIMMER 40 MINUTES---ADD THE CARROTS-SIMMER FOR 20 MINUTES –ADD THE CHUNKED CELERY AND THE POTATOES---AND 2 CUPS CHOPPED OR DICED TOMATOS— ADD 2 CUPS V-8 JUICE—SIMMER 30 MINUTES—Taste it  see if it needs more salt.  If so, ADD SALT AND PEPPER---- SERVE WITH CORNBREAD OR SALTINES---- **yield =8 to 10 servings**

### Potato Soup:

1 large baking potato, (peeled and cut into ½ inch pieces), 3 slices of thick sliced hickory smoked bacon, (micro-waved, drained on paper towel, and chopped in 1inch pieces), ½ cup finely chopped onion, 2 cups whole milk, 1 stick butter, or margarine, (cut in half), 2 tsp seasoned salt, 1 tsp black pepper, water to boil the potatoes.

In a 2 quart stew pot, place the cooked pieces of bacon, ½ stick of the butter and the finely chopped onion, sauté' this over medium heat, until the onion is clear, add the potatoes---put in just enough water to cover them----bring this mixture to a boil and cook until the potatoes are tender, **do not drain the potato water,** add the milk then the rest of the butter and spices---turn fire to low and bring back to a very slow boil. **Serves 4**—to make more servings increase by doubling recipe, except for bacon, butter, and onion.

I have developed or stolen many other recipes that our family is fond of, but these certainly are a number of our favorites, if I put out a second edition, I probably will enlarge this section

*Elizabeth Jene`(Beth) Clevenger, my gardening buddy helping me gather cherry tomatoes, and helping me eat them also! What a joy she is!*

*Riding the Osage with my wonderful brothers, and sisters— checking out the woolies in Phil`s Cadillac What great times we`ve had!*

*There they are! Never thought we'd live to see this, deer everywhere, buffalo aplenty, no fences as far as the eye can see and us still here to enjoy it together.*

*Ki-yi-ye-yike-us, nobody like us, we are the kids from Pawhuska high! I knew he knows the words!*

*Delores Jane (Redwine) Bartlett with our mother Clarice I, Berryhill- Cooper-Redwine. No one loved our mother more or better!!*

*L to R, Melanie Gill-Emily Gill-Donna Bartlett (bride)-Bruce Bartlett (groom)-D. Jane Bartlett-Drew Gill—back row left John Gill—back right Bruce Bartlett—picture taken at wedding.2000*

*L to R; front row-Clarissa Redwine, Nicole Johnson Chase Reasoner, Carla Reasoner, Katherine Redwine--Back row-Terry Redwine Shirley (Momma) Redwine, Carroll Redwine (Dad) Redwine, David Redwine, Dennis Redwine, D. Arron Redwine. Our family celebrating Mother's Day 1998*

*Tonya and Sam did not make this one. .*

*Philip, W. -James M. & Carroll E. Redwine*

*Same guys on July 4th 2004*

*L to R; James M. Redwine, Carroll E. Redwine, Philip W. Redwine, With Sister D. Jane Bartlett. Picture taken at Missouri University Sandwich shop in late 90's*

*L to R-- Sarah A. Redwine, Philip W. Redwine, Peg Redwine, James M. (Jim) Redwine, Carroll E. Redwine Shirley J. Redwine, and bottom front D. Jane Bartlett*

These few pictures easily would tell what memories I will take with me as my prized possessions.

*L. Kylee Hoskins December2005-- Kristie, "Maxwell" Hoskins`s daughter, David L. Redwine`s granddaughter and my 1st Great grandchild*

*Above L.-- Clarissa & Dennis Redwine, My grand-daughter and Son— above R. -- D. Aaron Redwine& David Redwine My oldest grandson & son with Nicole Johnson, Dave`s step-daughter and my oldest granddaughter.*

*Above L.-- Chase T. Reasoner & Carla R. "Redwine" Reasoner, My grandson and oldest daughter, R--Tonya M. "Redwine" Clevenger, holding Elizabeth J. Clevenger, my youngest daughter and youngest granddaughter & Tonya`s son Beau Casson Clevenger, my youngest grandson.*

# A Few Thoughts on the Important Things

There are few times in life that anyone gets the opportunity to say thank you simultaneously to all those he loves, this is one of those times.  Thank you family for making my life completely happy and so rich and full of accomplishment.  I have complete faith that for many future years our branch of the Redwines and their off spring will have a heavy impact for good in this world.  Therefore David Aaron, you must now carry the line forward, as it is your destiny, as the only Redwine male left in this limb of the family, **Wild oats, randomly sewn; do not count!**  A few words of advice to all the rest of the future generations, I freely give advice, as all you know.  It is your responsibility, as it was mine to set the bar even higher for your progeny, this will require much fore thought and sacrifice and at times you will not think it can be possible, just remember the ant and the rubber tree plant, never give up!  Supreme faith will really make a difference, I can tell you from personal experience it works, so pray about your problems, they will not go away, but adequate solutions will come about in surprising ways.  I have a true story to reveal that certainly illustrates this last point.

About thirty eight years ago during one cold and very bleak day the writer and his young family were traveling from one set of parents to the other to celebrate the Christmas holiday.  They had left Pryor, Oklahoma in full sunshine and expected to travel to Pawhuska without any weather problems.  However, they began to encounter a serious ice storm a few miles from Pryor and just west of Claremore they had to cross the Verdigris River on a very long rickety bridge, then immediately climb a very steep hill to leave the

421

river valley. They skidded across the bridge, and began their assent up the treacherous incline and about one hundred yards above the bridge, the car's motor appeared to no longer be propelling the vehicle up the hill and it began to slide slowly backward and dangerously sideways toward a cliff on the outer side of the hill. The author and his young wife watched in horror as they had no control of the skidding car, but their horror turned to awe as suddenly, the vehicle with their beautiful family began to roll evenly up the steep hill as though propelled by a giant hand pushing from behind it. When they reached the top and firm snow, the cars gears took over again and the ordeal was over. There is only one way to describe this event (devine intervention)

Trust and listen mostly to the people who love you, and think hard about turning your back on them for the advice of others. Books are just the written words of others who are most likely making the same mistakes as you and just because it is on the printed page does not make it a truth. The pursuit of wealth alone will bring you much misery, but if you strive to do all you can to accomplish your job or avocation better than anyone around you, it will pay great financial rewards, as well as make you happy. Giving of your time is always more generous than giving of your wealth, but sharing of your wealth will nearly always give you great pleasure in the long term. When meeting a person for the first time always remember, even though the persons attitude seems negative or abrasive, that this person in front of you is someone's little girl, daughter, wife, niece, granddaughter, etc. and likewise if the person is male it is someone's little boy, son and so on. Try hard to see them in this light, it is amazing how this will change the complexion of the moment into a positive situation for you both.

And for God's sake do not vote republican, it will haunt you forever, and so will I.

Still not quite ready for bottling, keep the corks handy---To Be Continued

*Absolutely the best decision I made in my life was to ask Shirley to walk side by side with me, sometimes I leaned heavily on her, sometimes she carried me, feisty, smart, sometimes really tough, but always on my side though every storm, and the worse the storm the tighter our bond became, how could I say all that needs to be said about this love story, forty- nine years and counting.*

*Carroll E. Redwine & Shirley J. Redwine picture taken April 2004*

# About the Author

Carroll E. Redwine was born in the last years of the great depression, he grew up in the dust bowl years of the southwest's worst drought in our nation's history and observed five declared wars and a police action that should have been declared a war. His family considered education and a strong belief in God to be extremely important to the well being of the individual and the Nation. Born in a dirt floor, two room cabin; he and his siblings are living proof that this country, its freedom to excell in all areas, and the intestinal fortitude of its determined people have been and will continue to be a beacon of light for a happy, kind, and considerate planet, where all peoples can exist together peacefully with equal oportunities in all areas of life. His story and those he chooses to tell in this short history of his family,most readers will find refreshing and although sometimes serious, nearly always comical.

Printed in the United States
55930LVS00004B/163-189